Islam in South Africa

Islam in South Africa

Mosques, Imams, and Sermons

ABDULKADER TAYOB

*Published in association with Religion in Africa, a series of
the African Association for the Study of Religions*

University Press of Florida
Gainesville · Tallahassee · Tampa · Boca Raton
Pensacola · Orlando · Miami · Jacksonville

04 03 02 01 00 99 6 5 4 3 2 1

Library of Congress Cataloging-in-Publication Data

Tayob, Abdulkader.
Islam in South Africa: mosques, imams, and sermons /
Abdulkader Tayob.
p. cm. — (Religion in Africa)
Includes bibliographical references (p.) and index.
ISBN 0-8130-1651-7   0-8130-2485-4 (pbk)
1. Islam—South Africa. I. Title. II. Series: Religions of Africa.
BP64.S63T39 1999
297'.0968—dc21 98-29933

The University Press of Florida is the scholarly publishing agency
for the State University System of Florida, comprising Florida
A&M University, Florida Atlantic University, Florida International
University, Florida State University, University of Central Florida,
University of Florida, University of North Florida, University of
South Florida, and University of West Florida.

University Press of Florida
15 Northwest 15th Street
Gainesville, FL 32611
http://nersp.nerdc.ufl.edu/~upf

CONTENTS

Preface   viii

1. The Sermon in Islam:
A Discursive and Religious Symbol in History 1

2. Creation of the Cape Mosque Discourse 21

3. The Claremont Main Road Mosque:
Redrawing the Cape Tradition 40

4. Transvaal Mosques: The Production of Orthodoxy 60

5. The Brits Mosque: Orthodoxy and Its Periphery 77

6. The Sermons: Ritual Inscription of Space 102

7. Sermons and the Re-citation of Discourses 115

8. Conclusions 137

Notes 149

Works Cited 161

Index   173

PREFACE

Friday worship is a particularly important event in the weekly calendar of a Muslim. Mosques overflow as worshipers perform ablutions and rush to participate in the weekly service. This can last for only a few minutes or may take up to an hour. The Friday service in a majority Muslim country cannot be missed. Friday is usually the weekly holiday, and amplification systems calling the faithful to prayer become louder. When the time for prayers comes, mosques fill to capacity and many worshipers often squeeze into places on a sidewalk or even a street adjoining the mosque. Friday worship in the middle of "normal" working day in a minority Muslim country such as South Africa is sometimes regarded as an intrusion that has to be tolerated and respected. In terms of the new democratic constitution, however, it can demand unusual rescheduling of office meetings and may make demands on schools to allow Muslim children to attend religious services.

This "intrusion" in any context is multiplied tenfold if the sermon comes under the guidance and control of political protagonists of one sort or another. Internal Muslim conflicts may be obscured from the outsider as petty or queer, but the rise of Islamism in global politics often means that the Friday flow to and from the mosque is continuous. Before the service, the flow of men in clean, often white outfits may resemble a stream, sometimes rushing, sometimes meandering, from a source. And then, about an hour later, the flow can be reversed, sometimes to an equally compelling goal. Anything can flow from a Friday sermon: a Khomeini-like audiocassette that reaches out to followers who have not made it on that day; a march against an embassy; a manifesto for an Islamic state; or a program of action against a perceived problem or threat.

Clearly, this is an onlooker's view, even if a legitimate and sympathetic one, which sees a religious symbol of multiple meanings and references that beckon to be examined. In a snapshot analysis, the Friday sermon could be deciphered in the power of the word and the mosque, the charisma of the individual preacher, the commitment of the worshipers, and the significance of order and regulation in the world around the mosque. This would be an affirmative analysis of the snapshot. It could also be formulated in a more incriminating appraisal, however. The Friday service may serve to highlight and encapsulate the segregation of the sexes, the manipulation of the text, the conformity or indifference of the crowd, and the simultaneous confusion of ablutions, prayers, and sermon. Either way, snapshot analyses disregard the history of the event, the multiple layering of the discourses woven temporarily into a seamless whole.

With the politicization of sermons in Iran, occupied Palestine, and southern Lebanon, it would seem that the depth of this important religious event has no chance of being revealed. The mullah brandishing a Kalashnikov at his side in the pulpit makes an indelible and frightening image. For many Muslims, that image evokes the power of Islam finally standing up to a bully, while observers see the terror of religious wars that should have been over long ago. And yet, both the proud—and sometimes arrogant—Muslim and the horrified observer have missed the deeper levels of this symbol. In the predominant images occupied by Khomeini's tape-recorded sermons bringing about a revolution, and the Cairene mosque preachers watched closely by security forces, the sermons remain obscured. In the modern world, thousands of people making space for a traditional practice remain incredulous. It can only be understood in terms of the political intrigues of Muslim clerics or the instability of the Third World.

In this study I propose to analyze the Friday sermon in the fascinating context of South Africa. It seems to me clear that each Friday sermon takes place within a number of overlapping contexts and corresponding discourses. The history of Muslims in South Africa has had a decided impact on the discourses, which have produced institutions, organizations, and leaders. One of the prominent signs of these discourses is the Friday sermon, which for its variety, aurality, and sheer presence compels greater attention and analysis. As soon as one starts looking more carefully at the sermon, it becomes clear that one cannot separate it from the leaders who produce it or from the mosques within which it is produced. The mosques are not simply brick and mortar, nor are the leaders mere veins and sinews. Mosques and leaders are both products and creators of religious discourse that radiates, now from the vast corpus of Islam, now from the particular history of South Africa. Religious corpus and historical contexts create possibilities and impose limits on the sermon in South Africa.

In one sense, since much of the material is not known outside small circles in South African academic scholarship, the symbols, discourses, and histories that I propose to unpack may be interesting for their novelty. I do not see the telling of these stories as an end in itself, however. As someone involved in the processes discussed in this study, I was not a classical participant-observer but a shameless participant, and I continue to be so. Hence, I began with a symbol of which, to a greater or lesser extent, I was a part. My attempt at unpacking its layers began from the inside and moved out, rather than the usual outsider moving in. I hope to use the opportunity to reflect on the comparative study of modern Islamic societies by using the advantages and disadvantages of this inverse order of investigation and reflection. As will become clear as the text proceeds, I am personally implicated in the mosques and sermons. It concerns me immensely to understand what takes place. Nevertheless, I hope that I have distanced myself sufficiently for others to appreciate the dynamics involved.

My second reason for not simply telling an interesting story lies in the conviction that stories—all of them, and especially academic ones—are carefully constructed out of particular interests and methodologies. There is no interesting story that does not originate from somewhere, rooted in interests and prejudices. I do not want to obscure the roots of my story, namely, the exploration of the sermon-symbol as I participated in it. Third, I choose not to tell a simple story because I deliberately want to deny it the privilege of replacing the lives of Muslims and their histories. This study is not the definitive account of mosques, *imāms*, and sermons in South Africa, from a Muslim viewpoint that no one from the outside could have. Like other accounts, it is born of particular concerns and interests.

I hope to unpack two key mosque traditions in South Africa within which Islamic sermons are located. I have had the opportunity to observe and participate in the Friday services of mosques in each of these traditions: the Claremont Main Road Mosque in Cape Town, center of the Cape tradition, is my religious and intellectual home, where I feel most comfortable even though I often mutter at some of its foibles and trendy flourishes. This mosque has become a symbol of iconoclasm in South Africa, but it is nevertheless part of a history of Islamic institutionalization in the Cape that began at the end of the eighteenth century. The other mosque tradition, represented here by the Brits Mosque in the region of South Africa formerly known as the Transvaal, is the community where I was born and raised. Since 1994, the Transvaal has been divided into four new administrative provinces, and Brits lies in the North West Province. The mosques in the greater region have emerged over a hundred years, and I refer to them as the Transvaal mosques. I take up the challenge of elucidating the contrasting sermons in each mosque within their respective histories and making comparisons within these two Islamic traditions.

Chapter 1 is a methodological framework for understanding Islamic religious symbols as used in this study. Chapters 2 and 3 are devoted to the Cape mosque discourse in the nineteenth and twentieth centuries, with particular focus on locating the Claremont Main Road Mosque. Chapters 4 and 5 repeat the exercise for the Transvaal and the Brits Mosque, and show how a mosque discourse and orthodoxy were constructed in a different historical context. In chapters 6 and 7, I analyze the sermons in the light of the historical and discursive contexts; the focus in chapter 6 is on the ritual inscription of space, while analysis in chapter 7 covers the formal aspects of the sermon as well its rhetoric in the contexts of apartheid and transition to democracy. The final chapter brings together my conclusions on the nature of sermon in historical and discursive contexts; the efficacy of religious institutions in a democratic civil society; and the location of religious change and reinterpretation.

It is my privilege at this point to thank the people of Brits and Claremont who have not shown any consternation at my questions or my sometimes dogged insistence on feigning being on the outside. There are probably many people I will forget, and I ask for their forgiveness, but I would like to express my appreciation for the histories remembered by the people of Brits. I want to single out the imāms, the committee members, and a host of informants mentioned in my notes. I was given access to their time as well as the carefully kept minutes which I used extensively to reconstruct key events in the history of the religious institutions. Most important, however, I want to mention especially the vivid memories of my father, who became my major source. Often, when I approached elders in the community, they were surprised that I was asking them for help when he was the best known for remembering the history of the town. As for Claremont, I want to thank especially Cassiem Saban, Ahmad Bilali Gamieldien, Abu Bakar Hattas, and the Imām A. Rashied Omar for their valuable time. As in Brits, I was also granted access to documents and pamphlets produced by the very active mosque secretary, Fahmi Gamieldien. Some board members, notably M. S. Kagee and Yusuf Omardien, also took the time to read earlier drafts of the manuscript and make valuable comments. The Jamāt Committee of Brits and the Claremont Main Road Mosque Board turned my research inquiries into a pleasant experience.

I have discussed the material presented here with students at both the University of Cape Town and the Islamic College of South Africa. Colleagues across the continents have given of their time and comments. I want to mention especially Dr. Robert Launay, whose patience and criticism helped me to persist with this study; David Westerlund, who read through the manuscript and saw its place in the study of religions in Africa by Africans; and Louis Brenner, who pointed out major gaps in a previous draft but encouraged me not to give up. In the first half of 1998, I also had the privilege of sharing my thoughts with a group of scholars at the University of Virginia. I hope that the work presented here is worthy of their comments. David Chidester, Ebrahim Moosa, and Shamil Jeppie in their unassuming manner always offered a reassuring ear and further review. Our own griot and community historian, Achmat Davids, has helped with his useful comments. My wife, Hawa, and children, Shaheed, Huda, and Tahseen, have once again shown great understanding and patience throughout the process. Finally, I would like to thank the University Research Committee of the University of Cape Town for financial assistance for the research conducted over the years. Naturally, I express my debt to all who were consulted, but I take responsibility for errors and omissions.

1

The Sermon in Islam: A Discursive and Religious Symbol in History

Discerning and interpreting the relationships of Quranic cosmology, worldview and ethos—symbolization between text and context—is a task that invites history of religions research.

Richard Martin

The Islamic sermon has become a useful instrument in sociopolitical praxis. It was used by nationalist movements during anticolonial struggles and then by postcolonial states for legitimating and justifying development, modernization, or simply power. Islamic movements have since recog- *Use of* nized the utility of the sermon and have used it for spreading their mes- *the sermon* sages, organizing campaigns, and charting programs. The sermon seemed *in post* to provide at once an audience, a symbolic place, and a malleable message, *colonial* a combination that leaders, reformers, and visionaries could not resist. As *development,* a symbol, however, the sermon is deeper than its message and more *modernisation,* penetrating than its effects. It is a public platform for a leader to make a *power* weekly statement, but it is much more than that. It may be an occasion for religious people to listen to some words of wisdom, admonition, and re- *Before that* membrance, but it is likewise much more than that. More than an occasion *used to/for* for propaganda, it calls for greater consideration. More than just familiar *anti-colonial* advice, it calls for greater sensitivity and appreciation. For the present *struggle* study, the sermon provided an ideal occasion for appreciating how a reli- gious symbol reflects its varied historical contexts and discourses.

The sermon as symbol as used here benefits from some of the theoretical reflections in the field of religious studies, particularly those pertaining to understanding Islam and Islamic practices. In this chapter I propose a model for understanding the symbol in its historical, social, and religious ramifications. Before setting out on this methodological journey, it may be useful at the outset to state briefly where the discussion is headed. The

Symbols of Islam

symbols of Islam in this study include the major rituals like prayer, fasting, and pilgrimage but also the celebration of the birthday of the Prophet (*mawlid*) and the ritual remembrance of God (*dhikr*). On the one hand, such religious symbols are codes, which can be compared with technical and functional codes used in everyday life. Religious codes are not by nature and essence an entirely separate category from nonreligious codes. Using the resources of the particular religious tradition, religious symbols perform important psychological and social functions for groups and communities: things get done, ideas thought, individual actions defined, and social groups formed. Each of the major practices in Islam may thus be regarded as a discursive practice, always linked to other practices in the tradition. The sermon, in particular, is a discursive practice inextricably linked to mosques and *imāms*. Symbols, however, are more than social strategies. They also point to the metaphysical beings or presence that a particular religious tradition posits. They refer to and draw strength from their connectedness with absolutes. In this sense, I propose that the sermon be related to the re-citation of the Qur'ān, *the* symbol of the divine irruption into the world within Islam. The sermon, I argue, is in fact a re-citation of the Qur'ān on Fridays through which revelation in Islam is extended and renewed.

Practical Purpose of sermon

In the discussion that follows, hence, the symbols of Islam are first placed in a historical context. In particular, South African sermons are symbols shaped and constructed in the context of colonialism and apartheid. Symbols, second, are located in discursive practices within these historical contexts. From Talal Asad, I develop the notion of an Islamic symbol as part of a discourse, which in this case includes imāms and mosques. This understanding of symbols expands the Geertzian conception of a symbolic map by focusing also on acts and statements as strategies and patterns within groups. Third, the discussion moves beyond Asad to suggest a third dimension for an Islamic symbol. A case is made for the religious location and relation of a symbol within a tradition. The sermon, in particular, is more than the sum of its effects. It is linked to the recitation of the Qur'ān and itself identified as a re-citation.

Sermons shaped by colonialism + apartheid

The Historical Location of the Sermon

Religious evaluations and analyses have often been accused of ignoring the historical location of symbols and rituals. Rituals, beliefs, and practices are often thought of as immutable symbols, which escape the positive and deleterious effects of history. Abu-Lughod addressed this when she recalled

Bourdieu's contention that symbols, rituals, and myths were not simply "dispositions that generate and structure practices and representations but are themselves structured by such things as material conditions characteristic of a class condition."[1] Symbols were themselves dynamic and changing, subject to the historical, dynamic forces of change. In the present study, then, the sermon is explored as a historically grounded institution.

At first sight, South Africa may appear a most unlikely place to trace and develop the role of the sermon in Muslim society. If we take into consideration the recent history of the country, Christianity and its enigmatic relationship with both apartheid and the liberation struggle seems a more likely candidate for analysis. More than Islam, it would present a variety of religious sermons for analysis and reflection. The fact is, however, that the history of Islam in South Africa is as long as the history of Christianity, European settlement, and colonialism in the region. The first group of Muslims in the Cape were Amboyan Mardyckers from the Southeast Asian islands, arriving only six years after the Dutch East India Company (Vereenigde Oostindische Campagnie) established a supply outpost in South Africa in 1652. The Cape was only supposed to be a halfway station between Europe and the East, provisioning ships that went around the Cape of Good Hope. Before long, however, it was considered a valuable possession in its own right and was colonized and exploited for its resources.

Since then, South Africa has undergone various forms of European occupation and control. Dutch company rule was followed by English colonization. The occupation of the Cape in 1806 and then the colonization of Natal in 1845 ensured that the entire coastline of present-day South Africa fell under the cloak of the British Empire. Faced with the English presence at the Cape, disgruntled European farmers left the Cape settlement and moved into the interior. They, in turn, subjugated most of the country by the end of the nineteenth century. These trekkers established two republics, which the British promptly took when diamonds and gold were discovered in the second half of the nineteenth century. And most recently, and crowning the long history of conquest and subjugation, apartheid led the country into one of humankind's greatest and most painful tragedies. Throughout this sometimes tragic, sometimes heroic history, Muslims continued to come into the country under varied circumstances. During Dutch company rule, most were brought as slaves, but there were also some prominent political prisoners. The British were responsible for Indian indentured workers, hawkers, Malawian mineworkers, Somali cooks and waiters in their army, and some intrepid international traders. Intermittently, there

Conversions

have also been many conversions from among the indigenous peoples. In one way or another, Muslims have been deeply enmeshed in the 350-year settlement history of South Africa. It would be a mistake to assume that the nature of Islam had little to do with the nature of South Africa.

Islamic practices, institutions, aspirations, and values were not simply a loosely held collage of African, Indian, and Southeast Asian influences. The latter are no doubt present, but they have become as South African as the soccer or rugby played in all parts of the country. Muslims established religious communities in the varying circumstances of South African history. Under Dutch rule, the first Southeast Asian and Bengali slaves were not allowed to observe Islamic practices publicly and thus developed rituals and practices in homes, often drawing on Sufi practices. When businessmen arrived at the east coast port of Durban, they built the first mosque near the Indian market. And when Malawians worked deep in the forests of the eastern Transvaal, they organized Mawlid celebrations on makeshift platforms. In their own ways, Muslims established Islamic practices and institutions within their particular political, legal, and social conditions. Mosques and schools, rituals and leadership, women's practices and youth aspirations all came under the sway of the historical context. The complex relationship between religion and social context is here investigated as expressed through the South African sermon. As a significant practice in Islam, it refracts the social contexts and the religious sense of South African Islam.

Sufi influences

The Sermon as Discursive Symbol

The sermon may be immediately appreciated as a symbol in the most direct sense. If we leave aside the complex application of the term, the sermon may simply mean a sign of Islam as a whole or of the Friday service specifically. For a person who knows little about Islam, the former may more easily come to mind, while more detailed knowledge of the tradition tends to produce a more specific relation. Speculating on what people could associate with the sermon may lead to some creative appropriations. Based on experience, hearsay, or sheer imagination, sermons could be linked to male hegemony, hierarchy, or the importance of the spoken word in Islam. This fantastic play of symbols and referents could go on forever, creatively generating a plethora of associated images. The result, unfortunately, may say much about the process of imagination but have only a tenuous link with the symbols as perceived and conceptualized by Muslims themselves. This employment of symbols as signs or associated references may work well for advertising agencies but not for understanding how Muslims relate to sermons within Islam.

Taking a giant leap from this notion of symbols simply as associations, Geertz developed one of the most persuasive models for understanding symbols in religions. For Geertz, symbols stood at the heart of a religion in society, as is clearly expressed in his famous definition: "religion is a system of symbols which acts to establish powerful, pervasive, and long-lasting moods and motivations in men by formulating conceptions of a general order of existence and clothing these conceptions with such an aura of factuality that the moods and motivations seem uniquely realistic."[2] According to Geertz, symbols formed a complex system that produced a complete map of reality. Symbols performed both the structural task of presenting a worldview, closely associated with the belief system of the religion in question, as well as establishing justification for certain behavior: "[symbols] link these [world view and ethos] in such a way that they mutually confirm one another. Such symbols render the world view believable and the ethos justifiable, and they do it by invoking each in support of the other."[3] Symbols linked beliefs, worldviews, and ethos in a persuasive and "factual" kind of way. In his well-known book *Islam Observed*, Geertz suggested enduring symbolic complexes that captured the essential traits of Islam in Moroccan and Indonesian settings. Sīdī Laḥsen Lyusi, the intemperate, brazen marabout, represented Moroccan Islam, while Kalidjaga's inner contemplative spirit did that for Indonesia. In Geertz's formulation, "Indonesian illuminationism portrays reality as a style of life celebrating mental poise. Moroccan maraboutism portrays reality as a field of spiritual energies nucleating in the persons of individual men, and it projects a style of life celebrating moral passion."[4] Geertz's theory is insightful for illustrating that symbols are not simply signs but complex maps providing the justifications for actions and behavior. Geertz does not ignore the context of Indonesia and Morocco, but shows how symbols were developed in very different histories. He seems to focus on and emphasize the specific cultural assumptions by which people think of the world and then come to act.

However, Geertz's theory, particularly its application in the Islamic context, does not make provision for the symbols and rites within Islam. He does not develop a typical Islamic symbol as part of a conceptual map of reality, nor does he show elements within Islam to be a part of the symbolic complexes like Kalidjaga and Sīdī Lyusi. Generally, Geertz regarded the purely Islamic elements as part of a "universal, in theory standardized and essentially unchangeable, and unusually well-integrated system of ritual and belief."[5] Islamic symbols were simply part of a scripturalist tendency, at once marginal among traders in coastal regions or in the cities of Indonesia and Morocco and disruptive as foreign intrusions. If one were to extend and apply Geertz's theory to scripturalist Islam, then one would have to take more seriously the conceptual map of Islamic scripturalism as it took shape in Indonesia or Morocco. Islamic scripturalism in both countries would be a product of the textual discourse of Islam and the local cultural and historical experience. Geertz, however, is happy to relegate the unchanging Islamic tradition to the periphery of society.

His proposal for a symbolic approach also does not pay sufficient attention to the meanings intended by the actors themselves. Taking their acts and stories as signs, Geertz is more creative than analytical. He resourcefully and competently presents his insights in the form of a key symbolic complex. Such an approach, however, reveals more about the skill of the interpreter than about the participants. It tells us little about the mechanism—old, new, or imperfect—that the religious actors used to shape these symbols or about how they confronted modern challenges. For my purpose, moreover, Geertz's approach totally ignores the symbol's relationship with the sacred in religion.

Combs-Schilling's study of the Moroccan Mawlid celebration of the birthday of the Prophet Muḥammad provides us with an important example of a symbolic approach to a particular Islamic practice. Her approach to symbols differs in key aspects from that of Geertz and provides an opportunity to consider the meaning of symbols in the study of religion from an entirely different perspective. For Combs-Schilling, symbols were functional and effective in society. Their effectiveness was due to their deep resonance in the human condition. The production of Mawlid rituals in the fifteenth century was the most effective cause for the legitimacy and endurance of the Moroccan royal household, the "most durable legacy, the sustaining foundation that renewed Sharifi legitimacy and power when all else faltered."[6] This may appear to be a particular illustration of the political function of Geertz's notion of symbolic systems. But Combs-Schilling's interpretation of the Mawlid performance in Morocco goes much further. For her, symbols, and she focuses particularly on ritual complexes, were essentialist communicative events "conjuring the great rhythmic processes of the universe." The Mawlid poem in Morocco employed such deep human conditions in the service of politics, "institutionaliz[ing] eros . . . [and] turn[ing] sexual passion into religious fervor and political loyalty."[7] The Mawlid celebration established pairs of dominance: humans over animals; men over women; marabouts over ordinary men; and the caliph over all the marabouts. The place of blood, movement, and color (especially red) at key points in the ritual confirmed and sustained such dominance in Moroccan society.

Rituals for Combs-Schilling had a direct effect on history for their resonance in the human condition. She drew attention to scientific theories to support her claims. Thus, for example, the brain recognized eleven basic units of color, which showed that it did not simply work in abstract categories. But Combs-Schilling went even further, arguing that this constituted sufficient justification to suggest a primordial, essentialist use of color in rituals. Using other such similar notions, Combs-Schilling posited fundamental structures of the mind and body and their particular reflections in color, categories, and movements. Religious symbols and rituals employed these fundamental categories to produce worldviews. The symbols were socially and politically effective because they evoked deep human characteristics.[8]

There are basically two interrelated problems with this conception of symbols. Scientific theories suggesting that the mind responded to colors and movements were not sufficient grounds for assuming that the variety of ways in which these colors and movements were used in rituals meant something enduring and unchanging. The scientific theory suggests that the mind was not a collection of abstract ideas, but Combs-Schilling argued that the ritual use of concrete shapes and colors in a particular context corresponded with these neural characteristics. Second, this conception of ritual has to ignore its actual practice. The historical accidents of the ritual in practice may have to be completely ignored to focus on the eternal, primordial worth of the rituals. Hence, the theory would have to assume that individuals and societies have no choice in the kinds of rituals and symbols they adopt and adapt. Habits and political and social contingencies must be ignored when focusing on the eternal resonance of the symbols.

Combs-Schilling's approach to symbols in the study of religion is well recognized, though increasingly criticized. In general, it has affinity with the work of a long list of scholars who seek to ground religion as a category in an essentialist religiosity. Otto called this the holy, while Eliade called it the sensus numinus. Generally, this approach is criticized for "religionizing" the study of religion by introducing unsubstantiated, untestable notions into a disciplined, cross-cultural study of religions in social contexts. Religions ought to be studied as social and empirical phenomena, no more and no less.[9] I reserve judgment on this debate between social context and sensus numinus until later. At this point, this approach must be evaluated in terms of its utility for elucidating and illuminating our understanding of an Islamic symbol, the Mawlid celebration of Morocco. Combs-Schilling connects the Mawlid to the great feast of sacrifice and the first night of marriage. These celebrations together entrench and confirm patriarchy, political legitimacy, and male sexuality. Patriarchy fired the imagination of early Islam and its conquests. Ritual sacrifice in Islam and its rich symbolism celebrated the hierarchy and "rightful domination of father over son, of senior men over junior men, of all males over females and children."[10] As in other Islamic societies, the deep contradiction in Moroccan society lay with female passion: at once loved and despised. On the one hand, the daughter was a potential source of power: "In a daughter, a man has a person who is part of his blood essence, but not a competitor for his blood-earned position of patrilineal dominance, as are sons, and not a potential sexual threat, as are wives and concubines."[11] On the other hand, women in Islam and in Morocco symbolized the threat to the enduring bond with God, truth, and Muḥammad. The rituals, using the symbolism of blood, sexuality, and redness, continually re-created Moroccan monarchy and male supremacy. For Islamic culture, Combs-Schilling imposes a permanent and unchanging interpretation of the Qur'ān on male and female relations and ignores the contradictions inherent in how men interpret them. To take one example, according to Combs-Schilling, the myth of the sacrifice of Abraham "undergirds" domination of father over son, of senior over junior men, and of males over females and children. Yet she fails to mention the power of God over men so central to the sacrifice and so pondered upon by Muslim exegesis. Combs-Schilling does not simply sublimate the hidden agenda of real male hegemony; she conceals the equally liberating notion that men should not arrogate the status of God to themselves.[12]

Whether one accepts the ingenuity of Combs-Schilling's interpretation of the Moroccan Mawlid or not, it is clear that, unlike Geertz, she takes into consideration the specific symbols of Islam and discusses their particular place in a ritual drama and social context. It seems to me, though, that she too failed to take sufficient note of the debates and the discussions that Muslims engaged in about these symbols and ideas. As a good anthropologist, she checked and double-checked her observations with Moroccan informants.[13] What was missing, however, was what Asad has called the discourses generated by Muslims over the centuries and through which they produced worldviews and aspirations. For Asad, the anthropological study of Islam as the primary object "should be approached as a discursive tradition that connects variously with the formation of moral selves, the manipulation of populations (or resistance to it), and the production of appropriate knowledges."[14] Geertz had unfortunately dismissed these traditions as a nebulous scripturalism, while Combs-Schilling saw eternal, timeless symbols where there were elaborate and complex historical practices. By not taking sufficient note of the many different interpretations of texts, rituals, and selves, Combs-Schilling missed some of the most creative human features of the ritual drama.

The study of religion as a discourse approaches religious symbols in a unique manner. They are neither merely the symbols of Geertz constructing a conceptual map of reality nor the essentialist symbols of the human condition as used by Combs-Schilling. The symbols of religions are codes, which can be compared with technical and functional codes used in everyday life, through which things get done, ideas thought, and social groups formed. The formation of a conceptual map and the entrenchment of male hegemony were products of a discursive symbol system. Religious codes were not a completely separate category by nature and essence. They could be placed within a single continuum of symbolic, expressive, and sacred codes at one extreme and technical, functional, and profane codes at the other. For Asad, rites and symbols in religions are "disciplinary practices" of which actors are aware, and with which they practice their religion.[15] Asad certainly placed religious symbols in their social space, but unlike Geertz, he placed the study of Islam, and religious symbols and rites generally, in the context of their production. The discursive practices of Islam included its legal, theological, and exegetical strategies, which had to be brought into the discussion of specifically Islamic societies, communities, and practices. Hence, it was not sufficient to read the sermon as a symbol of male power without discussing this significance in the rubric of legal prohibitions, conditions, and social spaces. This kind of discursive study should not ignore or deny the male dominance in the ritual but should locate it within the mechanisms by which it was produced by Muslim actors, using specific modes of engagement, justifications, and reasons.

An examination of Asad's application of his ideas in a chapter in *Genealogies of Religions* helps to clarify its particular relevance for the study of the sermon here. Asad's analysis pertains to the Saudi sermon, which he correctly identified as part of a political critique in Islamic society. This criticism was produced by young 'ulamā' graduates of Saudi universities in recent years. Asad called it "morally corrective criticism" and contrasted it with the criticism of the Enlightenment tradition of Europe.[16] He then differentiated this particular Islamic practice of admonition from those of two other groups in Saudi society. The first, the elder 'ulamā', many of whom were the teachers of the critics, were asked and expected by the king to respond to them. The senior 'ulamā' had become a long-standing part of the legitimating apparatus employed by the Saudi monarchy.[17] On the other hand, the Western-educated intellectuals discussed their criticism in private, approaching Saudi princes through direct contact. According to Asad, these two groups, unlike the first, did "not characterize their criticism in terms of the Islamic concept of nasīhah (admonishment)."[18]

For Asad, the sermon as admonishment was a useful example to illustrate how a tradition constructed a critical discourse, one distinctively different from the Enlightenment tradition. According to Asad, the discourse of the Enlightenment could not be extricated from the peculiar and particular history and politics of Europe. Religion, as understood by anthropologists and most social scientists, Asad argued, was part of this tradition. In this regard, the core of religion could only be related to the affirmation of spiritual beings, beliefs connected to this, and appropriate attitudes; it excluded practices with social and political intent. Asad illustrated this development in Europe through a systematic study of the definitions of religion, especially as formulated by Geertz and the key encyclopedias of Europe. Religion as political practice or religion as social action could not constitute its core, essential characteristic. Any religious act that had a direct political intention was regarded as the political abuse of religion and not part of its chief function. From this Enlightenment perspective of religion, the political engagement of a religious sermon, as illustrated in the Saudi example, could only be conceived as a manipulation. For the Saudis, acting as they did within the discursive practice of Islamic politics in context, the sermon as admonition was part of religion and not incidental to it.

While Asad's analyses served to illustrate the Islamic case as different from that of the Enlightenment, he did not take seriously the varieties of readings among Muslims themselves. By recognizing the sermon of the young 'ulamā' as nasīhah in the Islamic tradition, admittedly different from the Enlightenment, he omitted its actual location in the context of modern Saudi society. During the past century, many more developments have taken place, particularly in terms of the major actors defining the nature and limits of what is religious in the Muslim society. These developments include, among other things, the different interpretations and location of traditional Wahhābī supporters of the state, as opposed to those of the new graduates of Islamic universities. To these must be added the proponents of increased modernization. They include rapid modernization, even though this has been guided by an autocratic regime. In the face of this complexity, Asad elevated the admonition of the young 'ulamā' at the expense of the subservient and discreet advice and counsel of the court 'ulamā' and Western-educated intellectuals respectively. Like the young puritan 'ulamā', surely, the intellectuals could also be described as providing naṣīḥah in terms of classical Islamic models. They were recognizable traditions within the society, even though discredited by the political positions they held in legitimation of the Saudi state.

Asad's focus on the discourse of Islam and his reference to the discursive traditions of Muslims themselves is a useful model. However, in highlighting the differences between Islamic and Enlightenment discourses, he seems ambivalent about modern Islamic discourses. On the one hand, he excludes them: "And I refer here primarily not to the programmatic discourses of 'modernist' and 'fundamentalist' Islamic movements, but to the established practices of unlettered Muslims."[19] On the other hand, he accepts that the Islamic tradition will change under the impact of industrial capitalism and suggests that "an anthropology of Islam will therefore seek to understand the historical conditions that enable the production and maintenance of specific discursive traditions, or their transformation—and the efforts of practitioners to achieve coherence."[20] Modernist and fundamentalist Islamic discourses, as well as a host of other contextual religious and political Islamic discourses, should in principle be included in this assessment of Islamic discursive traditions in the modern world. The new discourses cannot be dissociated from the traditional discourses, but their modern productions too must not be overlooked.

Nevertheless, Asad's approach to naṣīḥah, admonition, as a disciplinary practice within society, may usefully be applied to an examination of other religious practices. In this study of the sermon in South Africa, a similar approach is followed in exploring the disciplinary dimension of sermons. Principally, it is shown that in the South African context, more than admonishment is produced in the discursive practices of mosque rhetoric. These additional discursive features of the sermon are uncovered by paying close attention to the mosque and imām traditions in South Africa. No sermon can take place without a preacher, a position which is itself a disciplinary product. Neither is a preacher possible without a mosque, its location, its particular religious orientation, and its management. Sermons in two very different kinds of South African mosques are examined as discursive events expressed in mosques and preachers.

As a place for worship, the mosque has come under considerable scrutiny in recent studies. Following Eickelman's insights on the place of the shrine in the context of extreme segmentation in Boujad, Morocco, mosques have been identified as neutral zones where differences were temporarily resolved or at least held in tense balance.[21] Using this model, Gilsenan's study of the organization of space in a Lebanese village described the older mosque as "a meeting point, the only possible meeting point, of this highly stratified community."[22] In contrast to the older mosques in Lebanon, he described the new mosques as ostentatious signs of power and authority claimed by a new religiopolitical presence. This presence was not really a true religious form, according to Gilsenan, as much as a product of a political and bourgeois expression of Islam. Gilsenan's judgment on the newer mosque marks the mosque as a symbol of identity and has also been used in a host of other contexts.[23] This negative judgment of new mosques and their deliberate attempts to make a statement in society, however, reflects the Enlightenment notion of religion as pointed out by Asad. But Gilsenan's study also matched the two mosques with two different kinds of meeting places in the village. The village mosque corresponded to the *majlis* while the ostentatious mosques corresponded to the salon. Gilsenan noted that the contrasting acts inside the majlis and salon created the places. The majlis was "characterized by the wide range of transformation that can occur within it," including sleeping, eating, and card playing, while the salon was "one-dimensional, full of objects rather than significations, desacralized—shoes are kept on; carpets show wealth and taste and are not for sitting on or for prayer; the Quranic verses on the walls are decorations rather than powerful signs."[24] Both majlis and salon were produced by signs and significations and suggest that their mosque counterparts were equally responsive to the acts and rituals that took place inside them. Sermons, as well as prayers, individual devotions, and communal gatherings in their variety, created special characteristics of mosque spaces. These acts were discursive practices that literally created unique mosque spaces.

Like the mosques, the religious leadership serving the mosques and delivering the sermons were also subject to discursive determination. In classical models, research on Muslims has used Weberian ideal-type categories to distinguish between Sufis as charismatic leaders, jurists as rational bureaucrats, and Sharifs as the quintessential traditionalists. The Sufi's charismatic authority rested on the spiritual feats performed by himself or his teacher; the jurist proved his mettle in Islamic legal discourse; while the descendant basked in the glory of pure blood flowing through his veins.[25] In a particular locality, Muslim communities would recognize the jurists, the Sufi, or the Sharif and would respect, condemn, or celebrate them. I regard the ideal types not simply as classifications by social theorists but as recognizable and identifiable patterns in a mosque community. A leader becomes a leader when he or she conforms, more or less, to the pattern or discourse established. Both historical context and religious values produce recognizable ideal types for prospective leaders and communities. Recent political developments in Iran illustrate these changing expectations. The Iranian mullah in the wake of the Islamic revolution would be constituted by a combination of three discursive traditions: his Shi'ite legacy as a jurist, prayer leader, or charismatic ayatollah; Iranian national history; and the revolutionary expectations thrust upon leaders since 1979. Like the mosques, discourses guided the expectations, the limits, and the possibilities of what might be expected of leaders.

An examination of the sermon cannot ignore the historical context and discursive strategies employed in the formation of the mosques and leaders. They represent the immediate conditions for the sermon and are directly reflected in it. As I show in this study, the sermon in Cape Town produced individuality and uniqueness in the particular authoritative status of the preacher, in the administrative organization of the mosques, and in the sermon's delivery and metaphors. All of these—leadership models, space, performance, and metaphors—were products of discursive practices in the Cape and came into play when the imām ascended the pulpit to deliver his sermon. The Transvaal sermon is shown to produce orthodoxy using similar disciplinary practices and strategies.

Metaphysical Ambitions

The historical location and the discursive power of a sermon do not exhaust the study of its symbolic dimension. When the particular contextual bias of the preacher has been revealed, and the discursive mechanisms unpacked, we would still be left guessing as to the particular value of the sermon in relation to Islam as religion. The historical location and discursive practices are important social dimensions of the religion. The sociological analysis of the sermons indicates how religions create maps for reality (Geertz) or create powerful disciplinary selves, groups, and institutions (Asad). However, it does not reflect the place and power of the sermon in relation to its specifically religious dimension. Thus, for example, daily worship (ṣalāh) may be interpreted and analyzed in its complex social and psychological dimensions. However, within the religion, it would be taught as the way of worship, adoring God in humble submission. In short, ṣalāh is worship. Whether one accepts the reality of God or not, the analysis of ṣalāh cannot exclude this devotional dimension.

This aspect of the sermon takes account of the debates in the study of religion pertaining to the reality or otherwise of its metaphysical dimension. Platvoet calls this the multi-tiered notion of reality posited by most religions, which cannot be subject to scrutiny and examination by the single-tier discourse of the comparative study of religions. Platvoet's proposed operational definition for religion addresses the problem by highlighting its problematic. Religion for Platvoet is "postulated communicative events within believed networks of relationships between believers and their non-verifiable/non-falsifiable beings or addressable reality."[26] "Non-verifiable/non-falsifiable beings or addressable reality" refers to ultimate reality, gods or God. Since this reality is not testable by an empirical science of religion, it cannot be made the object of disciplined investigations. In many instances, this means that the dimension of the religious practices directly connected to the nonverifiable/nonfalsifiable beings is bracketed and is often ignored in the conclusions that follow. Durkheim's famous example of "religion as cohesion" subsumed the efficacy of nonverifiable/nonfalsifiable beings or addressable reality into society. Using his definition, Platvoet proposes that balancing positivism and nonreductionism may solve the reductionist problem.[27] Alas, he does not provide an example of this neat solution.

I do believe that one can and should go beyond reductionism without having to make substantial religious pronouncements. On the basis of empirical observations, the orientation and meaning of symbols and rituals in a particular religion should be analyzed for their relation to nonverifiable/nonfalsifiable beings or addressable reality. This would not necessarily deny their social or personal implications, but it would at least recognize and take into account the "fact" of these nonverifiable/nonfalsifiable beings or addressable realities. For worship in Islam, for example, such a dimension may lead to an awareness of the relation established between God and the believer. Such a relationship may be compared fruitfully with ṣalāh in different Islamic contexts and under the influence of different schools of thought. More widely, fruitful comparisons may also be made in this particular religious dimension with worship and prayer in other religions. In the case of the sermon, the significance of this religious dimension may not be immediately apparent. A ritual speech has an immediate social and psychological impact, which would seem to obviate the importance of searching for a deeper religious significance. However, a closer look at the sermon discloses and clarifies this religious significance apart from its social significance. In fact, a brief survey of studies on the Islamic sermon illustrates the gaps left by social analyses of the sermon that neglect the dimension to which I am referring.

The potential of the sermon as a rhetorical instrument, and its competition among protagonists of every hue, has drawn the attention of scholars to its role in modern Islamic society. The sermon as a speech directed to an audience has been recognized and noted as a prescribed feature in Islamic ritual. In addition, the frequent citation of the Qur'ān in the sermons has been noted. However, the focus of the analyses has rested on the social effects of the sermon in relation to modernization, the legitimacy of the state, and Islamization. Recognizing the social function of the sermon and the preacher in Muslim society, scholars have tried to appraise their effect in the transformation of Muslim society. The key question engaging most observers has been the effect of the Islamic sermon in promoting or retarding modernization. The results have not been very conclusive. Some preachers were found to be promoting modernization, while others were obstacles to that end.

One of the earliest essays on the modern Islamic sermon, by Borthwick in 1967, categorically stated that the Islamic sermon could not promote development. As a rhetorical device expressed in formalized speech, the sermon maintained the established hierarchy in society. Moreover, because of its citation and use of formulaic and archaic patterns, it was not able to deal with specific, potentially divisive issues.[28] Since Borthwick's study in the 1960s, the role of Islam in politics has changed dramatically. The effectiveness of Islam as a political ideology can no longer be denied, and subsequent studies reversed Borthwick's judgment. In particular, Antoun's seminal 1989 work on the sermon in a Jordanian village found that, beyond its potential for political mobilization, the sermon was able to mediate and promote social change. Contrary to Borthwick, Antoun in an extensive study of a village preacher in Jordan recorded the use of colloquial Arabic in the sermons as well as finding willingness to depart from classical sermon models. He also showed how the preacher dealt with contentious issues like kinship relations and political parties.[29] More directly, Antoun related the effectiveness of the sermon in promoting development by using a religious idiom. Appreciating the place and significance of Islam in the village of Kufr al-Ma, Antoun proposed that the preacher was a culture broker who stood midway between the textual tradition of the religious scholars (the 'ulamā') and village customs. Antoun argued that the preacher in Jordan was able to reproduce religious values from the great tradition of Islam in the village community. He actively promoted a greater degree of conformity toward Islamic practices, attending regular worship and going on pilgrimage to Mecca. Social and political problems in the village were appraised in terms of their standard textual felicity. Village customs and traditions that resisted change were marginalized by scripturalist religious principles. According to Antoun, the sermon in the

Jordanian village was always in favor of modernization—but not Western-ization. Modernization in the Jordanian village took place in a particular sociocultural framework.[30]

Antoun's positive appraisal of the Islamic sermon in general, and the Islamist sermon in particular, does not account for the preachers in the Middle East standing with rifles at their sides. Replacing the rod with a dangerous weapon, they seemed to project a dreadful image of the Friday sermon. Gaffney's study of preachers in Egypt has accounted for Antoun's more moderate preachers as well as these radicals. Like Antoun, he found that some preachers promoted development, while others inhibited it. Gaffney showed that only the sermons of preachers broadly committed to the Egyptian state promoted development by supplying relevant religious justifications. When this political compliance and acquiescence was absent, however, the sermons were easily turned against the state; in such cases, preachers elevated the ordinary and inconsequential lives of the masses in Egypt to epic roles of good against evil. Exploiting the binary contrasts of "us" and "them," and "believer" and "disbeliever," they increased the po-tential for conflict as they painted a utopian ideal in which ordinary people could vicariously participate. Such sermons, according to Gaffney, did not change the lives of the people but created attitudes with which the modern Egyptian state could not deal.[31]

In a more extensive study, Gaffney related these two types of sermons to literary models. Moderate sermons, supporting development and address-ing the social and political needs of society, were identified as metaphors. In these sermons, the founding texts of Islam (the Qurʾān and the Prophetic examples) were carefully applied to new contexts. The metaphorical ten-sion between the texts of classical Islam and the context of modern Egypt were carefully controlled by those concerned about the desperate needs of Egypt. Emphasis was placed upon the application of values and principles from one context to another. In contrast, radical sermons were metonymic in the literary sense of the word, where the identities of text, contexts, and modern preachers were completely fused. According to Gaffney, met-onymic sermons rendered God, the Qurʾānic text, and modern society com-pletely indistinguishable.[32] Sermons formulated utopian and radical revi-sionist programs in the emotionally charged contexts of mosques. In the sermon, the Prophet himself urged the faithful to march against the secular national state.

The identification of rhetorical strategies of the preachers, and their po-tency for promoting or thwarting the goals of social and political develop-ment, were important for understanding what sermons actually achieved in different contexts. However, these particularly functionalist questions posed about sermons in a modern state have almost completely obscured their religious dimensions. The title of Gaffney's study, *The Prophet's Pulpit: Islamic Preaching in Contemporary Egypt*, suggests that the preachers were occupying an important religious space. Gaffney traced the sermon's principal office in Islam to the leadership of Prophet Muḥammad. He then showed how succeeding political leaders manipulated this powerful position, deteriorating in later periods to formulaic statements on behalf of caliphs and sultans.[33] In Gaffney, it seems that only the radical preacher, in his misappropriation of the Prophetic role, took on a purely religious dimension. Only he dared to break all boundaries between texts, context, and first recipient and thus become the Prophet. Antoun revealed even less of the religious dimensions of the sermon. He pointed to its religious significance in early Islam but offered nothing much about the modern sermon as a religious element within Islamic practices and beliefs. Observers of the modern Islamic sermon, then, bracketed the religious element in the sermon but ended up either ignoring it or warning against its negative effects for development or effective government control. The religious or metaphysical object or value of the sermon remained obscured.

The key to appreciating the religious and metaphysical object and value of the sermon lay in understanding the meaning of the Qur'ān in Islam and in Islamic society. The sermon in this dimension reflected the aural and oral recitation of the Qur'ān, the importance of which in Muslim society has been pointed out in numerous studies. Graham at least has focused on the nature and appreciation of the Qur'ān beyond its role as a rulebook and a text to be read, commented upon, and analyzed. He has located it broadly within a family of religious texts that are heard and appreciated orally and aurally.[34] The Qur'ān is not only the text but also its recitation, according to Graham. Recitation was a rereading, even a recall, of the revelation given to the Prophet Muḥammad. Thus, for Hodgson, the Qur'ānic recitation was "an act of commitment in worship" in which "the event of revelation is renewed."[35] Wilfred Cantwell Smith, in a recent work on religious scripture, confirmed this Qur'ānic presence in recitation. The Qur'ān, he said, was "the ipsissima verba of God Himself; God speaking to humankind not merely in seventh-century Arabia to Muḥammad, but from all eternity to every man and woman throughout the world—including the individual Muslim as he or she reads or recites it or devoutly holds it, or vividly or dimly or even unconsciously remembers a passage or phrase from it."[36] This recitation could be located in many Islamic practices, including but not exclusively the Qur'ān recitals that Muslims all over the world appreciate in beautiful and masterful renderings. In modern times, the names of competitions in Indonesia, Egypt, and Iran have become household words, evoking contests where the world's best reciters compete at reciting the word of God.[37] The recited Qur'ān has not been missed by Antoun or Gaffney in the Friday sermon. As Antoun recalled for the Jordanian village, "the Qur'ānic verses, traditions of the Prophet, and prayer formulae ... lac[ing] the sermons together are the ultimate reality for both the preacher and his listeners." Referring to the experience of Qur'ānic recitation as the ultimate encounter with God, Antoun believed that the Friday service best provided this opportunity: "But the most regular and significant recitation of the Qur'ān is on the occasion of the Friday congregational prayer service. Recitation precedes the Friday sermon and follows it, and the preacher punctuates his sermons with appropriate verses as does the worshiper in the culminating Friday congregational prayer."[38]

The memory of the Qur'ān appeared to repeat that first event. In reality, however, every recitation was also a re-citation when the contexts and complex resources of the Qur'ān in society were taken into account. I use hyphenation to emphasize the spaces and the interference between different recitations, whether that of Gabriel, the Prophet Muḥammad, or any other subsequent reader. Both spaces and interferences are dynamically positive attributes. The only threats they may pose are not to the text as such but to rigid notions of recitation. The "oral, performative, dialogic Qur'ān [was] encoded" in a list of debates, dogmas, and narratives like the illiteracy (ummiyyah) of the Prophet, the theory of revelation, script, and teacher.[39] This hermeneutical, dialogic nature of the Qur'ān cannot be understated, because the recitation, memorization, and transmission of the Qur'ān was deceptive in the way it appeared to reproduce itself. In the sermon, then, the Qur'ān resonated not only in the numerous quotations from it, although no doubt preachers cited the Qur'ān profusely and drew all kinds of lessons, allegories, and analogies from its chapters and verses. But they did much more than recite when they did so. As they related the Qur'ān to new contexts and new teachings, they re-cited the texts for these contexts. In sermons, preachers literally re-cited the Qur'ān by producing, in form and performance, their own compositions. They not only repeated the first act of revelation and recitation from Gabriel to Muḥammad but continued it. The sermon was not simply a speech act or admonishment. In terms of the nonverifiable/nonfalsifiable reality that Islam posited as a religion, the sermon was an occasion for a divine irruption. It recalled and reproduced, however dimly, the divine irruption in seventh-century Arabia. This does not preclude the function and role of the sermon as a speech act. As an oral and aural statement, the sermon may admonish, justify, threaten, or teach. Like any other speech, it can also induce a compelling urge to sleep. The recognition of these social functions, however, cannot ignore its religious value. One could possibly study the social effects of a sermon without taking into consideration this religious dimension, but it would be eliminating an important dimension of a sermon within a mosque in Islam.

The contrasting pair of recitation and re-citation has a distant echo in the theological debate on the nature of the Qur'ān. The Mu'tazilites opted for its createdness as a text and book, even as they believed in its divine origin. The Sunnite position, championed by Aḥmad b. Ḥanbal (d. 241/855), was that it was not created but was the word of God, pure and simple. Some of the later scholars reflected on the recitation of the Qur'ān and made a distinction between a recitation (qirā'ah), "the oral reading or recitation on one side, which is our material action," and maqrū', "that which is read or recited on the other; that which is brought to expression, God's intention, His thinking as we might say." This, according to van Ess, was the view of Ibn Kullāb, who rejected the Mu'tazilite position but still opened the space for human recitation. Van Ess produced a list of subsequent authorities who took a similar position, thereby introducing a consideration of the human element in the recitation of a divine tract.[40] Both qirā'ah and maqrū' were derived from the root qr', the one a verbal noun and the other a passive noun. In Islamic theological discussion, an attempt was being made to keep apart God's word and the human retelling of it. In the discourse of modern religious studies, I am trying not to ignore the metaphysical dimension. This can be done by appealing to the classical theological discussion, the notion that either form of recitation, an act of subjectivity, is always rooted in a hermeneutic. Thus emerges a delicate balance between recitation and re-citation. The boundaries between qirā'ah and maqrū' converge at the level of performance in a ritual context as they converge around the root verb.

So far, a case has been made for simply recognizing the metaphysical and religious dimension of the religious symbol or ritual. As far as the sermon is concerned, this religious dimension is also the source of creativity. This cannot remain at the level of theological speculation, because it yields opportunities for the reciters. The sermon has the responsibility to disseminate and formulate the discourses of the mosques and the imāms. While it would be expected to reflect the context and discourses as a historical phenomenon, its revelatory dimension provides an opportunity for creativity as well. The sermons, through this powerful notion of re-citation, provide a vehicle for determining how a particular social practice was articulated. In the two mosque traditions under investigation here, the sermons produced metaphors for elaborating the dominant discourses in context. The Claremont Main Road Mosque sermon re-cited the dilemmas and opportunities of a progressive Islam, while the Brits mosque articulated orthodoxy. In Asad's example, the sermon re-cited the Saudi critique of the king, and Gaffney's preachers re-cited legitimation and delegitimation of the state in Egypt.

The model for understanding an Islamic ritual as proposed in this chapter, then, has to begin with the historical context, which provides the important crucible within which a discourse of authority, correct practices, identities, and communities is founded. Such a discourse is produced by the historical conditions prevailing in a given situation as well as by the religious resources of individuals and groups. The disciplinary patterns within religions are rich and varied. They range from received knowledge of correct procedure in a ritual, intricate ramifications of legal philosophy, and elaborate detail and implications in theology to the deep secrets of mystical experience. These disciplinary practices take shape in a particular context, and give shape to the context in turn. In spite of the social significance of this complex, moreover, the ritual still has a religious and metaphysical dimension. As far as the religious tradition is concerned, this dimension of the symbolic may be the source of creativity. In the following chapters, I propose to apply this model to two mosque traditions in South Africa.

2

Creation of the Cape Mosque Discourse

Shaykh Abu Bakr Najjar, *Sufi Shaykh* one of the most illustrious leaders of a prominent District Six Mosque in Cape Town, never tired of reminding his friends in Johannesburg that he would not exchange his low-paying position for a lucrative one in the city of gold. Compared to the religious leaders in this rich city, the Cape imām enjoyed the honor, respect, and deference befitting a king, he would say. Shaykh Najjar felt and enjoyed what had developed in the Cape over two hundred years, during which Muslims produced a distinctive discursive tradition in mosque establishment. In this tradition, the Cape imām enjoyed the status of nothing less than a revered Sufi shaykh. In the context of colonialism and apartheid, the mosque and imām discourse defined leadership and authority in patterns of education, ritual, and community participation.

The Foundations *Mosque sermons provided leadership + authority in education, rituals, + community participation*

In 1652, after many years of passing the Cape of Good Hope on the way to the East, the Dutch Vereenigde Oostindische Campagnie established a refreshment station at the southern tip of Africa, the southwestern peninsula of what is now South Africa. The station was expected to supply ships with fresh food and water on their long journeys. The local inhabitants, the indigenous Khoi and the San, called Hottentots by the settlers, soon realized the station's insatiable hunger for land and cattle and resisted its expansion. This conflict became the context in which the first Muslims arrived in South Africa. In 1658, the Mardyckers from Amboya were brought to protect the settlement against the San and Khoi. It was a context steeped in irony, though, as the Mardyckers, brought to serve the interests of European colonists, were still regarded as second-class residents in relation to the free European burghers. The Mardyckers' position between the colonizers and the indigenous people has become an enigma and often a dilemma experienced by many Muslims since. Even the more recent apartheid ideology in South Africa ensured that most Muslims, classified as Indian and "Coloured" (officially meaning of mixed race), escaped the brunt of the worst forms of discrimination but were nevertheless second-class citizens like the Mardyckers.[1] This awkward political position is often reflected in the religious discourses developed by Muslims.

The vast majority of Muslims arrived at the Cape under much more adverse conditions than the Mardyckers. The Dutch company in the Cape depended heavily on slaves, who were bought from all over Africa and Asia but especially Madagascar, India, and the Southeast Asian islands, all having significant Muslim populations.[2] The company also used the Cape as a place of exile for political prisoners from the Southeast Asian islands. From 1667 onward, some of these exiles were prominent Muslim leaders. Brought in 1694 after a long and bitter struggle against the Dutch and its surrogates in the East, Shaykh Yusuf of Macassar was the most prominent of such exiles. He was not allowed to live inside Cape Town for fear of any possible influence he might exert over the small slave population. On the other hand, the Dutch governors treated him with great respect and decorum. Shaykh Yusuf was stationed on the farm Zandvliet at the mouth of the Storms River and lived there until his death in 1699.

Since the Mardyckers were not permitted to practice their religion in public, we have no record of the kind of religious activities they must have nurtured in private. Some contemporary Muslim scholars, therefore, have suggested that Shaykh Yusuf established the first Muslim community in South Africa, attracted runaway slaves who converted to Islam, and represented a symbol of resistance to European colonialism. In a book marking three hundred years of Muslim history in the Cape, Dangor had this to say of the first community: "Under the leadership of Shaykh Yusuf, who was 68 years of age when he arrived here, the group of Zandvliet formed one of the first very elementary structures of a Muslim community, and they came to represent the first area of resistance to colonization at the Cape."[3]

From this perspective, the foundation of the mosque tradition in South Africa should begin with Shaykh Yusuf. The figure of Shaykh Yusuf, however, is shrouded in the contemporary perceptions of Muslims and their long history in the country. Rafudeen's review of the primary and secondary documents revealed that the foundation of this earliest community is based on some tenuous evidence, plagued by numerous unsubstantiated claims and by mistranslation. The only significant statement referring to conversion, for example, was a Dutch reference to the high birth rate among Muslims. The phrase "dese Mohmetanen, door geboorte in getal, hoe langer, hoe meerder, zyn toenemende" has been creatively translated as meaning "multiplying" Muslims through conversion.[4] Moreover, company officials would have prevented influential exiles like Shaykh Yusuf, who had offered dogged resistance to the Dutch in the East, from founding any significant resistance groups in the Cape.

There is no doubt, though, that the memory of these political exiles and prominent personalities became an important part of Muslim religious consciousness and practices. It is not clear how soon this took place. Shaykh Yusuf's gravesite was at least a place of veneration in the first half of the nineteenth century.[5] This continued until an elaborate tomb was built around his grave in 1909.[6] Veneration of the shaykh has continued to grow in this century so that even today, Cape Muslims would not go to Mecca without first visiting the shrine of Shaykh Yusuf. Contemporary references to his anti-Dutch resistance as well as his foundation of anticolonialist activities inside the Cape cannot be extricated from this religious veneration. It was a social and political appropriation of a religious symbol. Shaykh Yusuf has become a key symbol of Muslim presence in South Africa.[7] Ignoring the Mardyckers, a Tri-Centenary Committee used the arrival of Shaykh Yusuf as the foundation of the first Muslim community. On the eve of the first democratic elections in the country, Muslims in Cape Town turned out in their thousands to celebrate three hundred years in South Africa. The high point of the celebration was a mass encampment around Shaykh Yusuf's tomb. It was a significant indication of how Shaykh Yusuf had been adopted as a symbol of Muslim presence in the country and Islamic resistance to colonialism and apartheid.

In spite of the importance of Shaykh Yusuf for contemporary Muslim identity, the search for the development of a mosque discourse must begin elsewhere. It lay neither in the first Muslims who came to the country nor in the prominent symbol of Islamic presence in South Africa. The institutionalization of Islam took shape during the second half of the eighteenth century when another group of Muslims were sent to the Cape as Banndieten (convicts) who conspired against the British. Some also came with authoritative Islamic credentials and set the foundations of Islamic institutions. Unlike the early exiles, who were often scattered in isolation outside the city, the convicts lived among the slaves and free black people.

Consequently, they had a better chance to develop institutions for the early Islamic community.

Political developments in Europe and South Africa provided unexpected opportunities for the establishment of Islam in public. In 1795, when Napoleon invaded the Netherlands, the Dutch House of Orange asked the English to occupy the Cape on their behalf.[8] Once in the Cape, the British introduced relatively more liberal measures with regard to the practice of religion, thus providing the political climate for the foundation of the first mosque. From within the Muslim community, the person directly involved in the establishment of the first religious school and mosque was one of the convicts brought to the Cape. He was Imām Abdullah Kadi Abdus Salaam, who was brought to the Cape in 1780 and imprisoned on Robben Island. Known as Tuan Guru, he was an able scholar and, while in prison, wrote the Qur'ān from memory as well as a book on jurisprudence and theology, *Ma'rifah al-Islam wa al-Imān*.[9] Upon his release in 1793, Tuan Guru devoted himself to teaching and also led the Muslims in congregational prayers, sometimes in the quarries of the city.[10] According to Davids, he was also responsible for the foundation of the first mosque, called Awwal Mosque, in 1798 on a piece of land that belonged to Saartjie van de Kaap, the wife of one of his students, Achmat van Bengalen.[11] Permission for such a building was obtained by the Muslim leaders from General Craig immediately after the English took control of the Cape.

The Central Role of the Imām

This narrative of the first institution of Islam at the Cape calls for some examination in order to delineate the particular mosque tradition that began to take shape. The Cape mosque was led by one prominent imām to the exclusion of any other contenders. The emergence of this focus on a single person can be gleaned from the foundation of the Awwal Mosque, particularly in the role of Tuan Guru and the exclusion of another prominent personality, Frans van Bengalen. Tuan Guru became the legendary first teacher and imām in the community, which concealed the mechanism by which the discursive tradition took root. Contrary to popular belief, the institutionalization of Islam in the Cape was not led by only one man. Frank Bradlow's examination of the evidence from the early nineteenth century reveals the prominence of Frans van Bengalen, with a slightly different interest and approach to the foundation of the mosque. Van Bengalen was a prominent slave "who purchased his own freedom and went [on] to become rich and himself a slave-owner."[12] His failed ambition underscores the uniqueness of the

Cape Islamic leadership tradition. His failure to acquire a prominent position in the Awwal Mosque reveals one of the key components of the Cape mosque discourse: imāms share leadership only grudgingly with other interest groups in the mosque.

In his statement to the Colebrooke and Brigge Commission investigating the conditions of black people in the Cape in 1825, the then imām of the Awwal Mosque, Achmat van Bengalen, stated that his predecessor, "who died about three years ago . . . was the first who had been allowed to officiate and build a place of worship."[13] Since Tuan Guru died in 1807, Bradlow argued that this person was Frans van Bengalen, who died sometime in 1821 or 1822.[14] Davids, on the other hand, suggested that "the principal Imams in 1797 applied for a mosque," and he reconstructed a corresponding line of succession consisting of these "principal" leaders. Thus, according to Davids, Tuan Guru was followed by Abdulalim (d. circa 1810), who in turn was followed by Sourdeen (who "probably" died in 1822).[15] Achmat van Bengalen's statement to the Colebrooke and Brigge Commission, however, referred to only one person who was "allowed to officiate and build a place of worship," and David's theory of a group applying for a mosque seems unlikely.

In my view, Frans van Bengalen had probably applied for the foundation of the mosque but had not been an imām as such. My argument for this position is based on a number of observations. First, it is not impossible to conceive that the Awwal Mosque was established soon after General Craig had granted permission, a point Bradlow seems to doubt. This establishment may have meant setting aside a place especially for prayer—not necessarily equipped with the domes and minarets and other such characteristic features easily identified by visitors and travelers. In Bradlow's analysis of the available literary evidence, it is clear that visitors in the nineteenth century, on whom he relies for the presence of mosques, repeatedly mistook houses for the kinds of mosques they expected in Islamic cities. The first mosque in the Cape may not have symbolized the presence of Muslims to outsiders. This is a case in which the search for the mosque as a symbol of Muslim presence obscured the mosque as a meeting place for organization and religious devotion. The absence of a mosque as a clear, unequivocal symbol of Muslim status for the public did not preclude its presence as a place of worship, equally important for the elaboration of Muslim institutions. It is quite plausible that the liberal atmosphere of the time led the Muslims to set aside a house or a site in 1798 as the first mosque. Simultaneously, they would have continued to seek more suitable land on which to construct a mosque.

Having taken note of this possibility, it becomes clearer what Frans van Bengalen's role in the establishment of the first mosque might have been. Both Bradlow and Davids agree on his role in the Muslim community in relation to the state. In particular, both agree that he appealed to Sir George Yonge in 1800 for permission to build a mosque, permission that was granted but was then thwarted by the Cape Burgher Senate. After 1804, when Batavian representatives took over the Cape from the English, Frans van Bengalen approached them too and negotiated land for a mosque in return for preparing two Javaansche artillery emplacements in defense of the Cape against an impending English attack. This time, the English had their eyes on the Cape not as temporary caretakers but as a new colonial power.[16] The Muslims fought bravely for the Dutch but could not prevent the Cape becoming the latest English colony. As far as leadership among the Muslims is concerned, the artillery installations provided yet another opportunity for leadership by Frans van Bengalen. Since he had applied for mosque premises from Yonge, and had negotiated for land in return for military duties with the Dutch, he may also have been the person to approach General Craig earlier. It is quite likely that Frans van Bengalen, as an influential person, approached the state authorities first for permission to establish a mosque (Craig) and then for land from Yonge and the Batavian authorities.

In the light of these negotiations, Frans van Bengalen emerges as the person principally concerned about obtaining state recognition for Muslims and negotiating on their behalf. He was not only a leader recognized by the state. He was also close to Tuan Guru, and we are told that he was present at the reading of the will when the Awwal Mosque imām's successor was announced. At the same time, it is clear that he approached the state on behalf of the Muslim community and with their knowledge. All these indicate the status of a leader who was not a religious scholar but someone who played an important part in the establishment of a religious institution. In earlier Islamic contexts, this role would sometimes have been played by the caliph, an influential minister, or a wealthy trader. Such patrons would establish a mosque and then invite religious scholars to serve the mosque and the community. The mosque would then reflect the particular religious orientation of the scholar but would also have to bear the direct or indirect social and political pressure of the patron involved.[17] In Cape Town, the development of this model seemed unlikely, given the particular conditions of slavery as well as the key roles taken by the early imāms. Slavery precluded the emergence of a class or group of influential traders, for example, who might build mosques and then maintain an influential role in relation to them. But Frans van Bengalen was an exception in Cape slave society and therefore the most likely candidate. As man of relatively considerable means, he could have played the role of patron in the classical Islamic model.

At the death of Tuan Guru in 1807, Frans van Bengalen tried to assert his leadership by suggesting his own choice of successor, Jan van Boughies. Achmat van Bengalen refused to bow to this pressure and appealed to the wishes of Tuan Guru: "Remember that Jan van Boughies can never, as long as he lives, take my place, and whoever gives him my place must answer on the day of judgment, and not to me."[18] When this did not work, Frans van Bengalen and Jan van Boughies purchased land on Long Street in 1807, with the intention of establishing another mosque. Long Street was within the city and not far from Awwal Mosque. This second mosque came to be known as the Palm Tree Mosque. Based on these developments, it is plausible to assume that tension existed within the Awwal Mosque. Achmat van Bengalen may have feared the loss of his own position if the team of Frans and Jan took over the Awwal Mosque. His rejection of Frans van Bengalen's demand, however, had long-lasting implications for the Cape mosque. Frans van Bengalen, who had gone out of his way to establish the Awwal Mosque, had to bow to Tuan Guru's and then Achmat van Bengalen's religious leadership in Cape society. The Cape mosque tradition would not tolerate nonclerical leaders in the community who were not patronized by religious leaders as such.

Teaching, Ritual Service, and Loyalty

Like the prominent leadership of the mosque, the role and function of the Cape imām within the Cape mosque was also constructed within the history of its institutionalization. In this regard, both the Awwal and Palm Tree mosques and their disputes provide us with opportunities for uncovering and delineating the basic expectations of a mosque leader in the Cape. Unlike Frans van Bengalen, Jan van Boughies emerged as a serious contender for religious leadership in Cape Muslim society. He was brought to the Cape at the end of the eighteenth century as a slave and later bought by Salia van Macassar, whom he had married by 1800. Jan claimed to have been the oldest "priest" in the service of the community since 1798 and also to have taught Achmat van Bengalen the "Mohammedan language."[19] This date coincides with the founding of the Awwal Mosque and attests to Jan van Boughies's long association with leadership in the Muslim community. Davids portrays him as a man who manumitted a considerable number of slaves but who also lost support due to his troublesome character.[20] A closer look at these and other characteristics of mosques headed by Jan van Boughies and Achmat van Bengalen indicates a deeper process than simply personal idiosyncrasies. More important, an examination of their mosque leadership methods suggests the chief roles created for imāms and later expected of them in the Cape mosque.

Jan van Boughies enjoyed a reputation as a teacher—also one of the hallmarks of Tuan Guru, who established the first classroom in 1793. This school grew enormously in the next few years, until in 1825, it had over 491 students.[21] The religious school established by Tuan Guru flourished as slaves sent their children to learn the basics of the Qur'ān, Islamic theology, and ritual performance. Numerous educational materials were developed, including textbooks for memorization called *koples* books and eventually catechisms by the teachers specifically for the people of Cape Town. The Islamic school in Cape Town was also responsible for texts and later published books on religious instruction for students in the local Dutch patois, later to be called Afrikaans. Using the Arabic orthography developed for Malay, they adopted an Arabic orthography for Afrikaans. The first such texts in what Davids calls Arabic-Afrikaans appeared in 1856, preceding campaigns to use the Roman script for the language.[22]

The implications of this school system for the Cape leadership model can hardly be underestimated. It appears in the descriptions and disputes of every mosque that has been established in the Cape since the Awwal Mosque. Even though the Cape imām had many duties beyond teaching, he was often thought of first and foremost as a teacher. Teaching, however, was more than just the transmission of knowledge. In his study of the education of a religious scholar in Morocco, Eickelman has paid careful attention to how an intellectual tradition was constructed in a culture-specific context. Education was an important part of the transmission, creation, and consolidation of a worldview that placed the teacher, the student, and the materials in their proper cosmological relations. In the Cape Islamic case, this meant—briefly but succinctly—"learning to be human and Muslim" in Cape Town. Eickelman also identified how the educational system created a particular place for religious scholars. Intellectuals in Morocco, the *fgihs*, as he called them, were essentially the common possession of a number of villages.[23] As strangers, they did not belong to any one particular group. Education in the Cape also had this cosmological and social significance. As in Morocco, being a student in a Cape school signaled in fact that one was being groomed as a teacher and could eventually head a mosque. In the examples of the numerous mosques in the Cape, we shall see how this educational element permeates the leadership expectations of the imām.

Mosque leadership enjoyed total dedication from the congregation through other kinds of social mechanisms as well. To the Colebrooke and Brigge Commission of 1825, Achmat van Bengalen reported the ownership but humane treatment of slaves in the Muslim community.[24] Jan van Boughies's reputation for freeing slaves suggests the distinctiveness of a mosque congregation in the Cape. While Van Boughies may have lost members due to his leadership conflict with the Awwal Mosque, he may have gained others by manumission. His buying of slaves for freedom, especially between 1800 and 1818, may be linked to the Rev. Campbell's description of a mosque service attended by "about a hundred men, chiefly slaves, Malays and Madagascars." Bradlow and Cairns connected this description to the Awwal Mosque on account of the "long staff with a silver head" used in the service. This popular staff, called a *tonka* in the Cape, is still used in the Awwal Mosque and is regarded as one of its key heirlooms.[25] However, Campbell's description of the "Mozambican" slaves inside the mosque coincides with a popular name for the Palm Tree Mosque as a "Mozbieker's" mosque during the nineteenth century. Mozambican slaves were imported to the Cape after a ban was placed on Eastern slaves at the end of the eighteenth century.[26] Jan van Boughies's reputation for manumission of slaves may account for the greater number of Mozambicans in the mosque. On the other hand, the presence of the tonka on that particular occasion cannot be explained inside the Palm Tree Mosque.

The distinctiveness of a particular congregation may not necessarily indicate a committed following in most mosques in the Muslim world. Calling the Palm Tree Mosque the Mozbieker mosque, thus, may not have had much significance. However, in the Cape mosque tradition, a close relationship developed between leaders and communities. The Mozbieker association of the Palm Tree Mosque of Jan van Boughies was deeper than simply a name. The terms used for belonging to the mosque and recognizing the authority of the imām denoted the strong bond between leader and follower. The regular attendants at a mosque were said to soembaai there, meaning that they worshiped there and went to other mosques only on rare occasions. More tellingly, however, these followers of an imām were called *murids*, a technical term in Sufism meaning a "seeker" who attached him- or herself to an accomplished spiritual master. Desiring their own spiritual development, the murids were novitiates who presented themselves to the master like corpses to a funeral undertaker.[27] The murids of the Cape imāms did not register their intent to undertake a spiritual journey; nor did the Cape imāms claim such spiritual accomplishments themselves. However, the use of the term murid was apt for describing the deep commitment of the worshiper to his or her imām in the Cape mosque.

The relationship between the imām and the murid was cemented by ritual services provided by the imām, and not by the promise of spiritual renewal or enlightenment reminiscent of the Sufis. Shell has masterfully shown the crucial importance of the Cape imāms in innovative rites of passage. Life's journey began with an elaborate birth ceremony, called *doepmaal* (literally a baptismal meal), where the parents would invite the imām to give the newborn child a name and protect the baby from evil forces in the society. The next landmark was when boys (and later also girls) concluded the complete recitation of the Qur'ān in the religious school. On the occasion of this accomplishment, a *tamat* ceremony acted as a kind of initiation rite for children entering adult Muslim life. The marriage ceremony where both bride and bridegroom attended emphasized the place of both parties but especially that of women in the society. The presence of women was apparently a response to vigorous Christian proselytization at the time. And finally, an elaborate and dignified burial ceremony, including a solemn march through the streets of Cape Town, declared the imām's commitment to his flock. The rites of passage were an important part of the service offered by Cape imāms to the community. On the one hand, the members of the congregation were provided a sense of belonging during slavery and afterward. On the other hand, the ritual service affirmed the leadership and authority of the imām in the mosque.[28]

At first, the Cape mosque discourse did not pay much attention to the desires of the congregation. It seems that this was more a discourse among leaders who were able to form a group of peers that controlled standards and expectations for potential and future leaders. However, during the second half of the nineteenth century, the people who attended the mosques began to express their ideas and expectations for mosque organization as well. This new development was spurred by the numerous disputes among the imāms, many often leading to the state court. The Palm Tree Mosque, in particular, was subject to contentious leadership disputes on charges of incompetence leveled against the imāms by some members of the congregation. In one such case heard in the Supreme Court in 1866, the court proposed a departure for the organization of the mosque. The court seemed to hint at a new approach when it commented on the prevailing tradition of succession: "no custom or law was proved whereby the imām had the sole right to appoint a successor; and that no custom or law was proved whereby the senior *gatiep* [preacher] should succeed the imām."[29] This judgment suggested that the community, or a part of it, could exercise some right to the choice of leadership in the mosque. The court, it seems, tried to make room for the community to share some role in determining the nature of the mosque.

This legal judgment was soon pursued by another Cape Muslim, Hadjie Salie Jacobs, who applied to the Supreme Court to force Imām Hassiem of the Jameah Mosque to appoint an assistant. The Hadjie lost his case but, not unpredictably, established his own mosque on Vos Street and called it the Nurul Mohamedia Congregation. What was unusual, however, was that he attached a detailed deed of transfer to the new property, which stipulated that an updated registry of members be kept. The registry, among other things, would define the eligible voters for the next imām. In a similar case, the Pilgrim Mosque was forced by the court in 1908 to form a "body of trustees" to administer the mosque.[30] These examples of mosque organization point in the direction of greater community participation. The latter could be achieved when the community was clearly defined in legal or bureaucratic terms. This body of members represented another force in the Cape mosque, one which often threatened the central place of the imām. As will be seen in the next chapter, imāms were not easily deposed from their central place in the mosque. Usually, through education and ritual service, they ensured that they gained the support of the new bodies thus created. By the end of nineteenth century, teaching, ritual service, and community loyalty were important components in the mosque discourse in the Cape. The imām created a conceptual worldview through education, and provided support in the form of ritual service, to which most members in the congregation responded with loyalty and commitment.

Pilgrimage

Pilgrimage to Mecca was yet another practice recognized in mosque leadership. Pilgrimage may have gained prominence as a means by which knowledge was acquired. Knowledge had enabled leadership in the community since the foundation of the Awwal Mosque in the Cape. Access to the Arab world through pilgrimage and extended periods of study reinforced this tradition.[31] It was not uncommon for pilgrims to stay in Mecca or Cairo for a long period, during which time they could study Arabic and other Islamic disciplines. Pilgrimage became a distinct means for acquiring greater access to authentic knowledge gained in Mecca, as opposed to being instructed in the schools of Cape Town. As a component in the battery of leadership claims, however, pilgrimage evolved into a discursive symbol, a mechanism, for the incumbent's right to leadership. Both as a means to education and the distinction of having stayed in the holy land, pilgrimage became part of the discursive definition of the Cape mosque.

Pilgrimage featured prominently in two cases, first appearing in the Mosque Shafee or Imām Hadjie Mosque. The third imām in this particular mosque, Abdol Gasiep, appointed two assistants, Hadjie Salie and Shaykh Abdol Azizi, an Arab, to conduct the Friday service. The former's eminence seemed to rest on the fact that he had made the pilgrimage to Mecca and was consequently called a *hadjie* (a pilgrim). Shaykh Abdol Azizi's command of Arabic, on the other hand, threatened the leadership of Abdol Gasiep. When the shaykh went to Arabia for a while, the imām decided summarily to relieve him of his responsibilities and denied him access to the pulpit on his return. In response, Shaykh Azizi, supported by Hadjie Salie, opposed the imām's decision. They brought a large number of Muslims from Claremont to depose the old imām. The imām responded with a restraining order from the court. During the subsequent court hearing, Abdol Gasiep was referred to as the "imām of the sick and the dead" alluding to the rites of passage (birth, marriage, burial) that the imāms of Cape Town administered to their congregants. However, Chief Justice Buchanan also alluded to the eminence enjoyed by pilgrimage in mosque leadership claims.[32] In this case, it seems, Hadjie Salie and Shaykh Azizi were unsuccessful in challenging ritual services with pilgrimage and superior knowledge claims. There is no doubt, however, that the performance of such an important rite as the pilgrimage was clearly recognized for leadership in the society.

The importance of pilgrimage for the leadership of a mosque was even more crucial to a dispute in the Jameah Queen Victoria Mosque. When Shahibo appointed his young son Hassiem to the leadership of the mosque, he was opposed by a Pilgrim Congregation, consisting apparently of men who had performed the pilgrimage. Their leader, Hadjie Abdol Kalil, decided to break away from the Jameah Queen Victoria Mosque to establish his own mosque. He bought premises and became the imām of the Pilgrim Mosque.[33] This particular mechanism of pilgrimage as a leadership claim, whether indirectly as a reflection of knowledge to be acquired in Arabia or directly for its own sake, shows how the mosque in the Cape constructed a discourse out of the Islamic rituals. As one of the five pillars of Islam, pilgrimage was not an intrusion of universal Islam into South African Islam, as Geertz and other modern scholars since Hurgronje have suggested for Indonesian Islam.[34] In the context of the mosque discourses, it was not even an important reorientation of the Muslims toward the universal Islamic center in Mecca.[35] As a discursive strategy in the Cape, pilgrimage joined teaching, ritual, and loyalty as the symbolic capital by which mosques could be created.

The Political and Social Effects of the Discourse

The discourse of the Cape mosque was not confined to the four walls of the mosques. Even though constructed within the mosque, the discourse had powerful effects in a number of important social and political contexts. As an Islamic discourse created within the city, it even had a powerful influence on traditions that came into the city from more central Islamic lands. The influence of the periphery on the center was clearly illustrated in the case of Abu Bakr Effendi, to be discussed shortly. Second, a discourse that generated loyalty and commitment to a leader could also be employed in the broader political and social spheres. Not surprisingly, it was less successful than in the mosque, but it nevertheless influenced the relationship between Muslims and the general public, the state, and civil society.

The Cape mosque discourse left an indelible impression on the representatives of the great Islamic tradition who came to the city. The example of Abū Bakr Effendi in the nineteenth century represents a pattern that has since repeated itself in the Cape. Abu Bakr Effendi was sent to Cape Town from one of the most powerful centers of the Islamic world, the Ottoman Empire. He was a special emissary sent to the Cape to help settle religious disputes in the Cape Town Supreme Court. On his arrival in Cape Town, Effendi was immediately sought by Cape Muslim leaders to teach their wards. By engaging in teaching, and not confining himself to his official judicial duties, Abu Bakr Effendi was locked into the Cape mosque discourse and achieved prominence and success through its specific mechanisms. Effendi taught students who used their new possibilities to claim leadership roles, often against the wishes of the Cape Shāfiʿī sensibilities. The Cape Muslims generally followed the Shāfiʿī legal school while Effendi belonged to the Ḥanafī tradition. He also wrote one of the first religious catechisms in Afrikaans using Arabic characters, thus becoming one of the many religious leaders who developed Arabic-Afrikaans.[36] But most important, shortly after Effendi's death, his followers bought land for the Moslem sect Aghanaf in 1881, to establish the first Ḥanafī mosque. It was only a matter of time before Ḥanafī teachings, shaped in the familiar Cape discourse, were concretized in a mosque. When Muslims were making their way to Mecca on pilgrimage, it appeared that they were drawing inspiration, information, and orientation from the center. However, the experience of Abu Bakr Effendi illustrates the power the local Cape discourse exerted on the dominant Islamic powers and authorities.

This is good example of how a peripheral or "little" tradition had an effect on the central or "great" tradition—an issue that one finds in a number of transregional religions or traditions that have a central dogma to promote, share, or impose. While apparently being imposed onto the periphery, the dogma is simultaneously transformed by it. The periphery is not necessarily spared by this subversion, but it imposes its own conditions on the center. In his study of the Jordanian preacher, Antoun used this central-periphery model to suggest how modern Islamization was a particular effect of the imposition of modernization in the Arab world. The little tradition, in this case Islam, was transformed—but not before leaving an indelible mark on the modernization process itself. Comaroff and Comaroff have developed this notion in the context of rituals in Africa. Rituals, they said, were "constitutive modes of practice" that subverted modernity and hegemonic Christianity. The malcontent of modernity was evident in local ritual practice.[37] The Islamic discourse from the center, Egypt or Istanbul or India, anywhere outside Cape Town, was also transformed, vulgarized, and perhaps liberated, when it tried to impose change on local contexts. In order to appreciate this, we must begin to appreciate Islamic materials not simply for their contents but in the local discursive forms into which they were received. The relationship between the Cape discourse and an Ottoman emissary illustrates this very well.

It is, however, not sufficient to identify and formulate the mechanism for a peripheral Islam or its possible effects on central traditions. The discourses must also be examined for the social and political effects and limitations within the periphery. They ought not to be celebrated for how they subvert the central and dominating traditions. The analyses must be ever alert to the creation of new centers and new orthodoxies on the periphery. In the context of South Africa, thus, the Cape Muslim discourse and its ability to generate support and loyalty within a mosque also sought to represent the Muslims as a community in Cape Town. With the disappearance of Frans van Bengalen, the imām wanted to represent Islam and Muslims in public. In the Cape Islamic tradition, Davids has suggested that Tuan Guru enjoyed this eminence and then bequeathed it to Achmat van Bengalen.[38] In 1836, on the eve of liberation of slaves, however, Jan van Boughies claimed the honor for himself against Achmat van Bengalen. The leadership of the slaves and freed slaves was one thing inside a particular mosque; but another matter when the entire Muslim population had to be taken into account. How did this discourse assist or hinder the powerful imām in this new challenge? What were the consequences of these attempts for the society as a whole? The dispute between Jan van Boughies and Achmat van Bengalen, played out particularly in the letter pages of local newspapers, is instructive as regards the role and function of the Cape mosque and imām in civil society.

When Achmat van Bengalen used the title "Chief Priest" in a pamphlet, Jan van Boughies challenged this usage in the pages of the *South African Commercial Advertiser*.[39] Davids argued that Van Boughies was disputing a status that Achmat van Bengalen had enjoyed since the death of Tuan Guru. It was a status recognized by the state when Achmat was asked to appear before the 1825 Colebrooke and Brigge Commission investigating slave and free black conditions. Furthermore, Tuan Guru had called him to witness the announcement of the future leadership of the community. For Davids, these distinctions pointed to Achmat van Bengalen's leadership within the community and thus his chief priest status. Davids argued that this was the status of *qāḍī* (judge), which Achmat van Bengalen enjoyed within the Muslim community. However, the words used in greater Cape Town for the positions were priest and chief priest, in contrast to *tuan* (teacher) or *emaum* (imām) within the mosque congregation. The distinction between the two sets of terms revealed their particular usage in the mosque discourse. In the evidence available for this issue, "priest" and "chief priest" appear in the exchange of letters in the newspaper and when the state was the object of a petition. But "priest" and "imām" identified two very different groups and communities. The imām was a leader in a particular mosque, while "priest" was a title used for announcing that authority in public. Leadership of a mosque as an imām provided the basis for representing Muslims at official levels as priest. Such a leadership claim was not a sufficient basis for actual recognition, however, as other imāms from other mosques could and did claim the same authority. The appearance of Achmat van Bengalen at the 1825 Colebrooke and Brigge Commission as chief priest was only a claim, not necessarily recognized in the entire Muslim community. Had Achmat van Bengalen's 1825 representation and then 1836 claim gone undisputed, we would probably have had a chief imām family in Cape Town that controlled all social, political, and religious matters in the wider community. But since this position was disputed by at least Jan van Boughies, we know that Cape Town may have had a chief priest claimant but not a chief imām.

For an effective chief priest, Muslims had to find a source and justification of authority that transcended the mosque and its rituals. Jan van

Boughies's letter to the *South African Commercial Advertiser* appealed to such a mosque-transcending claim when he delineated his position as a teacher in the Awwal Mosque. His role in the first community was not fortuitous. It was an attempt to claim leadership of the entire Muslim community, irrespective of the particular mosque to which one belonged. Ritual and educational services were mosque- or school-specific, which the appeal to the first community tried to transcend. However, Achmat van Bengalen had equally strong credentials. He had been the student of the first teacher, and his wife had donated the land for the Awwal Mosque. Moreover, both leaders' appeal to the first community of Cape Town found a challenge from one of the sons of Tuan Guru, Abdol Roef, who sent a dubious letter of support for Achmat van Bengalen to the newspaper:

> I also take this opportunity, Sir, to say that it is my duty to stand above all because Imām Achmet promised my father, Imām Abdullah [Tuan Guru], that he would not stand above us until we are forty years; but Sir, because I have not studied through the books enough, I have given this place to Imām Achmet until such time I am capable to occupy it.[40]

Ostensibly in support of Achmat van Bengalen, Roef's letter made his own claim to the foundational status of the Cape mosque. Unlike his senior counterparts, Roef's was a genealogical claim to the first community. The plural claims and counterclaims rendered this attempt at finding a mosque-transcendent discourse ineffective. The appeal to the first community was not decisive enough to lead the entire community. Each claim, even when it appealed to a higher authority, only reinforced and remained effective within the confines of a single mosque. Like Jan van Boughies and Achmat van Bengalen, Abdol Roef went on to found a succession of mosques that continued into the twentieth century.[41] His claim for genealogical priority against Achmat van Bengalen and Jan van Boughies was not sufficient for public leadership.

There existed a basic contradiction between the kind of leadership cultivated by the imāms inside the mosques and the leadership claims they made in the broader Cape public. On the one hand, leadership within the mosque through education, rituals, and spiritual commitment was cultivated with people on a personal basis. Its effectiveness in generating loyalty remained within a confined group of followers and could not transcend the mosque as such. Jan van Boughies could not expect loyalty from the followers of Achmat van Bengalen, and vice versa. The appeal to Tuan Guru as a mosque-transcending criterion faced many problems. Like early Islam, when there was more than one road leading to Medina, there was more than one road leading to Tuan Guru. Only an approach that did not have any direct interest in the local mosque could provide that platform. The fact that so many mosques went to the courts to settle disputes indicated that they were searching for such a neutral arbiter. The Cape discourse itself was unable to deliver that neutral space.

The Muslims of Cape Town were not going to give up so easily. Imāms who enjoyed support and loyalty in their mosques tried to assert that authority in broader society. Their continued attempts did not lead to a better platform for public leadership and representation of all Muslims. On the contrary, these public representations became an important feature of certain ambitious mosques. Imāms who aspired to general Muslim leadership imprinted such a function onto their mosques. As in the cases of Achmat van Bengalen, Jan van Boughies, and Abdol Roef, moreover, their attempts ensured the public role of the Cape mosque. These attempts ensured that Cape mosques were not permanently insulated from social and political issues in the broader society. Since the leadership was based on discursive formations within the confines of the mosque, public representation often resulted in a confusion of boundaries between local mosque and wider community. Sometimes, what appeared to be a public representation was only a specific contribution from a specific mosque congregation. Groups and individuals utilized social and political ventures representing the wider Muslim public to produce the sense of a singular Cape mosque community. At other times, Muslim public responses appearing to represent general Muslim interests were reactions to pressures on the Cape mosque discourse. In the nineteenth century, the first was illustrated by Muslim colonial collusion on the eastern frontier and the second by the 1880s riots against smallpox vaccination.

The fourth mosque in the Cape was granted to the Muslims by the state in return for participation in its war effort against the Xhosa in the Battle of the Axe. White colonial settlement was continually expanding in search of more land and resources. Once the Khoi and the San were subdued, the Xhosa in the Eastern Cape were threatened. As when Frans van Bengalen turned to military matters in 1804, a "Malay Corps" consisting of a medley of 250 volunteers and conscripts served the British with a standard "exhibiting the crescent on a green field with the Union Jack in the corner."[42] This amounted again to a Muslim readiness to assist colonial expansion in South Africa. In this case, Muslim volunteers were prepared to serve British colonial interests in return for land for a mosque. Davids seems eager to stress that not all the members were enthusiastic about the war effort when they arrived at the front and that the corps was disbanded after only four months.[43] More important to note, however, is that representation with the state, a public entity, was sought on behalf of the Muslim community to found a mosque. From the perspective of the mosque discourse, the nature of the war as a form of colonialist expansion was secondary. The mosque discourse was not an anticolonial discourse; neither was the Cape mosque a colonialist wing of the state. The mosque discourse in the Cape was simply concerned about establishing a mosque, which included the possibility of supporting or opposing colonialism. What appeared to be general support for the British was the hapless appropriation of Muslim sentiments for a mosque. Even more ironically, the communitywide participation of the Malay Corps was utilized for the production of a mosque for one group within the Muslim community.

After the Malay Corps was disbanded, some of the Muslims stayed on in the Eastern Cape and joined the small Muslim community there. Others returned and immediately campaigned for the land for which they had volunteered. A trust was formed by Abdol Bazier, Abdol Wahab, Daries, and Salies, and a mosque was built in 1854. Abdol Bazier, as the principal negotiator with the state, became the first imām of the Jameah Mosque, also known as the Queen Victoria Mosque.[44] The latter name, bowing to the reigning British monarch, confirmed the peculiar political position the Muslims chose. Representation with the state, however, in this case in a military sense, was for an imām one important component in the foundation of the mosques. Like Achmat van Bengalen in 1825, the imām Abdol Bazier was the chief negotiator with the state and the chief beneficiary. The mosque, with its unique discourse favoring one powerful imām, was founded in the public representation of Muslims in a colonialist war of expansion.

The mosque discourse of Muslims in the nineteenth century was implicated in the colonialist fabric well beyond military adventures. Generally, the establishment of mosques took place in the midst of mistrust and suspicion from the state and colonial society. There was one particular event in the nineteenth century that epitomized Muslim rejection of the political order. This was the Muslim rejection of quarantine measures adopted by Cape Town's authorities to combat an outbreak of smallpox. Muslims, supported by imāms, opposed taking vaccinations, refused to observe quarantine measures against those who were afflicted, and planned to oppose the proposed relocation of cemeteries outside Cape Town. It is clear that the municipality could have been more tactful or more considerate toward the religious sensibilities of its citizens, particularly those, like the Muslims, living in some of the worst parts of the city. However, the cemetery uprisings revealed aspects of the mosque discourse that went beyond clashing perceptions of medicine and proper city management. Funeral preparations were important rituals administered by the imāms, who refused to curtail these to comply with the special quarantine measures. Moreover, relocation of the cemeteries threatened an important dimension of the funeral rite, namely the practice of carrying the body of the deceased to its final resting place. Muslims insisted that it was part of the Islamic practice to carry the dead without the use of "mechanical transport, such as trains or horse-drawn carts, as this, too, was a violation of their religion."[45] In 1886, when the cemeteries were declared closed, Muslims defied the council and went ahead with burying their dead there. Rioting broke out when a burial was stopped by police, and the volunteer reserve force of Cape Town was called up to maintain peace and enforce the council's decision.[46] The riots of 1886 illustrate how the mosque discourse reacted to a measure that threatened one of its key practices and rituals. The patterns of mosque practices, in this case its ritual dimensions, defined the conceptual world within which Muslims lived. The conceptual world was neither supportive of colonialism nor opposed to it. It defined its own priorities and reactions. In the context of British colonialism in the Cape, it was remarkable for both its adaptability and its pathos.

Conclusion

The nineteenth century bequeathed to Cape Muslims a rich mosque tradition. The mosques were powerful and independent centers providing the sites for Muslim worship and leadership. Imāms established their authority in terms of expertise in Islamic knowledge, which could be obtained by periods of study inside Cape Town or during pilgrimage to Mecca. Imāms in the Cape ensured loyalty through ritual services offered to the community. These discursive practices of a typical Cape mosque provided the opportunities for establishing mosques. However, the effectiveness of the discourse was severely curtailed by its own constitution. The power that lay at the heart of individual mosque practices could not be transformed into communitywide leadership. An appeal to the early foundation of Islam in the Cape to act as such a transcendent criterion was inherently pluralist. The localized confinement of the discourse was confirmed even by apparently public representations. Muslim support for a colonial frontier war produced another mosque, and a citywide Muslim rejection of a public policy could only take shape in support of a localized ritual within the Cape Muslim discourse.

3

The Claremont Main Road Mosque:
Redrawing the Cape Tradition

We were full of nostalgia but were resolutely progressive.

Mariama Ba, *So Long a Letter*

Innovation in Claremont

On Friday, August 12, 1994, the imām of the Claremont Main Road Mosque, Abdul Rashied Omar, invited Professor Amina Wadud Muhsin of the Commonwealth University of Virginia to deliver the presermon lecture. She spoke to both men and women from the main floor of the mosque, and not from a special women's space on a mezzanine floor, in the basement, or in a completely different room. The mosque was separated into male and female sections but only by a thin rope, no more and no less. The response to the presermon was overwhelming. The mosque was flooded with local media to record the event. Mosque officials had made sure that such an event would not be lost to posterity, nor should this public statement for the place of women in Islam be ignored. While South African newspapers lauded the mosque's stand for women's rights, most Muslims were alarmed at this development. Religious scholars particularly organized a campaign to halt the new trend in Claremont. Their indignation took the form of pamphlets, lectures against Claremont's modernism, joint 'ulamā' meetings and conferences, and a petition calling for the imām's removal from office.[1] During the next Ramaḍān, moreover, the annual general meeting of the mosque was stormed by supporters of the Muslim Judicial Council to try to depose the imām.

The media and progressive political groups in South Africa welcomed the historic event, so soon after the first democratic elections in April of the same year.[2] South Africa was making yet another contribution to freedom and democracy.[3] On the other hand, Muslims were indignant that the West had achieved another victory, this time not on the battlefield but in the innermost sanctuary of Islam. The mosque's sanctity had been "desecrated" in a "historically unprecedented show of defiance" cried the *Muslim Views,* the local Muslim monthly, in its first issue after the event.[4] Both were correct to some extent. The South African experience of the struggle against apartheid had contributed immensely to developments in the Claremont Main Road Mosque, while modernity should also take some of the credit for this development. However, the Claremont Mosque was not simply a product of either, a symbol of liberation or of the encroachment of the West. Both the media and Muslim critics stopped short of a deeper appreciation of the mosque as a discursive space. From the observer's position, the mosque was a symbol of modernization and Westernization respectively. From the perspective of the Cape mosque discourse, however, it was not a passive recipient of new ideas. Like other mosques in Cape Town, it dealt creatively with these South African developments within the opportunities and limits of its own discourse.

The Claremont Mosque worked cautiously within the Cape tradition. Thus, for example, Amina Wadud Muhsin did not deliver the official Friday sermon but the presermon lecture. This parallel sermon supplementing the official Arabic sermon existed in most non-Arab countries. The Turks have even developed a separate pulpit for it in the mosque. Taking a lead from a Muslim conference held in Mecca in 1975, however, the Muslim Youth Movement had encouraged the delivering of the sermon in English or Afrikaans in South Africa: "In places where Arabic is not understood it is sufficient to have the prologue of the Khuṭbah and its essentials in Arabic, but the subject matter of the Khuṭbah must be in the language that is understood by the audience."[5]

Religious leaders in the Transvaal and Natal vehemently criticized the recommendations, but some Cape mosques, including Claremont, adopted this new measure. However, when Omar invited Amina Muhsin, he used the presermon tradition to introduce an innovation; that is, he used an older tradition, itself an innovation, to introduce another one.

The support for women's rights may be seen as only the first step in the direction of recovering the role that women had played in early Islam in the Cape. Women had always been part of the discourse as students and even financial contributors. More important, the emergence of imām leadership in Cape society obscured women's crucial role in early Islam in the Cape. Both the Awwal and Palm Tree mosques depended on the goodwill and financial support of women close to the leaders. According to Shell's study of the household in Cape slavery, women held prominent places in society. Their relatively smaller numbers throughout the period of slavery ensured their greater value, which resulted in greater legal and household advantages. Female slaves, often held in bondage in the homes of slave owners, achieved higher status thereby.[6] The prominence of Saartjie van de Kaap and Salia van Macassar in Cape Muslim society accords with this pattern of high status among women. Even though they did not play a direct role in the mosques themselves, both women were former slaves who acquired wealth and prominence. Saartjie van de Kaap, for example, was the daughter of Trijn van de Kaap, both of them manumitted slaves. Trijn van de Kaap possessed property that she passed on to her daughter, one part of which was used for the Awwal Mosque. In 1841, when Saartjie van de Kaap executed her will, she confirmed the use of the property for the mosque in perpetuity. But the remarkable woman was not simply watching from the sidelines while events were taking shape. By the time her husband died in 1843, her sons and the sons of Tuan Guru had established the Nurul Islam Mosque less than a hundred yards from the Awwal Mosque. Showing her rejection of their action, she amended her will and removed her three sons as executors, also stipulating that the successor to her husband in the mosque should bury her. Salia van Macassar was less influential, but she provided the means by which Jan van Boughies became a leader. It was only through marriage that Jan van Boughies was able to make a greater impact in society. Salia van Macassar gave him the financial independence to pursue his religious career.[7]

The absence of Saartjie van de Kaap and Salia van Macassar from the key leadership discourse was notable in the light of their earlier contributions. These two remarkable women seem to present a faint echo of what women may have been doing in the community. Given the importance of home-based Islam during the greater part of the era of slavery in the Cape, such roles may have been substantially larger than is assumed. As in early Islam, however, the institutionalization of Islam in the Cape led to a relative marginalization of the leadership role of women in the society. In the twentieth century, women in Cape Town still play an unrecognized but significant role in the mosque and religious institutions, sometimes even as members of mosque governing bodies. This latter leadership status has often been questioned and, in a few mosque communities, threatened. Amina Wadud Muhsin's presentation was a radical innovation, but it recalled the suppressed and unrecognized place of women in Cape Muslim society.

Twentieth-Century Mosques

In order to understand the Claremont innovations, we need to move a few steps back from the events in August 1994. As was suggested in the last chapter, Cape Town's mosques entered the twentieth century with a discourse that enabled leadership inside the mosque as well as providing an opportunity to represent all the Muslims in the Cape. The twentieth century in South Africa threw Muslims its own challenges, foremost among them being a greater degree of modernization and the scourge of forced removals under apartheid policies. A brief review of how mosques reacted to these challenges illustrates the developments in the Cape mosque discourse. In general, some mosques survived both modernization and apartheid, and imāms achieved even greater status and prominence than ever before. In many other mosques, imāms searched for new means of asserting their authority when the Group Areas Act of apartheid depleted their followers. The twentieth century also produced its own aspiring "chief priest," now however in an 'ulamā' fraternity, the Muslim Judicial Council. The latter tried to organize religious leadership in a more rational and bureaucratic manner. The relationship between this body and the mosque was often a difficult one, adding a new dynamic to Cape mosque history.

Da Costa's biographical study of Shaykh Muhammad Salih Hendricks (1871–1945) confirms the emergence of a religious leader in the twentieth century through the nineteenth-century Cape discourse. Originally from a family in Swellendam, the shaykh went abroad to study in Mecca for a period of fifteen years from 1888 to 1903. Religious leaders like Shaykh Muhammad Salih Hendricks returned with even greater competency in Islamic knowledge. In recognition of this excellence, such a leader was generally referred to as a *shaykh* to distinguish him from the imāms trained in the Cape. This higher qualification assured the shaykhs a special place in the leadership of the mosque. However, this did not mean that they could ignore the existing patterns of mosque leadership. Rather, as Abu Bakr Effendi had done, they had to establish their authority in terms of the discursive patterns and expectations in Cape Town. Da Costa reports that Shaykh Muhammad Salih Hendricks was initially received with mixed feelings in the city but then founded his authority in the familiar manner by teaching and preaching. He taught a group of women in the Palm Tree Mosque, while men heard him at the Nur al-Muhammadiyyah Mosque. He also conducted the Friday service at the Jameah Queen Victoria Mosque. Having established recognition of his knowledge and leadership credentials, Shaykh Hendricks set about building the Azzawiyah complex in 1919.

Later, in 1924, some of the shaykh's former supporters charged that he planned to build a mosque and not a hall, as had initially been planned, and that
he did not make a distinction between monies collected for his personal use
and those entrusted to him on behalf of the community. Shaykh Hendricks
won the ensuing court battle that established the hierarchy between the
imāms and the congregation for this institution.[8]

A survey of the Wynberg mosques provides another interesting example
of the continuing power of the Cape mosque discourse. Built in 1867 by an
English convert to Islam, Lord Joseph Ratcliffe, the Yusufiyyah Mosque was
administered by periodically elected trustees. The imām, though, enjoyed
absolute authority in the mosque through the normal ritual and educational
programs. Nazeem Mohammed, who went on to become one of the most
prominent presidents of the Muslim Judicial Council, was its the most successful imām.[9] This particular pattern, not unexpected in terms of the nineteenth-century history of mosques in the Cape, may be contrasted with
that at another Wynberg mosque, where a committee had more control.
The Darul Karar Mosque was established in 1922 by Hadjie Sulaiman Shah
Muhammad, a noted philanthropist who established a number of institutions in the Cape.[10] In terms of administration, Indian-controlled mosques
granted more power to the trustees and committees than to the imāms, re-
sulting in frequent clashes and disputes between the two. The Cape imām
usually expected far more freedom and status than the Indian traders who
headed the mosque committee were willing to accept. Interestingly, Shaykh
Nazeem Mohammed was first an imām at this mosque before he joined the
Yusufiyyah. During his term in the Darul Karar in the 1960s, his quarrels with
the mosque committee were endless. Even when he was discharged, Shaykh
Nazeem continued to lead his supporters in prayers while another imām
representing the committee led another group.[11] Shaykh Nazeem eventually
left for the Yusufiyyah, where he could enjoy more independence. In both the
Azzawiyah and Wynberg Yusufiyyah cases, it seems that some mosques of
the twentieth century maintained the absolute leadership of imāms against
trusts and committees.

Apartheid, particularly the Group Areas removals, had an important
impact on this relationship. The Group Areas Act of 1950 forced the relocation of most Muslims from the city center and from business areas in the
southern suburbs of Cape Town. The relocations favored the committees
and trusts against the imāms. When new mosques were built in the racially
segregated apartheid areas, the imāms generally found themselves in a
more vulnerable position. Committees raised funds for new buildings and

religious activities like schooling, and then sought religious leaders to serve them. This new condition had artificially created an advantage for trusts and mosque committees, often at the expense of the imāms.[12] In response, imāms held on doggedly to their special domains established in the nineteenth century. In particular, they continued to administer the rites of passage, which enjoyed greater popularity and interest as families were relocated. In the face of apartheid, religious rites provided a sense of order and normality. At the same time, imāms redoubled their efforts in the sphere of learning and teaching. Education, a key feature of religious authority and prestige, became an even more important means for inscribing the imāms' authority. Adult education programs became more prevalent than before. A survey of adult Islamic education in Cape Town in 1991 showed that almost all mosques regularly offered religious classes in Arabic, Islamic jurisprudence, Qur'ān, hadīth (prophetic statements and precepts), and especially hajj (pilgrimage).[13] While adult education supplemented the basic education of Muslims, it provided avenues for imāms to gain supporters and control. Without casting any general doubt on the erudition of the teachers, or on the utility of the training for people's religious needs, the classes must be seen as important sociological means to assert and reinforce leadership. By virtue of their educational and ritual services, then, the Cape imāms' visibility and prominence were reproduced in ritual service and, more prominently, in religious education.

Since the dispute between Achmat van Bengalen and Jan van Boughies in 1836, the public representation of Muslims had remained a vexed problem. The Muslim community in the twentieth century inherited a quarrelsome legacy in this regard. Continuous splintering of the Muslim community into numerous mosques aggravated the problem. Disputes on religious duties were regarded as the hallmark of the mosques and the particular imām and threw the community into obstinate juridical disputes. In a twentieth-century attempt to find a universal Muslim authority, the religious leaders in Cape Town formed the Muslim Judicial Council in 1945.[14] The formation of the council reopened the issue of there being a chief priest, an issue which had raged a hundred years earlier, and thus also the question of overall representation of the Muslim community. Like the nineteenth-century appeal to the Awwal Mosque, this new authority faced equally intractable problems. It too was unable to replace the locally founded mosque authorities in Cape Town. The twentieth-century experience of this central authority and a local mosque becomes much clearer in the history of the Claremont Main Road Mosque. The history of a central authority in Cape Islam illustrated the continuity of the mosque discourse; the power and limitation of Islamic law therein; and its ability to authorize new approaches to Islam.

Establishment of the Claremont Main Road Mosque

The central Main Road of Cape Town connected the city with Simon's Town, the naval base established at False Bay in 1814. Main Road attracted small settlements of houses and shops, one of them being the village of Claremont. Growing steadily, Claremont acquired a chapel in 1840. The establishment of a mosque is not usually mentioned in the popular accounts of Claremont, but it occurred in 1854, only one year after the first church was consecrated there.[15] The mosque building was a donation from a certain Slamdien who, as expected, established a trust that ceded and transferred "full and free property to Imām Abdol Roef Malay Priest, or his successors in office, of the Mosque in Buitengracht Cape Town, in trust for the Malay Community of Claremont in the Cape Division, certain pieces of land with a Mosque thereon situated at Claremont."[16] The imām in question was the son of Tuan Guru, Abdol Roef, who had earlier claimed his status as chief priest of Cape Town. When Slamdien granted him authority to the Claremont Mosque, Abdol Roef was already the imām of the Buitengracht Mosque. As religious leader and trustee of two mosques, Abdol Roef took the first steps toward chief priest status. He did not get possession of any more mosques, but when he died, he at least ensured the continuation of the family dynasty.[17] In Claremont, his son Abdullah (d. 1907) succeeded him, in turn appointing in succession his own three sons, Abu Bakr, Mohammed Amin, and Abdol Roef. These imāms followed their father's bequest until 1964, when the last-named passed away.

Shaykh Abdol Roef, the final undisputed leader in the Abdol Roef dynasty, enjoyed the prestige and status of the religious leaders in nineteenth- and twentieth-century Cape Town. For his murids, his teachings on Islamic jurisprudence and theology were beyond question. Only under extremely critical conditions would they venture to attend other mosques. Some would even forgo the Friday worship if they were out of Claremont and unable to get to their imām in time. Shaykh Abdol Roef particularly forbade his murīds to worship at the Stegman Road Mosque nearby. He argued that Shah Muhammad had donated the money for the mosque in memory of his daughter, who had died in a motorcar accident. The shaykh suspected that the mosque had been built from insurance monies paid out to Shah Muhammad, thus making the mosque unfit for worship. It is clear that, using Islamic legal teachings, the shaykh drew indelible boundaries between those inside and outside his congregation.[18] The Claremont Main Road congregation consisted of about sixty families, and each contributed one pound sterling per month for the imām and the mosque. This represented approximately 10 percent of the monthly salary of most members of the congregation. With the exception of two self-employed men, most were artisans in the building trade working for construction companies. The members also handed their annual Ramaḍān rice contributions to the shaykh. This charity was payable by every Muslim at the end of Ramaḍān and represented an offering for the expiation of minor infractions during the month of fasting. The shaykh collected the contributions in rice, which usually became huge mounds in his house. According to a Cape tradition, the shaykh could distribute it at his discretion.[19]

The devotion of the murids to the shaykh was reciprocated. Shaykh Abdol Roef, like the other religious leaders, was aware of the mutual obligations binding him and the worshipers. In particular, he devoted himself to the community, never absenting himself from the mosque and never turning down a member's request to officiate at the esteemed Muslim rites of passage. At funerals, for example, he would go down himself into the grave to inter the body. He made it quite clear to his murīds that he felt personally responsible for their salvation, and he promised that he would be with them on the Day of Judgment. In contrast, someone who was less committed to the shaykh and the mosque would not be given the same kind of consideration. When the shaykh was asked to officiate at a funeral service of a nonmurīd, he would not reject the invitation outright but would send one of his students to represent him.

The Claremont Mosque under the leadership of Abdol Roef was a classic model of the Cape mosque. Rituals constructed the bonds of commitment and loyalty between community and religious leaders that were the envy of other mosques. It is difficult to imagine how this idyllic relationship between imām and community could produce a modernist tradition in the Cape. However, a number of factors contributed to dramatic changes in Claremont. First, Abdol Roef failed to appoint a successor, which gave the community, or rather its influential members, the opportunity to assert themselves in this mosque. Second, the Muslim Judicial Council welcomed the end of an imām dynasty that competed with council authority in the Muslim community. And third, the Group Areas removals ensured that the Claremont community was relocated, creating space for students and youth to develop new Islamic concepts in the absence of any potential traditional opposition.

The End of a Dynasty

Abdol Roef's nephew Abdullah, supported by his brother Cassiem, claimed that he had been designated as imām of the mosque. Ahmad Savahl, a long-time and committed murid of the late Shaykh Abdol Roef, refused to accept this claim. He argued that the Abdol Roef family's deed of succession had come to an end and called a meeting at the Talfallah Moslem School to discuss the issue. There, many in the community agreed with him and believed that an elected committee would best serve the interests of the mosque. They also felt that this would be the best solution for the mosque in light of the pending implementation of apartheid. Muslims in and around Claremont were facing removals to "Coloured" areas in the Cape Flats outside Cape Town. Claremont had been declared a white residential and business area, and meager compensation was offered to those who owned property. Savahl and his supporters believed that a committee could most appropriately safeguard the interests of the mosque in such circumstances. Some even suspected that the new Abdol Roefs were seriously considering selling the property in Claremont and claiming its proceeds.[20] The meeting also decided to split the affairs of the mosque. A mosque committee was charged with maintaining the mosque, but religious affairs were handed over to Abdullah Abdol Roef and the Muslim Judicial Council. While confirming the Abdol Roef family's place in the mosque, the meeting introduced the authority of the Muslim Judicial Council into the equation. This was bound to lead to a major dispute.

At first, Abdullah Abdol Roef accepted this offer, but he later came to fear that mosque leadership was permanently slipping out of the family's hands. It appears, moreover, that his brother Cassiem Abdol Roef became the main protagonist for the rights of the family dynasty. As a mark of their independence, the two brothers announced that they did not intend collecting the monthly contributions from the families in Claremont. Tension rose between the Abdol Roefs and particularly Savahl, and an argument between the two was referred to the Muslim Judicial Council, as the meeting at the school had agreed. In principle, the council opposed Abdullah Abdol Roef's hereditary succession in the mosque, but it asked both parties to settle their differences. The council's recommendation for conciliation was understandably rejected by both the community and the Abdol Roef brothers. The imām continued to insist on his absolute authority in the affairs of the mosque, while the committee began to seek ways by which its role in the mosque would be firmly certified without the Muslim Judicial Council. As in many other mosques since the nineteenth century, the committee sought that support in the judicial system of the state. The committee went in search of the original trust deed of the mosque, which led it to the Buitengracht Mosque.

This mosque had been far less successful for the Abdol Roef legacy than had the Claremont Main Road Mosque. At Buitengracht, the first Abdol Roef passed on leadership to Hamien, who was followed by Abdol Rakieb, a grandson of Tuan Guru. Abdol Rakieb was only twenty years old when he became the imām. He was taught by Abu Bakr Effendi and insisted on performing the Friday worship in terms of Ḥanafī jurisprudence. Among other differences, this meant that the Friday service would go ahead even though forty worshipers were not present. This issue sparked off among Cape Muslims a Shāfiʿī-Ḥanafī dispute that raged during the latter half of the nineteenth century. In 1906, moreover, Abdol Rakieb was accused of bringing about financial crisis for the mosque by taking out a bond on it. Abdol Rakieb wanted to develop the land adjacent to the mosque in order to generate a stable income for its administration and maintenance. He raised the money from the bank in spite of a stipulation in the trust against doing so and was subsequently forced to vacate his place in the mosque. Hadjie Mogamat Taliep, imām of the Quawatul Islam Mosque bought the mosque and changed its name to the Nurul Islam Mosque.[21] Irregularities again surfaced in 1939, when the British Mizan of Afghanistan Society saved the property once again from liquidation. This time, the mosque was placed under the management of a committee, which was entrusted to appoint the imām.[22] In terms of the pattern of mosque traditions in the Cape, the Buitengracht Mosque moved from one in which the imām held complete sway to one in which a mosque committee was entrusted with final authority. Unlike the Claremont Mosque, the Abdol Roef imāms in the Buitengracht Mosque did not produce a succession of imāms as in Claremont. The Abdol Roef representative in this mosque lost his charismatic and powerful place in the mosque when he misread the needs of the community in the nineteenth century.

Armien Bassadien was the imām in the Buitengracht Mosque in 1967 when the Claremont congregation tried to unravel its legal history. Neither he nor his committee was aware of the legal link between the mosques. Considering the history of Buitengracht Mosque, it was not surprising that the committee supported the Claremont congregation against the imāms. As trustee of the Claremont Main Road Mosque, Imām Bassadien claimed his position in the mosque by virtue of the title deed of 1854. The Abdol Roefs challenged this claim, forcing the matter to court. The court decided that Bassadien, and not Abdullah Abdol Roef, was the trustee of the mosque in terms of the trust deed. The court, however, went further by suggesting that a constitution be drawn up to make provision for a fifteen-member board of governors and a board of trustees consisting of the imām and the president and vice president of the board. The community accepted these recommendations, Bassadien resigned as trustee, and the first board was elected. Abdullah Abdol Roef was appointed as imām and, according to the agreement, became one of the trustees. All the parties accepted this new arrangement except Cassiem Abdol Roef, who walked out of the judge's chambers in protest but without lodging an explicit objection at the time.[23] Nevertheless, the disempowerment of the imām, begun by the mosque committee, was further entrenched by the Supreme Court's registration of a constitution. Subsequently, other court hearings rendered this disempowerment irreversible.

Abdullah Abdol Roef served as imām until 1972. Then, ignoring the constitution and 1968 agreement, he resigned due to ill health and appointed his brother as successor. The board of governors opposed this decision and decided to exercise its legal power. Refusing to recognize the imām's resignation or appointment of his brother, the board instead fired him. It also demanded that both brothers vacate the mosque premises. When the brothers refused, the board brought a court interdict against them. The matter went through a five-year-long court proceeding, which was eventually decided in favor of the board. The Abdol Roefs appealed in vain against the judgment in 1978.[24] The court upheld the authority of the board in terms of the 1968 agreement. The long duration of the proceedings, and the Abdol Roef brothers' failure in the initial hearing as well as the appeal, entrenched the position of the board of governors against the Abdol Roefs. Cassiem Abdol Roef, however, continued to regard himself as the rightful imām of the Claremont Main Road Mosque. In 1992, when he heard that the mosque congregation was deliberating on a major renovation, he accused the new imām of incompetence for allowing the destruction of parts of the mosque and the house. Cassiem Abdol Roef threatened the imām and the board of governors with a Supreme Court hearing by arguing that they had violated Islamic law:

> We hereby call upon you to cease building operations forthwith. We have made an inspection and note that building operations are being undertaken contrary to the Sharīʿah. We require an undertaking from you to cease the building operations and this undertaking must be delivered to this office by 12 noon on 11 August 1992 failing which we shall move the Court for an urgent interdict to stop you from wrongfully and unlawfully continuing with building operations.[25]

Abdol Roef insisted that a mosque could be renovated only if it was restored to its original form and by using as many of the old building materials as possible. The board and the imām decided to oppose the motion, but on the day of the hearing, Abdol Roef withdrew his application, and the court ordered him to pay all costs.[26] In a press statement issued after the 1992 *Claremont Board v. Abdol Roef* case, the chairperson Adam Samie expressed his frustrations: "We resent the fact that a considerable amount of time and energy has been spent in resisting this application. The congregation is weary of the vexatious Court proceedings instituted by the Abdoorofts [Abdol Roefs] over so many years." The chairperson may have been justifiably frustrated by Cassiem Abdol Roef's persistence, but the board and the Muslim Judicial Council were instrumental in the destruction of a tradition.

The Claremont conflict disclosed some important institutional rearrangements in the Cape Mosque discourse. The dispute illuminated the relationship between the court, the local mosque, and the Muslim Judicial Council. While the community first called upon the council to settle their dispute, the 1968 court agreement between the mosque committee and the Abdol Roefs marginalized its role in the matter. The inability of the council to effect a decisive resolution to the conflict led the community to seek a more binding authority. Initially, this did not mean that the council was completely ignored. Examining this issue in terms of the judicial approach of the council, Lubbe has shown how it viewed hereditary succession as an "un-Islamic practice," which it "was determined to destroy by placing emphasis on election, to the exclusion of succession along family lines."[27] The court proceedings thus confirmed the textual traditions of the scholars against the tumultuous tradition of the family dynasties. Council representatives were present during the court proceedings throughout the 1970s, and both the Supreme Court and Appellate judges praised and commended the expert testimony of Abu Bakr Najjar, then president of the Muslim Judicial Council. They contrasted it with the evident lack of expertise on the part of the Abdol Roefs, especially Cassiem.[28] In his evidence, Najjar confirmed the earlier position of the council and categorically denied the notion of a hereditary mosque and imām tradition in Islam that the Abdol Roefs were claiming. In the words of Justice Watermeyer, "Sheikh Najjar conceded in cross-examination that in some mosques in Cape Town it had been the practice for the imāmship to be handed down from father to son, but there was no such thing as an hereditary imāmship. It was for the community to elect an imām with the approval of all, or the majority, of them. An imām has no right to appoint his successor."[29]

The Muslim Judicial Council, represented here by Najjar, displayed a consistent message against the imām tradition of Cape Town, placing it against an Islamic textual tradition that did not make provision for the hereditary leadership of charismatic imāms.

The approach of the Muslim Judicial Council, however, ought not to be considered simply as a product of a different interpretation or tradition in Islamic law. Between independent imāms and more demanding communities, the council was not simply implementing Islamic law. It attempted to use Islamic law to inscribe a new mosque subject. The attempt, however, was half-hearted as it constituted a fundamental threat to imāms in the classic Cape Muslim discourse, of which the leaders of the Muslim Judicial Council were also beneficiaries and subjects. In theory, the Muslim Judicial Council represented a tradition and a discourse quite distinct from the local mosque leadership represented by the Abdol Roefs. Its legal considerations and priorities tried to establish an authority distinct from the traditional power base of the imāms and the shaykhs. Founded on the textual traditions of Islam, the council presented the Sharī'ah (Islamic moral and legal code) as a decree that could act as the final arbiter and authority in the Islamic community. In this case, Islamic law was an attractive neutral ground. In the nineteenth century, Jan van Boughies and Achmat van Bengalen had posited their leadership on the basis of their link to the first Cape Muslim community. The Sharī'ah of the Muslim Judicial Council appeared to promise a more reliable, neutral foundation.

Independent imāms such as the Abdol Roefs understood the threat that such an authority posed to their positions. In the early 1960s, Cassiem Abdol Roef was expelled from the council because he refused to abide by its decision. Cassiem, in response, declared his independence by announcing his allegiance to the arch-architect of apartheid, Dr. Hendrik Verwoerd, stating that "on purely religious matters the ruling of the Prime Minister should be sought and not that of the Muslim Judicial Council" because "Dr. Verwoerd was the qāḍī, i.e. the real authority."[30] This statement was not simply a reflection of an arch-conservative. Cassiem had signed the 1961 Call of Islam manifesto rejecting apartheid in principle. The statement reflected the rejection of the Muslim Judicial Council's authority. It correctly recognized the council's ambition to assert its authority over all religious issues in the Cape, thereby reducing the special influence of the individual imāms in the mosques. The Abdol Roefs, from a family tracing its founding to the first imām of Cape Town, had claimed supreme authority in the mosque community. It is not surprising to find, therefore, how Cassiem Abdol Roef resisted the Muslim Judicial Council's centralization of imām authority by appealing to the authority of the state. Other imāms were not as dramatic or extreme in rejecting the authority of the Muslim Judicial Council, but they too were threatened by its decrees.

And yet, the council did not regard the Sharī'ah as an impersonal authority, to be used as final arbiter in all cases. The particular practice of the council in the Claremont case reveals how the authority of its leaders, especially its influential top hierarchy, could not be separated from the mosque-imām complex in Cape Town. They were themselves imāms in mosques, and understood the pressures placed upon them by the community. On the one hand, they were sympathetic to imāms challenged by the community. On the other hand, an independent imām was a potential and real threat to the council. The council was caught between its desire to be a representative body for independent imāms and the creation of a discursive authority of the Sharī'ah. Between the two, it has since been singularly unsuccessful in producing an effective alternative authority. The Muslim Judicial Council can act on issues of correct belief and practice that transcend the mosque contexts. But these mosque-transcending discourses have potentially made local mosque authorities vulnerable. The conflict between the general and the local spheres of authority has paralyzed the council, compromising decisive action on many an occasion. The Claremont case was one such occasion, and the council's political involvement against apartheid was another. Lubbe ascribed the inability of the council to take a decisive lead in political affairs to fear of losing support.[31] I submit that that support was institutionally bound within the discourse of the Cape mosque tradition.

The Return of the Imām?

The history of the Claremont Mosque, caught between the court, the Muslim Judicial Council, and the community, left equivocal suggestions for the Cape mosque discourse. At first, the council paved the way for an imām who would be accountable to the congregation. Deep down, however, the leaders of the Muslim Judicial Council could not undermine the Cape imām. This equivocation ensured the continuity of the Cape mosque discourse and, at Claremont, the rebirth of a new imām.

The Claremont Main Road Mosque revealed the creativity of the Cape mosque discourse in adopting a new approach to Islam. This new approach, singularly successful at Claremont in a way that it has not been anywhere else in the country, has been variously called political Islam, Islamism, and Islamic fundamentalism. I prefer calling this exceedingly varied phenomenon Islamic resurgence, which I regard as a new paradigm for constructing Islamic identities, practices, and authorities in the modern world.[32] In Cape Town, this new paradigm began to take shape in the 1950s when young Muslims started demanding a different approach to Islam from both the religious leaders and the mosque committees. Imām Abdullah Haron, who was the imām at the Stegman Road Mosque, provided opportunities and avenues for youth to participate in the affairs of the mosque. While introducing them to the Cape mosque discourse, Imām Haron himself came under their influence in terms of modern social and political thought. Together they bequeathed the Claremont Mosque a Cape discourse with a new emphasis. In this section of the chapter I trace its transfer from Stegman Road to Main Road, and how the Claremont Mosque developed further in the discursive context of the Cape mosque. The discursive formation of the new approach, and not only its contents, reveals the birth of a Cape imām clothed in progressive garb. First, a dispute in the Stegman Road Mosque and a leadership vacuum in the Main Road Mosque favored the development of the new discourse. Then the Group Areas removals played their part in ensuring a free space in which youth and students could experiment with new ideas.

Between 1964, when Abdol Roef II died, and 1968, when the constitution was adopted, older members vacillated between the two mosques during the dispute while most of the younger members became committed to Stegman Road Mosque. Haron, who understood and responded to the aspirations of the young, impressed them. Some were also overwhelmed by an imām who openly discussed the social and political challenges facing Muslims. Haron was a model imām, the kind they wished would be emulated at the Claremont Main Road Mosque. Islamic resurgence was able to establish an important place in the Claremont Main Road Mosque through this connection. Tragedy struck in 1969, when the South African security establishment arrested Haron. He was finally murdered, like many other anti-apartheid activists, on September 27, 1969.

In the Stegman Road Mosque, a dispute arose as to who should succeed the imām. There were two possible candidates: Ebrahim "Sep" Davids was favored by most of the trustees and members of the congregation, while Abu Bakr Fakier had won recognition for his critical and incisive approach to Muslim youth affairs.[33] Fakier was known as Imām Haron's mentor in the politics of South Africa. The choice of the trustees and community forced Fakier to move with his supporters to the Claremont Main Road Mosque. In this mosque, in the meanwhile, the congregation's challenge to the Abdol Roefs was creating a leadership vacuum, which Ahmad Savahl and the board of governors wished Fakier would fill. Here, the choice for Fakier was not directly prompted by his outspoken social and political rhetoric.[34] Interestingly, these credentials of Fakier's mattered less than his family relation with Savahl. Nevertheless, Fakier thus acted as the temporary imām and Friday preacher during the lengthy legal battle. Fakier did not serve the community as "an imām of the sick and dead" nor as an accomplished jurist; he was neither a typical Cape imām nor a member of the Muslim Judicial Council. During his term of office, he continued to espouse a sociopolitical interpretation of Islam and was different in that sense from both the Abdol Roefs and the mosque committee. This was encapsulated in the ritual changes introduced during his term. For the Friday sermon, Fakier dispensed with the presermon translation and presented the actual sermon in English from the top of the pulpit. In addition to replacing the Arabic sermon, Fakier's use of English instead of Afrikaans signaled his departure from the literary culture that the imāms dominated through texts and education.

These changes—the use of English and the reduction of the imām's ritual function—could not take place without a major demographic change in the congregation. This had been ensured by the Group Areas Act removals, effectively carried out during this period. When the act forced Muslim families to leave Claremont for areas further away from central Cape Town, it left the field open for a new tradition to flourish. The mosque dispute had placed the Claremont imām's position in jeopardy, and the forced removals ensured that potential followers relocated their religious loyalty to mosques in the new areas. In the absence of both imāms and families, the Claremont Main Road Mosque was particularly frequented by college and university students, who found the political messages of Fakier and his associates more relevant to the countrywide uprisings against apartheid. By the time the board of governors won the court battle in 1977 and the appeal in 1978, the mosque had become a key venue for Islamic resurgence in Cape Town. In a statement made to *Muslim News*, Fakier underlined the meaning of the victory in court for the struggle against apartheid:

> We have succeeded in getting the Abdol Roefs out. These were men working against the principles of waqf [pious endowments] and the Sharī'ah. The greatest challenge now is to see if we can build up a dynamic and progressive community. Men officiating at the Masjids were made the authority and are asserting themselves. People are worshipping them instead of Allah Ta'ālā.

As far as we are concerned this case was not only an indictment of the Abdol Roefs; it was an indictment of the community. My concern is not the Abdol Roefs but the appalling indifference of the community to commit itself to the struggle for justice. Justice should be the commitment of all Muslims.[35]

Fakier's statement was a categorical notice of the changes taking place in the discourse of the mosque. Like the Muslim Judicial Council, it was in favor of the Sharī'ah against the hereditary leadership of the imāms. In addition, though, it was committed to the renewal and reform of the community with which it found much fault, particularly in relation to the cause of justice against apartheid South Africa.

When Fakier departed for Saudi Arabia to pursue higher studies, Hassan Solomons and then Abdul Rashied Omar of the Muslim Youth Movement followed him successively as leaders in the mosque. During the 1980s, under both Solomons and Omar, the mosque became the place where apartheid was categorically condemned and opposed. The various political and social positions held by Muslim youth with respect to apartheid, the Islamic Revolution in Iran, and other national and international issues were debated in its sermons and lectures. In South Africa, Muslim youth were divided between positing Islam as an alternative ideology struggling against apartheid on its own, and engaging the injustice of apartheid together with anti-apartheid activists. The Muslim Youth Movement and Qiblah (established in 1980) of Achmat Cassiem supported the former position, while the Call of Islam popularized the latter. In terms of a specific revolutionary strategy, Qiblah supported the Iranian Islamic Revolution and adopted it as a model, while the Muslim Youth Movement was cautious of its Shi'ite proclivities. Like the juridical debates among the religious leaders, these struggle strategies became the most important points of discussion in the mosque sermons, camps, and debates. Together, they fostered a new interpretation of Islam.

The interpretation was located, however, within the familiar Cape discourse. Both Solomons and Omar were recognized authorities in the Cape mosque tradition. As result, they were expected to and did fulfill their role in the principal duties inside the mosques. For Cape Town, this included the Friday sermon and adult education as well as presiding at the important rites of passage developed in the nineteenth century. In 1986, moreover, Omar launched the 'Ibad al-Rahman Study Group to provide a venue for education and campaigns. True to its anti-apartheid inclination, the name was adopted from an organization Imām Haron had founded in the 1960s.[36] Nevertheless, the study group was not unlike similar adult classes offered by imāms throughout the city. Like the others, this one also established and promoted the imām's authority and support in the mosque. As imām, Omar also ventured views on religious issues. He went against a majority trend in Cape Town and joined a small group of imāms who decided to celebrate the second Eid in Islam with the people who concluded their pilgrimage rites in Mecca. It was within the all too familiar Cape discourse, then, that the new ideas of Islamic politics and anti-apartheid rhetoric were disseminated.

There was one aspect of the Cape discourse that the Claremont Mosque developed to unexpected dimensions. Since the nineteenth century, the communities had demanded more accountability from their imāms. This had led to two unfavorable situations: either the imāms had managed to gain complete, unquestioning allegiance from the community, and expelled dissident groups, or community groups and mosque committees had forced the imām into subservience. However, in the Claremont Mosque, this community role took on a different approach, partly as a result of the long court battles and partly as a result of an innovative reading of Islamic texts elevating community involvement. The lengthy court procedures—from when the first constitution was drawn up in 1968 to the final Abdol Roef attempt to unseat the imām in 1992—created a constitutional tradition in the Claremont Main Road Mosque. In effect, it gave the community much more prominence than in other mosques. Omar did not fight this new power but employed it effectively in an innovative approach to dealing with juridical and religious discussions and other social and strategic matters. Great care was taken to include the community in discussions and debates as the imām promoted a contextual and hermeneutic approach to reading Islamic texts. All views, including quotations from the Qur'ān and ḥadīth, were regarded as subjective interpretations and could in principle be debated. Omar, for example, led the congregation on a round of deliberations concerning the number of additional cycles (rak'a'āt) to be performed in the Ramaḍān tarawīḥ prayers at night. After many hours of discussions, the community decided by way of a vote to reduce the number to eight, following a tradition of the Prophet but going against a dominant Islamic tradition in South Africa insisting on twenty. Following a similar procedure, Omar invited Professor Amina Wadud Muhsin to present the presermon talk in August 1994. The democratic nature of these discussions has often led to great alarm in the wider community, for whom religious knowledge and expertise represented immutable facts and values. In a tradition where the imāms were the absolute arbiters of Islamic knowledge, the Claremont Mosque introduced a more inclusivist approach to matters. From the perspective of more authoritarian mosques, this mosque seems to be going against the notion that religious teachings and ideas were given to be obeyed and practiced, preferably through the offices of a respected imām or the Muslim Judicial Council. On the other hand, it was a logical conclusion to a Cape mosque tradition that had demanded greater community participation in the nineteenth century.

Conclusion

The innovations and changes in the Claremont Main Road Mosque must be understood in the light of how a twentieth-century mosque related to its inherited discourse. Mosques and particularly their imāms could and did create authoritative structures in the network of educational services, ritual sensitivity, and public representation. During the twentieth century, however, the rationalizing discourses of organizations and Sharī'ah authorities sometimes supported and sometimes threatened this organic link between community and imām. It claimed leadership for the entire community in the region on the basis of expertise in Islamic law and theology, posing thereby a potential threat to the power and authority of the imām in the local mosque. With the Sharī'ah, the Muslim Judicial Council could have established a discourse that countered or at least controlled the nineteenth-century discourse. Caught in the contradiction of popular support and an impersonal textual tradition, however, the council leadership did not act decisively against independent imāms. It left the courts to make the final decision, and thus ensured the continued vitality of the individual mosque. In the case of the Claremont Main Road Mosque, however, this choice has turned into a religious and theological nemesis for the Muslim Judicial Council.

The conditions of apartheid relocations and the persistent court proceedings of the Abdol Roefs placed the Claremont Main Road Mosque in a state of transition. Both these factors helped the success of another approach to Islam by providing it a place as well as a discourse within which it could thrive. The message of Islamic resistance to apartheid filled a leadership vacuum in Claremont at an opportune time. As the Muslim Judicial Council failed to take decisive action, it forced the community to seek support from the South African judicial system and, in the meantime, invited

Fakier to head the mosque. The context of Group Areas removals ensured in no small measure that the new message faced little resistance to its innovations. Most important, however, the Claremont Mosque charted new territory within the old forms. When the old imām gave way to Islamic politics, a new one replaced him, stronger than the old but thriving on the traditions that produced him.

4

Transvaal Mosques:
The Production of Orthodoxy

The trustees or the majority of them for the time being shall have the absolute power to appoint the *Imām* to officiate in the aforesaid mosque for such term as to them shall seem necessary, and to impose on him and his successors such conditions in writing as shall be necessary for the due and proper discharge of his office and for his good, moral and proper behavior in accordance with the laws of the Koran and the recognized customs of the Indian Sect worshipping in the said mosque and the said trustees either unanimously or by majority shall have the power either to remove or to suspend the said Imām from office for any breach of his contract.[1]

Thus reads the official trust deed establishing the Quawatul Islam Mosque in Cape Town in 1892, the first mosque built by the Indians who had recently arrived in South Africa. The Cape tradition had enabled the new arrivals to establish their first mosque, but it was clear from the outset that the Indian tradition was going to differ from the Cape's in one important respect. Unlike in the existing Cape mosques, the trustees in the Indian mosque enjoyed absolute power and authority. In the Transvaal, traders and hawkers would build mosques with similar preconceptions of how mosques should be governed, precipitating the emergence of an alternative mosque discourse in South Africa. The legal and political impediments of European prejudice further consolidated this pattern of mosque foundation. This chapter is devoted to the Transvaal mosque discourse that developed in this context.

Indians arrived in South Africa in 1860, some as indentured workers and a small group as traders and hawkers. By the time they arrived, the general outlines of South Africa had more or less been drawn. British policies in the

Cape had induced many settlers of European origin—by now called the Boers, meaning "farmers" in Dutch—to set out on the epic northward journey called the Great Trek. This movement was directly affected by the abolition of slavery and the missionary support for black emancipation. These conditions, inimical to white settler interests, convinced a large number of the Boers to seek a comfortable distance from British influence. Unfortunately, their search for freedom from British policies implied the subjugation of African peoples living along their newly created wagon paths. After a series of bloody wars of conquest and occupation, the trekkers founded two republics north of the Orange River. The Orange Free State Republic lay between the Orange and Vaal rivers, while the Zuid Afrikaanse Republiek that would become the Transvaal lay farther north, between the Vaal and the Limpopo rivers. Initially, the British followed their earlier subjects, and prevented their free access to a seaport. This meant the annexation of the eastern part of the country in 1845, the terrain known as Natal, lying between the Indian Ocean and the Drakensberg mountain range. When gold and diamonds were discovered in the two Afrikaner republics, British ambition was fired sufficiently for the complete colonization of South Africa. This was achieved after a series of political, military, and legal manipulations, but finally and decisively during the Anglo-Boer War from 1899 to 1901. Indians found themselves in the middle of this complex political map, caught between British colonial interests and an emerging Afrikaner identity.

Slavery being abolished, indentured workers from India were brought by the British, primarily to work on the sugar plantations in Natal. In addition, the British allowed a smaller number of "passenger" traders to follow, partly induced to come to South Africa to serve the indentured workers. Soon, Indians diversified their economic pursuits to include trading with both the white colonists and the indigenous people of South Africa. By 1874, Indians had moved into the other regions of the country as they followed the discovery of mineral deposits at Johannesburg and Kimberley respectively. Indians did not restrict themselves to the most prominent mining towns but ventured into the remotest towns and villages of the country, acting as an important agency through which British goods were delivered to these parts.[2] When the Indians proved to be more ambitious than the British had bargained for, numerous political and legal obstacles were imposed to prevent their release from indentured status or their expansion and prosperity as free Indians. The Afrikaners followed and perfected such British-invented racist legislation. In particular, the Orange Free State took the extreme measure of preventing Indians from entering and residing in its territory. Right until the fall of apartheid, it demanded special transit permits from Indians traveling through its territory. The Zuid Afrikaanse Republiek authorities were only inhibited by British pressure from completely preventing Indian settlement as well. Nevertheless, they too made every effort to restrict or prohibit Indian acquisition of land and access to trading rights.[3] This particular aspect of their policy had direct implications for the Transvaal mosques. The British used the treatment of Indians in the Boer republics to further their own colonial plans. Discrimination against Indians, who were technically British subjects, became one of the many grievances used as justification for colonizing the Boer republic with its rich mineral deposits.[4]

Muslims built mosques and established Islam under these difficult political conditions. From a legal perspective, the discrimination against people of color in South Africa is well-known and documented. Less fully known, however, is the Indian response to these conditions in terms of their community formation. Here I mean not only the history of resistance in political terms; from the Gandhian campaigns at the turn of the twentieth century to the role of the Natal and Transvaal Indian Congresses as allies of the African National Congress, such histories have been written.[5] What I propose to do, however, is uncover the discourses that gave rise to the Indian Muslim subject in South Africa. As a specific case, I explore the historical and discursive formation of mosques in the greater Zuid Afrikaanse Republiek that came to be known as the Transvaal. Muslims who established mosques, devised strategies, and expounded a peculiar political ethic of establishing Islam in the country. The mosque committees, generally called *jamāt* committees, became the most powerful brokers and mediators between the state and the Muslim communities. Their political ethic of accommodation and compliance with the state—Boer, Briton, or Afrikaner—was inscribed in the Transvaal mosque. The jamāt committees did not achieve their prominence simply through financial donations. They were constituted in the discriminatory legal history of land tenure for Indians. The context favored those who dealt directly with the political authorities, always potentially at the expense of the religious leaders. Unlike the Cape imāms, therefore, the Transvaal religious leaders were politically and socially defenseless employees receiving paltry wages. In response, they founded an orthodoxy and an orthopraxis by which to claim the mosques for themselves. While the traders built mosques during British colonialism and apartheid, the religious leaders responded by redefining the mosque in the rhetorical and bodily gestures of orthodoxy and orthopraxis. It is this discourse, created in response to mosque committees and the disempowerment of 'ulamā', that is reflected in the Transvaal sermon.

The Foundation of Islam in the Transvaal

The earliest mosque in the Transvaal capital of Pretoria dates to at least 1887.[6] Muslim traders established religious structures with enthusiasm, often in defiance of their precarious political position. The traders built mosques with such regularity and promptness that their antagonists, the white traders and government authorities, often suspected that the mosques were precursors of trading and residential settlements. This was explicitly mentioned in Heidelberg by the magistrate when he opposed the registration of a mosque on the grounds that "it would seem as if this was the thin edge of the wedge in getting a footing into the European quarter of the town."[7] For whites, the mosque was a symbol for the more threatening trading potential of Indians. While there may have been some truth in the charge, much more was taking place among the Muslims as they tried to find a niche for themselves in South Africa.

Jamāt committees consisted of the prominent individuals of the communities, generally traders. Organized into committees, traders provided the financial and organizational support and patronage for the infrastructure of Muslim activity. Throughout the Transvaal, there were only seven family trusts that administered mosques exclusively, without community involvement (see table 4.1). In the rest, the officials were elected on a regular basis. Women, however, were completely excluded—not deliberately excluded but simply ignored. The responsibilities of the committees included the rights to appoint, dismiss, and remunerate the imāms and religious scholars ('ulamā'). Sometimes, positions on the committees were considered to be particularly prestigious and evoked much competition. At other times, the responsibilities of raising funds and dealing with the authorities were regarded as particularly exacting, and few people were willing to volunteer. In any event, whether entailing more or less commitment, the jamāt committees have enjoyed considerable authority through their activities.

The jamāt committees' composition, their relationship with the state and religious leaders, and their conception of Islam defined the political praxis of Muslim communities. In order to establish mosques, committees had to deal directly with the state to obtain permission or find loopholes in legislation. Not surprisingly, therefore, the establishment of mosques followed the patterns of obtaining trading rights and licenses, thus providing

Table 4.1. Transvaal family trusts

Town	Family
Burgersfort	Tayob Fakir Muhammad
Carolina	Ismail Mohammed Dadabhay
Coligny	Nawlakhi
Mayfair (Jhb)	Ahmed Essop Patel
Nelspruit	Ismail Minty & Sons
Trichardt	Ebrahim Daya
White River	Muḥammad Ismail Gardee

the powerful lever for jamāt committees in the structure of the mosque. Mosque building in the Transvaal took place in the shadow of government decrees designed to minimize, and preferably eliminate, Indian ownership of property. Mosques were founded on concessions carefully extracted from the state or via loopholes detected in discriminatory legislation. Muslims often reminded the British and later the Afrikaner authorities of their right to freedom of worship; they lost no opportunity to benefit from legislation pertaining to places of worship.[8] When this did not work, trusts and committees used the services of white nominees, and on occasion even of state officials, to keep the discriminatory legislation outside the mosques. Many mosques were held under the name of a department or a cabinet minister or simply the South African State, instead of the community as such. In addition to white nominees and the state, Indians also used Cape "Malays"—who could be anything from wives, friends, or false declarations to ingenious genealogical creations—to register mosques. Land ownership restrictions did not apply to Cape Muslims, and some Indians were able to obtain such "Malay" rights. Of the mosques in official white areas in the Transvaal, for example, eleven were formally owned by the state, seven by white nominees, and four by Malay or Coloured persons, while one did not register at all (see table 4.2). In spite of the continuing legal problems of mosque ownership, mosque building mushroomed in the Transvaal, testifying to the community's resolve to find a niche in the country.

The use of nominees and these dubious racial "rights" was entrenched as a successful mechanism by which to establish mosques. Even the victory of the National Party in 1948, and their notorious Group Areas Act (no. 41 of 1950, amended in 1957) did not make a difference to this pattern. In terms of Nationalist ideology, Indians in the Transvaal were earmarked for reloca-

Table 4.2. Mosque nominees

Mosque /JK	Established Nominee
Barberton	Minister of Int. Donges
Belfast	Miss Hall
Benoni	City Council Lease
Bethal Town	Minister of Interior
Bloemhof	Patel (Malay rights)
Brits	Union of South Africa
Ermelo	Jacksons (Attorneys)
Jhb Newclare	Unknown Malay
Jhb Newlands	Mrs. Nathee (Malay wife)
Jhb Newtown	Mendelsohn (attorney)
Jhb 15th Street	City Council lease
Jhb 23rd St	City Council lease
Klerksdorp	No transfer taken
Leandra	(Leslie) Minister of Interior
Louis Trichardt	Minister of Interior
Lydenburg	Unnamed white nominee
Machadadorp	Mrs. Chotia (German wife of Mr. Chotia)
Middelburg	Salojee Ltd. Trust
Pietersburg	Union of South Africa
Pretoria Marabastad	City Council lease
Pretoria Queen St.	Mr. Bowyer
Standerton	Mrs. Valod (Malay wife)
Ventersdorp	Unnamed Coloured person
Vereeninging	a Mr. Vorster

tion from some of the prime spots in the central business districts. Trading districts built and developed over the past sixty or seventy years were summarily closed down and new areas were allocated for Indian trading. Many landowners suddenly found that properties and buildings purchased under permit or through nominees were summarily expropriated by the state, and inadequate compensation was paid. In spite of these drastic measures, jamāt committees whose communities were earmarked for relocation did not stop the building of mosques. As under previous laws, some mosques were built under official ownership and sometimes official sponsorship. For example, the Administrator of Transvaal opened the Krugersdorp mosque in 1948 on the eve of the Group Areas Act. The state, it appeared, condoned and even blessed the building of mosques in the early days of

Table 4.3. Mosques built in white areas after 1948

Town	Year established
Barberton	1952
J'burg 15th St.	1948
Krugersdorp	1948
Louis Trichardt	1954

apartheid (see table 4.3). Jamāt committee members thought the apartheid regime was not entirely serious about implementing its ideology. As with earlier legislation, some loophole would be found and a mosque would be built where needed.

However, when the Group Areas Act was implemented in earnest in the sixties, mosques in white areas, including the one founded in Krugersdorp in 1948, were marked for expropriation. Now, however, Muslims throughout the country resisted this by appealing again to the religious sensibilities of the Afrikaners. Themselves espousing ostensibly Christian values, Afrikaners were particularly vulnerable to the appeal to religion. Mr. Laher, a mosque committee member of the Nugget Street Mosque in Johannesburg, described in an interview in April 1990 how he pleaded with Group Areas inspectors that the preservation of religion would serve the anti-Communist interests of the state. He believes that he secured sympathy for the mosque by using the potency of an anti-Communist slogan at the time. However, such personal approaches were not going to be sufficient against the comprehensive ideology of apartheid. Therefore, citing the religious laws of *waqf* applicable to mosque property, Muslims took their grievances to court. In terms of the Islamic laws of waqf, mosques were religiously endowed properties that were not subject to sale and expropriation. In a landmark case of 1963, the Middelburg Muslim community successfully resisted the expropriation of its mosque.[9] The community had to move; and it also lost other land and buildings that the mosque committee had accumulated over the years for school facilities and investment purposes. Only the mosque was saved from destruction and expropriation.

Muslims maintained the mosques in white areas they were forced to abandon, and these became lonely testimonies against the pointlessness of apartheid. Probably the most poignant statement was made by the Muslims of Nylstroom, who refused to build a mosque in the residential area as a symbol of their rejection of forced removals. Five times a day, they called the faithful to prayer, and five times a day, Muslims worshiped at a mosque around which they were prohibited to live. Muslims did not actually hear the call to prayer but insisted on driving the five miles from where they were supposed to be safely tucked out of sight. In most other cases, Transvaal mosques were more passive reminders of relocation. As apartheid took shape, the mosques, their minarets, and their calls to prayer remained but stark reminders of once thriving communities.

From the perspective of mosque formation, Muslims remained generally accommodating toward the state. The jamāt committees, in particular, realized that they required the state to establish mosques in the newly designated Group Areas. Relying on the success of mosque establishment in the Transvaal, they preferred to negotiate concessions from the state rather than systematically resisting its destructive designs. In spite of repeated measures by which freedom of movement and ownership were curtailed and controlled by colonial and apartheid authorities, the jamāt committees were locked into accommodationist political practices, which even the most dreadful forced removals of apartheid could not change. They believed that they would somehow survive the onslaught of apartheid as they had survived British and Boer policies for a hundred years. As key actors in the establishment of mosques in the Transvaal, moreover, the jamāt committee benefited from this checkered legal history. Although the state enacted a list of restrictions, most laws were open to some petition and lax implementation.[10] Jamāt committee members established the necessary "influence" and "contact" with cooperative government officials. Difficulties with one or another discriminatory law could be alleviated or removed through mediation. While this type of state patronage inscribed a client status for Muslims, it translated into considerable power for individuals within the Muslim communities. Jamāt committees, as the dominant group in the Transvaal, did not acquire their authority and prestige simply by providing the finance for building the mosques. They were constituted as authorities in the legal history of Indian ownership in the country. Their authority was all the more effective precisely because it appeared that there was no other way of building a mosque except by approaching the state, cap in hand and feigning obeisance, preferably through one of the influential leaders.

The mosques in the Transvaal, then, were products of a particular legal history. The jamāt committees were the major beneficiaries in the process, wielding complete power and authority through their particular relations with the state. This does not mean that mosques were not symbols of ethnic and racial groupings among the Muslims, as is elsewhere well attested.

Muslims from India came from small villages and towns, representing a diverse range of linguistic and ethnic identities, which were also reflected in the mosques founded in South Africa. Transvaal mosques among Indians, however, were ethnically defined in a very imprecise manner. The example of the first mosque in Pretoria showed the extent of this ethnicity as well its limitation. This mosque was built and controlled entirely by the Memon-speaking group until Achmat Effendi persuaded trustees to draw up a constitution that included Surti- and Kokani-speaking members of the community. Effendi was dismissed for his interference, but the constitution was eventually changed to accommodate his suggestions.[11] Ethic identities of the mosques, therefore, were generally not as powerful a force as the legal constitution of the mosque in South Africa. The legal and political history of the mosque had a greater impact on the nature of the mosque organization than the ethnic and linguistic pecularities of the congregations.

The Mosques Redefined

The power of the mosque committees in the establishment and development of mosques was exerted over the religious leadership. In response, the latter advocated orthodoxy and orthopraxis in redefining the character of the mosques, particularly with regard to what took place inside the mosques. Religious leaders did not question the political relations with the state or the financial power with which the mosque committees exerted their influence. Religious leadership in the Transvaal was not a revolutionary rejection or representation of the underclasses. Unlike the Cape imāms, these religious leaders still relied on traders to build mosques under the particular political conditions prevailing. As a mark of their sphere of influence, however, the religious scholars posited the power of Islamic knowledge and orthodoxy to determine the religious discourse inside the mosque. An examination of this dimension of the mosque, its power and authority, and its promotion or demotion of particular religious practices reveals the most powerful religious discourse dominating the Islamic ethos of the Transvaal.

The first organized religious leadership in the Transvaal was initiated by Cape imāms. By 1888, Cape Muslims had established a mosque in Ferreirastown in what was known as the Malay quarter. This mosque was demolished in 1907 when it was condemned as insanitary, but the plot was incorporated into the Juma Masjid Society in 1916. Another Malay mosque in Johannesburg, known as the Twenty-Third Street Mosque, was established in 1895 in Pageview and continued to serve the "Malay" community until the Group Areas removals. The "Malay" mosques of the Transvaal maintained a direct link with the Cape Muslim community and followed the patterns of the Cape mosque discourse. Naudé lists a number of Cape imāms as the first religious leaders in the Transvaal: Imām Taib Japie (arrived 1870), Imām Khaliel (1899), Imām Abdul Malik (about 1905), Imām Kamalie (about 1910), Imām Biehardien (about 1918), Imām Ismail Japie (about 1918), and Imām Suraai (about 1926).[12] In 1922, these imāms formed the Jamiatul Ulama Transvaal and published a text in Arabic-Afrikaans, the linguistic tradition that flourished in the Cape. In the beginning, these religious leaders seemed more prominent than their Indian counterparts, and they seem to have been at the forefront of Islamic affairs in early stages in the Transvaal. At the turn of the century, a Shaykh Muṣṭafā from Johannesburg requested a juridical decree (fatwā) from the great Muḥammad Abduh in Egypt on the following questions:

1. Could Muslims wear or sell European clothing?

2. Could Muslims consume meat of animals slaughtered by Jews and Christians?

3. Could adherents of one legal school (madhhab) in Islam be led by an imām from another school?

From his reformist position, Abduh answered all three questions in the affirmative.[13] The first and third questions underscored the juridical differences between the Indian and Cape Muslims. Cape Muslims, especially under Effendi, had adopted Western clothing topped by a Turkish fez, in contrast to the Eastern clothing of the more recently settled Indians. Moreover, the Cape Muslims were Shāfiʿī while most of the Indians were Ḥanafī. The second question even suggests a more liberal tradition than that which has become dominant in either the Cape or the Transvaal. Most important, the questions posed to an authority in Cairo register the orientation of Muslim affairs. Under the dominance of the Indians, that direction has since changed toward India. Cape imāms were slowly marginalized by a dominant Ḥanafī leadership.

Indian communities preferred bringing religious teachers and officials from villages in India. Most of these imāms were brought as employees to the various mosques emerging in the region. An "Arabiese medikant" (Arab herbalist) mentioned by Bhana and Brain may have been self-employed.[14] Generally, however, Indian religious leaders remained under the patronage of the jamāt committees, sometimes under deeply ironic conditions. An example of the latter was the Smuts-Ghandi Agreement of 1914, which allowed a limited number of "educated entrants" to serve the cultural and religious needs of Indians. While a statutory act was designed to limit Indian immigration in 1913, the agreement of 1914 was responsible for many imāms coming to South Africa to serve the needs of the Muslims. The new imāms were indebted to the jamāt committees for political relations enabling their entry. The agreement stipulated that they were not permitted to engage in any form of independent economic activity, and residence permits were granted for brief temporary periods.[15] The situation for imāms in the Transvaal seems to have been a little worse than in Natal: in addition to the permission required to enter South Africa, they also required permits to enter the Transvaal. In both cases, jamāt committees had to apply for such permits on their behalf.[16]

On the basis of their more precarious political position, the Indian imāms established a different kind of religious leadership from that in the Cape. When they organized themselves, it was on the basis of 'ilm, Islamic knowledge, offered to the communities, rather than of ownership, administrative control, or loyalty. 'Ilm became the cornerstone of their intervention in the Transvaal mosque. The first person to organize the Indian religious leadership in the Transvaal was Mawlānā Ebrahim Sanjalvi, who revived the Jamiatul Ulama Transvaal in 1934 with the support of the Mia family, pledging to "give religious guidance to the Muslim community . . . concerning the Sharī'ah."[17] It established the Waterval Islamic Institute for training 'ulamā' and encouraged students to travel to Islamic centers of learning in India and Pakistan.[18] The status of the 'ulamā' in the Transvaal was enhanced in no small measure by the emergence of the Tablīghī Jamāt, a mass movement that originated in 1928 in India and reached South Africa in 1962. The Tablīghī Jamāt was founded on a simple message by which individuals committed themselves to re-creating, as far as possible, the lifestyle of the Prophet in the modern world. In terms of content, and as we shall see also of discourse, the goals of the Tablīghī Jamāt coincided with the religious reforms promoted by the 'ulamā'. The movement organized groups of individuals moving from one mosque to another, spreading their simple and appealing message.

Both the Tablīghī Jamāt and the Jamiatul Ulama were aligned to the Deobandi approach to Islam in India. Deoband is a town in India and the site where the first Islamic seminary of British colonial India was established in 1867. It was the seat where a distinct religious orientation was established in modern India, which has come to be known as Deobandi thought. Metcalf has identified this approach as an aloofness from the state but without overt opposition to its excesses; a careful balance between Sufism and legalism but with a puritan emphasis on the early authorities of Islam; and, more important, an alliance with the merchant class as opposed to subservience under political rulers.[19] Unlike in India, where many Deobandi 'ulamā' joined the Congress movement against British colonial occupation, the South African Deobandis generally accepted the particular political relations established by the mosque committees. The Deobandi outlook, a purist orthodoxy, was marshaled as a discourse inside Transvaal mosques in order to balance the power wielded by the mosque committees in building and establishing the mosques. It was never directed at questioning the political approach established by the prominent traders.

It was natural for the Transvaal 'ulamā' to transform and purify religious practices. As in many other Islamic societies, the elimination of *bid'ah* (innovation) became a rallying cry against numerous accretions that were deemed un-Islamic and non-Prophetic. As imāms and religious teachers, they redrew the curriculum for religious instruction in order to conform to this new orthodoxy. The Waterval Islamic Institute became a center for disseminating standardized textbooks and examination officers who visited the *madrasahs* (religious schools) in the region. Later, mass-circulated literature in the mosque also became a popular means through which these new ideas were presented and entrenched in the community.[20] The anti-bid'ah rhetoric of Islamic orthodoxy has been studied extensively, and it has its legendary advocates, from Aḥmad b. Ḥanbal (d. 241/855) and Ibn Taymiyyah (d. 728/1328) to Muḥammad b. 'Abd al-Wahhāb (d. 1206/1792). In an assessment of contemporary bid'ah controversies, Rispler-Chaim points out that the arguments have not changed significantly since the earliest times in Islamic history.[21] On the one hand, bid'ah practices remain popular and thus attractive for groups and even states wanting to exploit them for greater support and legitimacy, respectively. On the other hand, they have come under severe criticism from scholars, who judged their validity on the basis of their fidelity to the Qur'ān and Prophetic practices. Bowen has approached the subject with greater depth in a study of discourses, locating the arguments within competing discourses. In the case of supplication (*du 'ā'*), for example, modernist reformers in Indonesia charged that villagers were practicing bid'ah when their invocations were made loudly. While modernists regarded supplications as a means of addressing God, villagers were also addressing spirits. Bowen regarded both as discourses that defined a different meaning and place for Islamic supplication.[22] The bid'ah debate, then, was not simply a debate over textual fidelity; it was deeply embedded in competing discourses.

The anti-bidʿah rhetoric in the Transvaal was present in the ʿulamāʾ booklets, sermons, and school syllabi. However, the most effective rhetoric was not restricted to speech and the written word but took effect in specific gestures and acts by the protagonists of the particular viewpoint. This is an aspect ignored by Rispler-Chaim and by others who have focused entirely on the legal arguments.[23] Such arguments were a powerful weapon only in the arsenal of the ʿulamāʾ who wished to alter religious practices in a very specific context. The control of religious practices and ideas through ritual was more expressive than the debate over texts. Anti-bidʿah rituals were more effective in that they could not be as easily ignored as could speech or texts. More important, the gestures revealed the focus of the anti-bidʿah rhetoric. In the case of the Transvaal mosque, anti-bidʿah gestures were directed at the reclamation of the mosque from the jamāt committees. A few examples will illustrate the force and effect of these powerful ritual claims in Transvaal.

Marshaling the Qurʾān and the example of the Prophet Muhammad, ʿulamāʾ proposed and enacted different forms for popular religious practices. Reforms were introduced in the manner in which one could appeal to or remember God in a group, the particular dress code used inside the mosques, and the manner in which one celebrated official holy days. First, it was emphasized that religious supplications of all forms were to be recited inaudibly. This included the duʿāʾ (supplication) after the daily worship; the takbīr (proclamations of the greatness of God) on Eid festival days; and salutations to the Prophet (ṣalawāt). Usually, each of these expressions was recited loudly and then accompanied by equally formulaic responses, creating an action-response scenario between an imām and his audience. Now, Deobandi ʿulamāʾ insisted that apart from certain standard forms of prayers during the performance of worship, all other supplications and invocations and their responses had to be performed silently. On this point, they relied principally on the following verse: "Call upon your Lord with humility and in secret" (Qurʾān 7:55). Removed from context and competing interpretations, the Qurʾānic verse was advocated as an absolute decree.[24] The Qurʾānic citation, however, paled in significance compared to the ritual gestures that accompanied it. ʿUlamāʾ left worshipers guessing as they mumbled prayers and abandoned the familiar and elaborate supplication expressions. Sometimes, they simply said nothing; at other times, they rushed through the formulae in order to suppress any possible response from the audience. Where once mosques resounded with supplications, they now became muted places of confusion at worst and private meditation at best.

Dress code was another reform that elevated the role of the 'ulamā' in the Transvaal mosque. The 'ulamā' prescribed a certain form of Islamic dress at all times: a long white shirt (*kurta*) and head covering (*topi*). While this dress had always been appropriate for religious scholars in the Transvaal, it was now presented as the preferred dress for all Muslims. For those who did not conform to such dress in their everyday attire, some minimum requirement was deemed absolutely essential inside the mosque. Hats and long cloaks, as well as innovative pull-on sleeves, were provided for worshipers inside mosques. One particular dress item that took on a special significance in the Transvaal mosques was the length of men's trousers. All men were expected to fold their trousers above the ankles during prayers. Men in the Transvaal slowly developed a habit of folding their trousers as they walked into the mosques. Those who refused were identified, sometimes discreetly in the sermons or by less than discreet nudges in the ablution blocks.

Deobandi criticism was also directed at four popular celebrations in the Transvaal mosque calendar.[25] First, the birthday of the Prophet was celebrated on the twelfth of Rabīʿ al-Awwal, the third month of the Islamic calendar. Then the community observed the *Miʿrāj* (ascension) of the Prophet on the twenty-seventh eve of Rajab, the seventh month of the Islamic year, in memory and celebration of the night journey undertaken by the Prophet. The night of absolution (*Barāʾah*), also called *Laylat niṣf Shaʿbān* as it fell on the fifteenth of Shaʿbān, the eighth month of the Islamic calendar, was an occasion for asking forgiveness of God as well as of the person on whom an injury had been inflicted. Finally, the night of power, *Laylat al-Qadr*, was observed on the twenty-seventh night of Ramaḍān, the climax of devotion during the month of fasting. In the Transvaal, these events were observed by men attending the mosque for the night worship, which was usually followed by a special *khatam*, a ritual during which a few copies of the Qurʾān, each divided into thirty parts, were distributed for recitation. This would be followed by a special sermon for the occasion. The event concluded with sweets, fruits, and rose-scented milk or water distributed by a wealthy patron, often in fulfillment of a vow. These special nights in the town were known as "Big Nights"; attracting huge audiences, most often larger than the Friday gathering. 'Ulamā' were critical of the manner in which the events were celebrated as well as the inversion of priorities. They criticized the celebrations either for being innovations or for providing opportunities for introducing nontextual practices into the society. Such rhetoric, even though powerful, was supplemented by more purposeful gestures. Using their crucial positions in the mosques, the 'ulamā' most frequently refused to attend or, worse still, agreed to attend but not to preach. Sometimes they demanded that the recitation of the Qur'ān during the khatam be completely inaudible. At other times, they refused to conclude the event with the usual supplication. Again, even though the basic intellectual arguments were drawn from texts, the 'ulamā' expressed their displeasure through gestures articulated from the position they held at the head of the mosque. Hence, we find that in each case, criticism by the 'ulamā' of the innovations was accompanied by ritual gestures placing them in absolute control of the mosque. Inaudible supplications rendered the mosques available only for the preachers and ritual leaders. Dress codes forced a standard that the 'ulamā' had adopted; and the muted celebrations of the Big Nights robbed all but the 'ulamā' of a role therein.

The redefinition of the mosque was confirmed in the program and activity of the chief supporters of the 'ulamā', the Tablīghī Jamāt. For the latter, traveling and propagating their particular message was regarded as the pinnacle of going out in the "path of God" (fī sabīl Allah). As they moved from one mosque to another, Tablīghī Jamāt members became the mosques' most important and natural occupants. Mass gatherings (ijtimā') at regional and national levels were convened to reinforce this enveloping geographical inscription. By their presence and their fervent devotion inside the mosque, the members in the movement inscribed meaning in the mosques in the same way that the early traders had inscribed its political practice. The ritual moving from one mosque to another, and the Tablīghī members' invocation of the authority of the scholars for information, constituted a methodical recovery of the mosque from the jamāt committees. With their occupation of the mosques, they repossessed the mosque for themselves and the 'ulamā' most convincingly and emphatically.

Conclusion

Influential traders, then, played a significant role in the establishment of Islam in the Transvaal. At first, they simply set aside places for worship. Later, in their desire to erect recognizable places of worship, they found themselves faced with legal and political obstacles and prejudice. Against these obstacles, traders founded a discourse of mosque building in the region. Mosque committees, consisting mainly of influential male traders, stood at the head of the operations. They relied on their intimate knowledge of the law, on government officials, and sometimes on sheer dissimulation to establish and build mosques. The political conditions of British colonialism and then apartheid demanded the greatest attention and determined the nature and power of mosque officials.

This pattern of mosque building curbed or determined the effects of other possible constitutive discourses on Transvaal mosques. Thus, strong linguistic and ethnic identities among Indians, which could have had decisive influence in the nature of mosques, were and continue to be an insufficient basis for building and maintaining a mosque. Such ethnic emphases in mosques do exist in some communities, but they do not determine the manner in which mosques are founded, built, and then managed. Similarly, Islamic legal considerations were also secondary in the formation of a Transvaal mosque. Mosques were not founded on the basis of Islamic law. Islamic law was invoked only much later in response to apartheid threats to expropriate mosques. Earlier, for example, mosques were built on the basis of the freedom of worship accorded to British citizens. It may be argued that early Muslims went to such extraordinary lengths to register mosques on the assumption that mosques were ideally founded on inviolable land, which could not be subject to the whims of nominee owners or government decrees. They were supposed to be indefinite endowments (waqf), the function of which could not be changed.[26] There is no historical record extant that points to this Islamic legal consideration among the early Muslims. On the contrary, the willingness to found so many mosques in spite of unacceptable conditions points to the fact that Islamic legal considerations were not of primary importance. Mosques as places of worship could simply have been temporary prayer rooms, jamāt khānahs or muṣallahs, rather than formally designated and consecrated mosques as such. Such instances, however, were rare. Most communities founded mosques. The absence of strong ethnic and Islamic juridical foundations in the mosques can only be explained in terms of the powerful political praxis of founding mosques in the Transvaal.

The ʿulamāʾ in the Transvaal had to accommodate themselves to this structural and political context. They could have been subservient mosque employees and accepted the pressures of the mosque committee officials. In the Transvaal, however, the ʿulamāʾ accepted the mosque committees only insofar as their particular relations with the state were concerned. Inside the mosque, and thus in terms of religious dictates, the ʿulamāʾ appealed to Islamic knowledge in order to stake their own claims. The orthodoxy and orthopraxis they demanded were directed at redefining the mosque as regards its particular religious practices. In this chapter I have focused on the ritual transformation of the mosque ethos. Islamic puritanism—often regarded as simply the pronouncements of the authoritative Arabic texts of the Qur'ān and the Prophet—has here been shown to have had a highly specific target in the Transvaal mosque. Such textualism was not simply a form of Arabicization, as Sanneh seems to argue is the distinctive spirit of Islamic reform and puritanism.[27] 'Ulamā' puritanism was a Transvaal response to the discourse of how mosques were founded and established by traders in the context of colonialism and apartheid.

The 'ulamā', with powerful textual and ritual persuasion, were able to convince a large number of Muslims in the region that correct belief and practice within the mosque was their prerogative. The force of verses from the Qur'ān and statements from the Prophet Muḥammad would not have been sufficient. The gestures that redefined the activities of the mosque, by leaders appointed by mosque officials, could not be ignored. The ritual gestures were apparently derived from scriptural texts, but when they were enacted in ritual, they reinforced the transformative nature of the text as well as clarifying the target of this transformation. Mary Douglas, in a study of the importance of ritual, points to this nature of rituals felt by and accepted by particular mosque officials in the Transvaal. Ritual, she said, "comes first in formulating experience. It can permit knowledge of what would otherwise not be known at all. It does not merely externalize experience, bringing it out into the light of day, but it modifies experience in so expressing it."[28] The rituals made it absolutely clear that puritanism was directed at the particular control enjoyed by the traders.

The 'ulamā' were extremely successful, but only to the extent that they left the political relations intact. The 'ulamā' did not question or oppose the politics of accommodation or client status in mosque building in the Transvaal. Thus, unlike the Cape, the mosque remained a product of that political relationship, and Islamic rules and conduct within the mosque deftly avoided any issues that questioned this relationship. In fact, committed as they were to defining the practice of religion within the four walls of the mosque, Islamic rules and conduct created an aura of insularity and self-sufficiency against the political issues that raged in society. It was an ideal world where mosque committee and 'ulamā' could ignore competing discourses and political challenges. Divergent political and religious views could easily be domesticated.

5

The Brits Mosque:
Orthodoxy and Its Periphery

In a study of traditional and reformist modes of learning in Morocco, Eickelman identified the "prismatic nature of Islamic learning," in which certain subjects enjoyed prestige in terms of place and time over others.[1] In Morocco, peripheral subjects like Qur'ān exegesis were taught during nonprestigious times, always contending for better time slots. Bowen identified the peripheral nature of some Muslim discourses in an Indonesian community, where the traditional village discourse practiced a form of dissimulation for its inability to compete with the prestige of Islamic modernism.[2] In both Morocco and Indonesia, careful observation charted discordant and dissonant voices on the periphery of dominant voices. Both these cases point to the social location of peripheral interpretations and voices in Muslim society. When the mosque gives the semblance of timeless, unified practices, alternative interpretations are already at work on the periphery.

The mosque in Brits gave the semblance of one such discourse dominated by one single political praxis and religious interpretation. As in other towns in the Transvaal, the jamāt committee constructed the discourse for the purchase and building of the mosque, while 'ulamā' determined the religious dimensions inside the mosque. And as in other parts of the Transvaal, both were constructed in the context of Afrikaner settlement, cheap black labor, and apartheid ideology. Upon more careful observation, however, peripheral voices and interpretations of Islam were detectable. In a few cases in the Transvaal, these marginal interpretations of Islam reproduced mosques. Generally, unlike in the Cape, new interpretations alone were not sufficient for the foundation of a mosque. Marginal and alternate interpretations usually positioned themselves on the periphery of the mosque, waiting to make significant interventions whenever an opportunity presented itself.

In the town of Brits, there were two such peripheral interpretations of Islam. One of these was the voice of those who still believed in the efficacy of practices deemed bid'ah by Deobandi orthodoxy. This so-called Brelvi movement nurtured the condemned rituals and tried to propose an opposing orthodoxy for the town. The second interpretation of Islam was that of Islamic resurgence, cultivated and promoted by a number of youth organizations and, as we saw earlier, also by the Claremont Main Road Mosque. The Islamists publicized issues of liberation politics, conversion of African Muslims, and women's rights. Both the Brelvi movement and Islamic resurgence, each in its own way, constructed interpretations at a distance from the centrally occupied mosque. The following case study of the Brits Mosque presents the center-periphery dynamics in one Transvaal mosque.

Background

The town of Brits lies in a fertile valley, halfway between Pretoria and Rustenburg in the North West Province. The area is one of a number of extremely fertile valleys in the Magaliesberg mountain range, well-known for its excellent soil of turf and lime. The farms on which the town is located were called Roodjekopjes and Zwartkopjes and were owned by Johan Nicolaas Brits, from whom the town got its name. His farm was part of the vast rural *platteland* of the country dominated by conservative white farmers. Trekking from the Cape, these Boers had defeated the forces of Mzilikazi, the Zulu king Shaka's renegade general, and they considered the "central high veld theirs by right of conquest."[3] The 1974 *Souvenir Album* issued by the Afrikaners of Brits flaunted this claim by stating that they saved the local Tswana people under Chief Mogale from the military might of the Zulus. Whites, according to the *Album*, brought "peace" and "civilization" to the valley.[4] The town was totally dominated by Afrikaners, who regarded their hegemony as natural and self-evident. This is nowhere so clearly depicted as in the *Album*, which confirms the prominence of this group of people in the town and the relative marginalization and even obliteration of the Indian and African people. Once they were given "peace and civilization" in the nineteenth century, the latter seemed to have disappeared, featuring in neither the agricultural nor the industrial development of the town. Their disappearance, however, was more a reflection of Afrikaner ideology than of reality.

The experience of local African communities has been catastrophic. Africans seem to have been part of the town from its inception. However, as early as 1928, an African "location," as black residential areas were called, was earmarked for settlement to the north of Brits. This was the start of their literal removal that matched their ideological erasure. Slowly, this dusty, unserviced area called Oukasie became the cheap labor resource of the town. By 1953, the Afrikaners felt that Oukasie was too close for comfort and began to make plans for yet another removal. Nothing came of this decision until the 1970s, by which time Oukasie had expanded considerably as workers streamed to the town's industries. As white demand for land increased, the 1953 decision to relocate the Africans was recalled. The local black town council, appointed by the Brits municipality, was granted the "honor" of announcing the removal of the residents of Oukasie in 1985. People were expected to move to Lethlabile, about fifteen miles out of Brits. Some people did move, especially those who had better jobs and preferred the new serviced township to the neglected Oukasie. Temporary and domestic workers, however, unable to afford the higher rental and transportation costs, formed the Brits Action Committee to resist the forced removals. After a long and bitter struggle, Oukasie residents won their battle against the state in 1990, the year Nelson Mandela was released from prison.[5]

The Indians made a fleeting appearance in the *Album* when they bought the Afrikaner-owned businesses in an area proclaimed Indian in 1955. A closer look at the settlement of the town reveals a more complex picture. Oral accounts indicate that Indian hawkers visited the area from as early as 1890, one of the first being Joosub Soomar. More arrived after a dam was built in 1921 and some traders followed the irrigation canals that serviced the farmers in the region.[6] In fact, there was a big enough Indian group in 1921 to warrant the building of the first mosque, the land for which was donated by Hassim Soomar, a prominent businessman. The corrugated iron structure enjoyed the distinction of being the first place of worship in the town. Churches had preceded the mosque in the outlying rural areas around Brits, but the first church in the town was established only in 1925 and a synagogue in 1931.[7] If we judge a religious center as one of the significant marks of urban settlement, the Muslims appeared have to played a greater role than the *Album* suggests. While Afrikaners dominated the rural areas, Indians occupied an important place in the town itself. The relationship between the traders and the Afrikaner farmers was congenial. Illustrating the mutual exchange of goods and services, a Muslim called Rooibaard (redbeard) Patel was presumed by the Afrikaner farmers to possess occult powers. He became famous for helping farmers to find lost donkeys and cattle in the district of Brits. This relationship between a resourceful Indian businessman and credulous Afrikaner farmers was a more accurate depiction of the relationship between Indians and Afrikaners than the one advocated by the *Album*. Unlike the portrayal in the *Album*'s history of the town, the relationship underlined an inverse hierarchy of the political privilege of Afrikaners and the economic power of some Indian traders.

When the town was officially founded, a number of Indians explored the familiar loopholes of acquiring property. Most Indians purchased land using the name of a Mrs. Dolly Deenat, a Cape Muslim wife of one of the traders. As the pioneer Indian Muslim, however, Joosub Soomar campaigned for the "exemption" of the area under the Asiatic Land Tenure (Amendment) Bill of 1932, which restricted Indian land ownership. Soomar was convinced that his request would be heeded. Since this area of Brits fell outside the irrigation canal system, it would be "exempted" from the draconian effect of the law. In addition, lying on the lower part of the valley, it was more prone to flooding from the Hartebeespoort Dam overflow that ran into the Crocodile River to the south of the town.[8] As expected, the government agreed to exempt the area from the restrictions of the act. Land ownership by Indians in the town, then, began with a law designed to restrict that very process. Having secured this loophole, the earliest families bought tracts of land measuring approximately three acres, running north-south from the railway line to the Crocodile River. Each plot of land could easily accommodate an extended family consisting of five or six household units. When the area of exempt status was confirmed as an Indian Group Area in 1955, land ownership was fixed in the hands of these influential families. Consequently, land for residential use remained a major problem in the town. Some residents even believed that the removal of Indians and their relocation to an area outside town would have addressed this unequal situation. Thus, when the residential area was expanded later, in the 1970s, Indians regarded this as a blessing from the town council and not as a problem caused in principle by the policies of apartheid land use. The problem lay in the combination of possession of land by a few influential families and restriction of Indians to a designated and confined space. On the basis of a false perception of shortage, many supported apartheid legislation that ostensibly "solved" the land problem.

The jamāt committee and the 'ulamā' set down roots early in the town. Important though Muslims may have been in the history of Brits, my interest in the mosque lies in the production of a political and religious discourse that gave shape to this community and its relations with the state. While Muslims may justifiably claim a prominent place in the town's development, closer investigation yields a subsequent checkered history in relations with the dominant authority as well as with the African communities in and around the town. I begin with the production of the dominant mosque discourse between the mosque committee and the religious leaders.

The registered name of the jamāt committee in Brits was the Brits Mohamedan Madrasah, but it was simply called the Jamāt, and its officials Jamāt members. This institution has existed in one form or another since the first mosque was built in 1921. It convened meetings, organized elections, and kept some modicum of records. With a clear and underlined seven-eight-six, representing the numerological value of the Islamic invocation "In the Name of God, Most gracious, most merciful," the first recorded meeting followed proper procedure:

786

Committee meeting of the Brits Mohamedan Madressa held at Brits at the residence of the secretary Mohamed Tayob on the 23 rd January 1959.

Present: Mohammed Hassim (in the chair); Mohamed Ismail; Aboo Omar; Mohamed Tayob[9]

All subsequent meetings were recorded in this fashion in a large ledger book. Annual general meetings organized elections at regular intervals, usually once a year. All male members took part in the elections. Prominent traders occupied the key roles on the committee. Later, in chronological order, medical doctors, school teachers, and 'ulamā' followed them. Black Muslims living around the town were never represented on the jamāt committee. Even though women were often asked to contribute to the building of the mosque, they were completely excluded from elections, deliberations, and the mosque itself. Even when the newly renovated mosque was opened in September 1992, women were only allowed to view the mosque during nonprayer times. And that was permitted only after the 'ulamā' had expressed their grave reservations. It was not surprising that, when permission was eventually granted, most women had lost interest in taking that single peek into the mosque.

Jamāt activities together constituted a discourse of social and economic authority in the mosque. Regular elections conferred legitimacy to the group, and the raising of sufficient funds and establishing of relations with state officials defined a particular range of appropriate acts. Principally, the financial duties of the jamāt committee included paying salaries to the imāms and teachers and building and maintaining the mosque, the religious school (*madrasah*), and cemetery. In Brits, as in many other towns, the jamāt committee raised funds through donations, monthly subscriptions, school fees, and last but not least, through the purchase of business premises that could then be rented. The fund-raising was not simply collecting money for the maintenance of the building. These activities constituted an elaborate pattern that created unique representations of a Jamāt member. A few examples will illustrate the powerful discursive nature of fund-raising. The Jamāt raised money through monthly subscriptions and madrasah fees from each and every person in the community. In 1960, the community subscription began with one pound sterling per trade license holder and ten shillings per nontrading resident. This later became a uniform levy payable by all income earners and stood at four rand per month in 1991. Solly Moonda, a bicycle dealer, served the jamāt committee as a punctilious treasurer for seventeen years from 1970 to 1987. He would know exactly when to approach a new wage earner about his or her obligation to the coffers of the Jamāt.[10] In addition, the committee levied madrasah fees, which increased over the years: from fifty cents in 1964 to four rand in 1983. The fees for the madrasah were closely linked to the salaries of teachers.[11] Increases were demanded from the community when new imāms were appointed, the imāms often being expected to collect the fees. Like the monthly commitments, the fees were not paid regularly, and the Jamāt had considered barring nonpaying children from Islamic education and displaying the names of nonpaying members on the mosque board.[12] The monthly subscriptions and school fees had been agonized over, for they could not fulfill the needs of the Jamāt. Nevertheless, they gave the semblance of the whole community participating in the operation of its institutions. The threats to put names on the mosque boards or to exclude children from schools reflect a commitment to determining membership in the community through Jamāt activities. In this sense, the levying of fees was not merely a matter of balancing accounts and paying bills. It had implications for defining membership in the community.

The most effective means of raising funds in the community remained direct collection by way of pledges from prominent business families in the town and in the Transvaal region as a whole. The contributions were also discursive practices reinforcing the prominence of the wealthy. While the monthly contributions tried to define the nature of the local community, the contributions by wealthy families in town established the authority and prominence of traders. In Brits, there have been some dramatic and spectacular donations, especially during the building of a new mosque in 1962 and its renovation in 1992. No doubt personal religious motivations were involved, but the dominance of the donors determined the discourse of wealth and power in the Jamāt.[13] The personal religious motivations for the contributions, for instance, did not preclude making demands as to how these funds ought to be used. Many incidents may be cited, but the 1992 renovation provides some striking examples of the process involved in the building of a mosque. Renovation plans were drawn up, submitted for approval, and passed in 1983.[14] A new committee, however, shelved these plans and submitted another plan for the town council's consideration. The new plan, duly approved, was then advertised in the mosque before a contract was signed for the work. Until then, no objections were raised either against the million rand that needed to be raised for the renovation or against the kind of alterations proposed in the plan. The objections came when the existing mosque ceiling and walls were torn down. Few had visualized such drastic transformations to a thirty-year-old landmark. Some people objected to the specific changes and others to the enormous sum spent on the mosque. Complaints involved the poor quality of the bricks being used, the type of paving outside the mosque, the seats in the ablution block, and an obstructive beam across the mosque. At almost every step of the renovations, groups of men were engulfed in debating the detail. One dissatisfied member of the community changed his mind only when he saw the completed building in a dream and liked it. Eventually, after considerable argument both inside and outside Jamāt meetings, and after some costly modifications, the mosque received the community's approval. It was completed and opened for worship in September 1992.[15]

The fund-raising activities defined a particular sphere of influence enjoyed by the jamāt committee and by the prominent donors to the mosque. The latter were also important for another set of the Jamāt's principal duties, namely obtaining building permits, getting plans approved, and obtaining death certificates for burials. The jamāt committee could not manage the mosque without a particular political relation with the apartheid state. When the repugnant racial laws of apartheid were applied by the state, the Jamāt responded not by invoking ethical and moral principles but accommodating its demands. In the apartheid era, obtaining permits often meant going cap in hand to a government office set aside for black (nonwhite) matters. Government offices were regularly duplicated to keep whites and blacks apart. However, in this regard, Jamāt members were prominent business leaders, well-known to the small town's officials. When they went in for such official matters, therefore, they would be recognized and given much better service than the average black person. In addition to the personal deference shown to prominent members in government offices, the Jamāt routinely took advantage of loopholes and concessions in the law. Sometimes, this meant a deft changing of identities and accommodation to suit the legal complexity of the day. In 1958, for example, the state informed the jamāt committee that the school was not officially located in the Indian area of the town. Until then, the Jamāt had owned the building as part of the Roodjekopjes and Zwartkopjes farms on which Brits was founded. The Jamāt applied for the reproclamation of the school, but the state would only allow the transfer if the Jamāt was an "Indian" legal entity. This meant that the Jamāt's constitution had to specify that only Indians would be eligible for office in the organization. There was some discussion in a community meeting of transferring the school to the Ministry of Interior instead of adding a racist clause in the constitution. But eventually the demands of apartheid were acceded to, and the transfer took place in 1963.[16]

The fund-raising activities and political relations established by the Jamāt formed the foundation of its authority and gave it the justification for intervening in the religious affairs of the community. Here, however, it was challenged by the discourse of Islamic knowledge. Initially, the Jamāt desired control of the imāms and teachers in terms of the standards of education and general accountability, but the new Deobandi 'ulamā' were able to assert their control inside the mosque. More recently, they have even begun to make demands within the jamāt committees themselves. The earliest imāms in the Brits community served for brief periods, until Moosa Mohammed Nana (d. 1957), known as Moosa Pir, came to Brits.[17] He stayed long enough to become a prominent symbol of piety, commitment, and devotion. In addition to his teaching and mosque leadership, he was also visited by people in the town for his prayers and healing amulets (ta 'wīdh). His close relation with the community, especially the administration of Islamic medicine, recalled the relationship between a Cape imām and his congregation. However, Moosa Pir did not appoint his successor and remained in the employment of the Jamāt until his death. The committee, with the assistance of new religious scholars returning from Deoband, constructed a new leadership discourse in the town.

After Moosa Pir's death, his wife Khala, his daughter Zubaydah, and two sons continued to teach in the madrasah. The jamāt committee was not happy with their services, complaining about the material taught in the schools, the "unqualified" standard of teaching, and the fact that the Nana family was selling sweets and homemade condiments to the children, sometimes on credit. On the basis of these grievances, the Jamāt decided to take control of Islamic education.[18] In 1964, a committee of inspectors was appointed to investigate religious education. This committee dismissed the Nanas and accepted the syllabus of the Jamiatul Ulama Transvaal.[19] Further, the committee recommended that other home-based private madrasahs run generally by women be discouraged and positively curtailed.[20] Brits thus joined many other madrasahs in Transvaal in adopting the syllabus, books, and approach to Islamic education of the Deobandi school of thought, and in eliminating the prominent role of women in religious education. The collusion between the Brits Jamāt Committee and the rising Deobandi authority closed a chapter of the Nana family's influence in the town, and with it their representation of a particular type of religious leadership and education. These were henceforth to be centralized and bureaucratized, a development to benefit the ideology of Deobandism.

The 'ulamā' introduced some fundamental changes in the practice of Islam in order to embody and consolidate this leadership. These practices declared their independence from the jamāt committee and determined an orthodoxy and an orthopraxis within the mosques. In Brits, two issues initiated the 'ulamā' critique of religious practices. The first arose in 1969 with the death of Joosub Soomar, the pioneer of the town: the imām in charge refused to say the customary final prayer at his graveside, at the same time condemning the practice of joining the bereaved family for a meal after the burial. Both traditions were among of the common practices of Muslims throughout the region. The imām was summoned to a Jamāt meeting, where he declared both practices innovations (bid'ah) and vowed that he would change his position only if a juridical opinion to the contrary was brought from the Jamiatul Ulama Transvaal.[21] The second issue cropped up in 1973, when Mawlānā Mobin al-Haq insisted on reading the invocation after the ṣalāh (workshop) inaudibly. Both incidents clearly stated the prerogative of the 'ulamā' in deciding what was acceptable in matters pertaining to religion. Refusal to perform a prayer at the burial of a Muslim was indicative of the kind of leadership being cultivated. Certainly, the 'ulamā' were most competent and should be expected to make interventions in matters of religion. Upon closer inspection, however, it becomes clear that they intervened in the context of the powerful jamāt committee. They focused their attention on activities inside the mosque to define an alternative discourse to that inscribed by the Jamāt's political and financial prerogatives.

Table 5.1. Temporary appointments in Brits

Appointee	Date	Years of service
Haffejee Nana	April 1964–1968	4 years
Nana (second time)	1973–	20 years
Haffejee Bux	November 1964–February 1965	4 months
Haffejee Moolla	July 1965	6 months
Haffejee Ebrahim	September 1967	4 years
Hafiz Adamjee	August 1968–February 1978	10 years
Hafiz Ravat	March 1975–May 1976	1 year
Mr. Ellemdin (teacher)	1979	6 months
Hafiz Osman	June 1976–June 1979	3 years
Hafiz Osman (2d time)	June 1983–	10 years–

The rising authority of the 'ulamā' within the mosque can also be gauged by their progressive control of the Friday sermons. From the beginning of the 1960s up to 1973, the Jamāt insisted that the 'ulamā' desist from delivering extemporaneous lectures. In 1962, the Jamāt even purchased a book containing the English translations of sermons, from which the imāms were expected to read. Moreover, in 1965, the Jamāt demanded that all sermons by visitors be confirmed with them.[22] Since the 1973, when the 'ulamā' stood their ground on salaries, the situation has gradually changed to the advantage of the 'ulamā'. When a complaint was received from a worshiper in 1981 about the length of the lecture, the Jamāt decided to approach the imām "informally."[23] And more recently, the Jamāt has allowed the 'ulamā' to invite visitors, though reserving the right to object subsequent to the sermon.[24] While the jamāt committee still maintained some oversight, it was a far cry from the resolutions and decrees that had earlier characterized their relationship with the 'ulamā'. In short, then, in Brits as elsewhere in the Transvaal, religious leaders gained more prominence and authority. They projected leadership in terms of their roles as teachers and reformers and not as guides and soteriological pathways.

The focus on knowledge and epistemology introduced changes in the definition of what constituted a religious leader. In Brits, this was reflected in the titles used for the scholars. In the early 1960s, a religious scholar was called "haffejee," derived from the Arabic term ḥāfiẓ, which literally referred to someone who had memorized the Qur'ān. In Brits, haffejee was the designation for both those who had memorized the complete Qur'ān and those who were reasonably knowledgeable in Islamic studies. With the demand from the jamāt committee for better teachers, however, a degree of differentiation set in. The proper ḥāfiẓ was distinguished from the haffejee. For example, one of Moosa Pir's sons was called Haffejee Nana before he went abroad in 1968, and then Ḥāfiẓ when he returned in 1973. He was called ḥāfiẓ to distinguish him from the other haffejees who had not gone abroad and who had not memorized the Qur'ān. Similarly, Imām Kassiem Saib was invited and employed as a "qualified" scholar in 1969 for his considerable experience in teaching.[25] But he was not a ḥāfiẓ, nor had he studied for many years at an Islamic seminary in India or Pakistan. Had he come to Brits a few years earlier, he would have been called a haffejee.[26] "Imām" in this case granted Saib a degree of recognition he would have been denied before the Jamāt began its search for qualified scholars. Eventually, at the head of the leaders stood the *ʿālim*, called a *mawlānā* or *molvī*, which referred to a graduate of a religious institution in India or Pakistan. Such a person would have spent up to ten or even twelve years mastering Islamic law. Next came the imām, the ḥāfiẓ; the haffejee eventually disappeared altogether.

The hierarchy of titles eventually translated into a differentiated salary scale. In Islamic history, the extreme case of such a pecuniary hierarchy was stipulated by the Ottoman Qanūnname, where a candidate for the 'ulamā' establishment was expected first to "teach at a 20-akce madrasa . . . and shall then proceed to advance by 5-akce stages."[27] The *akce* was the standard Ottoman silver coin, and qualifications and salaries were significations of each other. A similar salaried hierarchy was only reluctantly established by the Brits Jamāt. Generally, the Jamāt found ways of appointing lower-salaried haffejees and ḥāfiẓes and was reluctant to reward good service (see table 5.1). Ḥāfiẓ Adamjee's case illustrated this anomaly. He was invited from Natal when the Jamāt was negotiating for the better qualified Mawlānā Abbas Jeena, returning to Brits from Pakistan, at a salary of R160. When the latter turned down the offer, Ḥāfiẓ Adamjee was appointed at R100 per month.[28] As somebody who had only memorized the Qur'ān, Adamjee received a lower salary than that offered to Jeena. Even Adamjee's successful ḥāfiẓ school for memorizing the Qur'ān did not increase his wages.[29]

Salaries represented an ambiguous measure of independence and worth for the 'ulamā', who were aware that a lower salary implied lower worth in the eyes of the community members. They knew that their salaries were well below those paid to similar professionals in the community. They also knew that salaries were a reflection of their subservience to employers. But the 'ulamā' insisted that they did not lead the prayers in the mosque as part

of their salaried duties. In terms of Islamic law, they argued, a person leading the worship was not entitled to payment.[30] This position was founded
on a phrase that appears repeatedly in many places in the Qur'ān: "Do not
sell the signs of God for a trifle sum" (e.g., Qur'ān 2:41). It is an issue that
bothers the conscience of every intellectual. However, as the above-men-
tioned Ottoman example and numerous other religious officials in the
employment of Islamic polities in the past and present attest, religious services were paid for directly or indirectly. For the 'ulamā' of Brits, though,
the refusal to accept payment was a vital stance, which they could not concede. Their determination did not always work in their favor; and sometimes, the value of their independence was completely lost. Community
members often complained that 'ulamā' were not always timely for the
daily worship and were often absent on bitterly cold winter mornings and
during school holidays. The Jamāt tried in vain to establish a system of
rotation or increased remuneration for anybody prepared to sacrifice his
vacation. The 'ulamā' tried to be present on a voluntary basis but refused to
take the financial bait.

As elsewhere in the Transvaal, the 'ulamā' in Brits also relied on the
support of the Tablīghī Jamāt in the town. There were only about ten active
members of the Tablīghī Jamāt in Brits, but they enjoyed much wider support and sympathy. Imran Muhammad, the leader of the Tablīghī Jamāt,
informed me that the movement had embarked upon a goal of making
the mosque "alive" twenty-four hours a day by performing various super-
erogatory prayers and recitations of the Qur'ān.[31] According to this plan,
somebody from the movement would be inside the mosque every minute
of the day. This signaled the central role the mosque played in the Tablīghī
Jamāt and confirmed the manner in which the movement tried to reclaim
it for the 'ulamā'. In fact, this occupation of space was felt by the jamāt
committee, as the movement's activities became a point of contention
among some jamāt committees in the Transvaal. The Tablīghī Jamāt's itin-
erant groups slept and ate in the mosques, leading to frequent friction with
the jamāt committees in the Transvaal. While there have been occasional
grumbles in Brits, especially as regards the newly renovated mosque, the
movement has never been refused permission to use the mosque facilities.

The 'ulamā' with the support of the Tablīghī Jamāt controlled the religious space in the town. Against the financial control and fund-raising activity of the jamāt committee, the 'ulamā' inscribed a religious space within
the mosque, principally achieving this by focusing on their expertise
in Islamic knowledge. The 'ulamā', however, remained employees of the
committee and subject to its economic and political clout. In order to dis-

tance themselves from the Jamāt's authority, the 'ulamā' tried resolutely to control the mosque sphere and to detach their service from salaries.

On the Margins of Orthodoxy

The dominant discourses of both the Jamāt and the 'ulamā' did not completely exclude opportunities for groups to articulate different Islamic discourses on the periphery. In Brits, both the Brelvis and the political message of Islamic resurgence gained ground from the mid-1980s. Both of these, however, thrived best on the margins of the mosque, seeking alternative avenues and means to promote their messages. Deobandi pronouncements on Islam did not go unchallenged. As expected, Deobandi objections to traditional celebrations and practices provoked Brelvi opposition in the town. The Brelvis also originated in India, reacting to the Deobandis with an almost militant reinstatement of tradition. They were called Brelvis in reference to the arch opponent of the Deoband school in India, Aḥmad Raza Khan of Bareilliy (1856–1921).[32] In South Africa, these counter-'ulamā' were strongest in Natal around the shrines of two prominent Sufis, Badsha Peer (d. 1885) and Soofie Saheb (d. 1910).[33] In the Transvaal, some jamāt committees and businessmen supported the Brelvis in reaction to the overzealous drive of the Deobandi 'ulamā' and the Tablīghī Jamāt. They insisted on organizing the Mīlād celebrations of the birth of the Prophet, which became the focal point around which the Deobandi and Brelvi textual and bodily discourses were contested.

From the mid-1980s, Mīlād celebrations were introduced by inviting Brelvi 'ulamā' to officiate at gatherings, especially when the local imāms refused to participate. The turning point against Deobandi hegemony in the Transvaal took place in Azaadville, the Indian area of Krugersdorp. The town was well-known for its Deobandi support, but a small group of Brelvis challenged this by arranging Mīlād celebrations in 1987 in the local town hall. The people of the town tried to deny the Brelvis the use of the hall but failed to convince the local management committee responsible for the public amenities of the township.[34] On the Saturday night before the actual celebrations, a number of people were preparing for the occasion. At the same time, a Deobandi group got together in the nearby mosque and deliberated on the intrusion. Accounts differ: the Deobandis say they were invited to a debate, while the Brelvis say that the masses in the Azaadville mosque were incited to root out the innovation by force. The ensuing march led to a fracas in which one of the Mīlād organizers was killed. A case of murder was opened, but a court hearing acquitted the Deobandi mob. The death of the Brelvi supporter revealed the overwhelming power of the Deobandis and brought those opposed to its hegemony closer together. Since then, in fact, the number of Mīlād celebrations in Transvaal has increased. Moreover, some Deobandi 'ulamā' themselves realized that their attacks on folk practices were proving counterproductive. In response, they introduced their own meetings, called Sīrat Jalsah, for celebrating the Prophet Muḥammad, to counter the Mīlād of the Brelvis. The gatherings and countergatherings present some estimation of the extent to which competing religious arguments were produced in ritual acts. They were, as David Chidester has pointed out, the battle over the symbol of the Prophet.[35]

In Brits, a group requested the jamāt committee in November 1986 to be allowed to recite the *salāmī* salutations to the Prophet in the mosque. This salutation to the Prophet was a characteristic Indian ritual, which included a poem of praise in honor of the Prophet in Urdu and the usual Arabic invocations for blessings upon the Prophet Muḥammad. The salāmī would be performed standing, and all events organized by the Brelvis were usually concluded this way. The Niaaz Committee threatened to disrupt the activities of the Tablīghī Jamāt in the mosque if such permission were not forthcoming.[36] The request was directed at the jamāt, but it recognized the alliance between the 'ulamā' and the Tablīghī Jamāt who controlled the ethos of the mosque. Permission was refused and no disruption ensued, but the Brelvi opposition has since emerged as a permanent feature on the margin of the Brits mosque.

Like the Deobandi discourse, the Brelvis included both intellectual arguments and ritual acts. Admitting the fact that un-Islamic practice did creep into the festivals, Brelvis defended the principles of the events themselves. Visiting saintly graves was based on the normative practice of the Prophet (*sunnah*). They rejected the purported "grave worshiping" at the Sufi shrines but insisted on the validity and desirability of visiting saints. They cited instances in early Islam in which intercession (*shafā'at*) by the pious had not been considered an innovation. Most significant, however, the Brelvis accused the Deobandis of selective criticisms of "innovations."[37] They pointed out that the Deobandi judgment of this event was extremely selective since the Deobandis themselves blessed and encouraged a range of other practices, including the Tablīghī Jamāt's annual mass gatherings over the Easter weekend. Like the Mīlād, these gatherings were also innovations that could not be defended in a literalist interpretation of Islam.[38] Like the Deobandis, the Brelvis also demanded more than intellectual acknowledgment of their arguments. As noted, all events organized by the Brelvis were concluded with the recitation of salāmī salutations to the Prophet, during which everybody was expected to stand in a show of respect. From a textual counterattack to a bodily gesture deemed to suggest respect for the Prophet, the Brelvi opposition marked a space for itself in the Transvaal. While the "origins" of the disputes were ostensibly textual interpretations, the force of the arguments was invoked by bodily, ritual gestures. A more detailed description of the Brelvis in the town confirms this comprehensive symbolic response.

In Brits, the Brelvis consisted of two distinct groups, both of whose activities underlined their secure but marginalized spatial locations around the Brits Mosque. The first, led by Ashraf and Iqbal Tayob, organized and financed the major celebrations of the birthday of the Prophet. Both Tayobs were prominent businessmen in the town, and Iqbal at one time also chaired the jamāt committee. In Brits, this group organized both a commemoration of the Big Night in the mosque and a special celebration of the Mīlād on a Sunday in the community hall. The event inside the mosque revived a tradition that had been eliminated during the 1970s; at that stage, before the rise of the Deobandi 'ulamā', it was sometimes also held in the local cinema.[39] With its reappearance in the 1980s, a compromise was reached whereby the 'ulamā' were prepared to deliver a short sermon on the Prophet, with the least amount of disruption to the normal night worship. The Mīlād supporters accepted this arrangement but distributed the traditional treats of bananas and rose-flavored milk without the permission of the 'ulamā'. The grand celebration of the Mīlād, moreover, was reserved for the special event in the community hall. Here, other Transvaal supporters attended and helped to swell the numbers of the local supporters. The event consisted of poetry recitals and lectures on the Prophet. Special provisions were made for women to listen to but not actively participate in the celebrations. Closing the proceedings was a sumptuous meal, to which all Muslims in the town was invited. One or two large pots were reserved for distribution to the indigent in local hospitals. As expected, there was much debate as to whether it was proper to attend this function, especially to partake of the meal. The organizers of the celebration, however, ensured that pots of food were also available for collection for families who did not want to be seen at the event. The ideological divisions were clearly drawn by the leaders and forced ordinary Muslims to take public positions. This did not mean, however, that the lines of demarcation were never crossed.

The second Brelvi group in the town consisted of about eight to ten men who came together on Thursday nights for reciting litanies in praise and remembrance of God (dhikr). This dhikr jamāt began holding their meetings in the mosque but then found that they clashed with the dominant Tablīghī Jamāt, whose greater support monopolized the mosque after the night worship. Any different but concurrent meeting after the evening prayers would have been regarded as too confrontational for the small town. Hājī Ismail, initiated into the Qādiri Sufi order, lead the dhikr. The gatherings on Thursday nights did not initiate anybody into the order, much less to the philosophy and mysteries of Sufism. The dhikr itself took a fixed form from week to week, lasting for about an hour. In one of the meetings that I attended, an additional section was read to bring some relief from the drought facing South Africa. The standard invocations in the dhikr of Brits began with placement of a jug of water in the center of the circle of partici-pants and continued with the following sequence of recitations:

1. Durūd ("O God, send peace and blessings on Muḥammad and his family") one hundred times;

2. Lā ilāha illa Allah ("There is no God but the God") one hundred times;

3. Illa Allah ("But the God") one hundred times;

4. Allah ("The God") one hundred times;

5. Durūd five hundred times.

The recitals began and ended with the salutations to the Prophet. The phrases containing God were progressively reduced, rising in a crescendo to God (Allah). It was as if the recitations led finally to the central awareness and experience of God. Moreover, symbolized by the salutations, both the beginning and the end of such a journey were mediated by the Prophet Muḥammad. At the end of the recitals, the jug was passed around and each person was given an opportunity to "transfer" his recitation into the water by blowing into it. The water was then passed around once again in small glasses to be drunk, followed by snacks. It was as if the recited blessings were passed through the breath and then consumed. It was clear that while the Deobandi 'ulamā' emphasized obligations and debt to God and Prophet in their sermons, the Mīlād and dhikr jamāts celebrated the pres-ence and efficacy of God and the Prophet. The Brelvis rallied people around the efficacy of the Prophet in Muslim society, while the Deobandis insisted on conforming to his behavioral norms.

The members of the dhikr jamāt inscribed a different social space for themselves in relation to the mosque. As mentioned earlier, they preferred to perform the dhikr away from the mosque even though they continued to perform all their other obligations there. Inside the mosque, they sought to distinguish themselves ritually through subtle symbols. For example, they made a point of greeting by shaking hands at the end of prayer. This practice may be commonplace in many other Muslim contexts, but it was a significant gesture in a town where even this was considered a religious innovation. For the group, though, it was a mark of belonging to a distinct fraternity.

The Brelvi approach to Islam was an orthodoxy and orthopraxis familiar to the people in town. However, the history of South Africa, especially as a result of apartheid, also generated a new paradigm of understanding Islam. In a study of the Muslim Youth Movement of South Africa (*Islamic Resurgence in South Africa*), I showed how the 1970s witnessed a protracted battle, exegetical and ritual, between Deobandi 'ulamā' and university- and college-educated youth. The Deobandis rejected the desire of such youth to render the texts of Islam accessible to all literate Muslims and to open the doors of Islamic institutions to women. As a broad movement, Islamic resurgence in the Transvaal was not as successful as in the Cape; in particular, it failed to mobilize support for a communitywide anti-apartheid movement. It could not substantially challenge or change the discourse of political accommodationism of the traders or the Islamic epistemology ('ilm) of religious leaders. Nevertheless, it was successful in pointing to the silenced world of women and African Muslims in the region. As champions of the Islamization of Africa and the liberation of Muslim women, it founded some marginalized interpretations in the Transvaal.

Islamic resurgence was first introduced into Brits by a well-attended address by Ḥāfiẓ Abu Bakr Muḥammad, the first president of the Muslim Youth Movement. For a brief period, a branch of the organization also operated in the town.[40] Islamic resurgence made a second and more durable appearance in 1983 when university students launched the Muslim Youth Movement's study circles: one for men and two for women. The male members were restricted to former students and graduates, while the women were a more diverse group, including housewives. The focus of the study circles, reading the Qur'ān in translation and discussion, was not attractive to the great majority of residents. A number of sermons, therefore, were delivered on Fridays to curb what was called "MYM modernism." Most of these were directed against those who refused to conform to the dress regulations of the 'ulamā' or who introduced too much "politics" into Islam. Even though the MYM group in Brits was small, its activities were seen as deviations not to be tolerated.

There was no fundamental objection to incorporating African Muslims into the community. The reality of integration between two different classes and their outlooks, however, proved more difficult than in the ideal teachings of Islam. Muslims of African origin have been in the Transvaal almost as long as Indian Muslims. Muslims from Malawi in particular were attracted to the industrial and mineral boom of the Transvaal at the end of the nineteenth century. Indian Muslims generally call all African Muslims from countries north of South Africa Somalis. Most of them are from Malawi since the British colonization of present-day Malawi in the nineteenth century. One of the earliest reference to African Somalis in the Transvaal emerged in the letters of Achmat Effendi. In 1903, as "Chief Priest for the Transvaal Colony," he urged the attorney general to reconsider the identity of eighty "Somalis" who had served the British military as cooks and waiters during the Anglo-Boer War. He argued that they ought to be regarded as South African Malays, so that they could be exempted from registration fees, pass regulations affecting Africans, and other discriminatory practices. (Since the days of slavery in the eighteenth century, pass laws in South Africa have restricted the free movement of indigenous people. During apartheid, this became the principal means of controlling the everyday lives of Africans. As part of the Coloureds and Indians, Muslims were not subject to these laws.) Effendi's suggestion was categorically rejected, with an insistence that the "Somalis" would most definitely be natives "subject to the disabilities imposed on Coloured persons" concerning liquor laws and walking on footpaths.[41] Effendi seemed, in the familiar Cape fashion, to identify Islam with Malays, which contrasted sharply with the emergent Indian character of the jamāt committees and the 'ulamā'. His failure to get Somalis reclassified as Malays, however, seemed to echo the failure of the Transvaal community to embrace not only the Cape Muslims but also the increasing number of Muslims of African origin.

African Muslims continued to arrive in South Africa as part of a migratory labor force attracted to the mining and forestry industries. Once present, they sought out the mosques, where they attended Friday worship services. The class difference between the Muslims in the towns and wealthier suburbs and the African Muslims was reflected in the religious institutions of the Transvaal. Many mosques in the Transvaal employed Malawians as caretakers and callers to prayer (bāngīs) and more recently, but reluctantly, as imāms. Malawians were preferred for their belonging to the same faith but also because they demanded less in wages. Jamāt committees have paid them wages in keeping with those usually reserved for the least skilled black workers in South Africa. The example of

Brits clearly illustrates the structural disadvantage of African Muslims. As elsewhere, Malawians were relegated to the lower rungs of the town's Islamic institutions. In 1959, when an Indian applied for the job of calling the faithful to prayer, he was turned down not because of any question regarding his competence but to avoid paying the higher "Indian" wages.[42] The assumption was that Malawian workers could comfortably be given "black" wages. As visitors to South Africa, Malawian bāngīs have also been at the mercy of the state. Like the 'ulamā', they have had to rely on the jamāt committee for jobs and for permits to live in Indian group areas. In this regard too, jamāt committees have not always been that helpful. In one case in 1975, an unnamed bāngī in Brits was asked to repay a fifty-rand application fee to the local Bantu commissioner.[43] This was an exorbitant burden upon the low wages of a bāngī earning thirty rand per month.[44] Bāngīs periodically petitioned for better wages and questioned their submissive roles. They were rarely successful and often sought alternative sources of income, even *fafi* running for gamblers and dispensing special healing cures they had learned in Malawi.[45] Occasionally, objections were raised inside the jamāt committee about the pitiful state of the bāngī's terms of employment or his living quarters. Sometimes, as in one meeting, an attempt was made to reduce the bāngī's workload by employing an even cheaper African "girl" (*sic*).[46] Clearly, Malawian workers could not expect anything from the Jamāt, trapped as they were in the political and economic conditions determined by apartheid capitalism. This particular master-servant relationship between Indian and Malawian Muslims was confirmed and entrenched in Islamic religious institutions.

The Islamic resurgent discourse, even in Brits, has occasionally stood by African Muslims in their plight. With its concern for social and economic rights in Islam, it has taken on the cause of the bāngīs and African Muslims. Improved working conditions and the discontinuation of the use of Urdu in the mosques have been the focus of the most pointed criticisms. The latter issue has affected African Muslims living in and around Brits as well as some Indian Muslims. The mosque on Friday was filling up with African Muslims, who sometimes comprised about fifty out of a total of four hundred men. Furthermore, an increasing number of younger Indian Muslims no longer understood Urdu. 'Ulamā' were adamant that Urdu was crucial for the cultural identity of Indian Muslims; they generally made many people feel that they ought to learn it to understand the mysteries and depths of the faith. A Dr. Ahmad, a medical doctor who had been part of the first study group in 1983, rejected the special place of Urdu in Islam and sometimes went to extraordinary lengths to show this. In particular,

being aware of African Muslims' feeling of rejection, and unable to do anything about the sermons, he removed his children from the religious school
for a while. The situation has not yet been resolved, but sermons are rarely
given in Urdu any longer. On the other hand, discriminatory practices and
the pitiable plight of African workers in the mosques still leave much to be
desired.

Islamic resurgent organizations also expressed their concern about Afri-
can-Indian relations through an increased commitment to conversion. This
may seem odd and even arrogant in that the acceptability of Africans was
conditional upon their conversion. However, conversion in the South African context meant a rejection of the "natural" boundaries between
South African groupings. The possibility of conversion underscored the
basic humanity of South Africans. Second, within the Muslim community,
conversion was ignored by the dominant discourses of the 'ulamā' of both
Deobandi and Brelvi inclinations. The 'ulamā' engaged in conversion
campaigns long after modern youth organizations had established a track
record. The Islamic Propagation Society founded in 1958 in Johannesburg
was one of the earliest movements to promote Islam among Africans.
Later, in the 1970s, conversion became one of the prominent objectives of
the Muslim Youth Movement. Conversion was projected as a political solution to the country's problems. Conversion, from the perspective of youth
organizations, was always directed at the social and political dimensions
of South Africa. Some Muslims were attracted to Islam because of the
dominant Christian theological support for apartheid. In this context, Islam
emerged as an alternative voice for Africans.[47] Even the purely theological
anti-Christian polemic of Ahmad Deedat's videos and cassettes had a
political echo. It was a polemic directed against a religion that supported
and justified apartheid. As far as the discursive map of Transvaal was
concerned, proselytization became the hallmark of Islamic resurgence protagonists in the Transvaal. It was the one area in which they were unhin-
dered by criticism from the Deobandi 'ulamā'.

Africans embraced Islam and founded communities and mosques, but
insufficient research exists on the nature of African Muslim communities
themselves. Fewer in number and less economically successful, their institutions are not as easily visible. There is no doubt, however, that like their
Transvaal and Cape counterparts, Malawian Muslims in particular established strong links with Islamic authorities in Central Africa. Sufi rituals
and Mīlād celebrations formed an integral part of their social manifestation
of Islam.[48] With the reintroduction of the Mīlād by the Brelvis, Malawian
Muslims have eagerly joined this familiar ritual in town as well. In spite of

the strong Indian character of these celebrations, most Malawians recognize this as a familiar celebration of the Prophet Muḥammad. The new communities, founded on the basis of the past forty years of conversion campaigns, are even less well known. These await greater appreciation from scholars.[49]

A brief assessment of conversion and township Islam in relation to the dominant discourse in Brits makes a small contribution. While Islamic resurgence as a discourse was ineffective in the Brits mosque, its contacts with African Muslims eventually led to the establishment of small communities in the townships around Brits. Frustrated by the lack of response in the Indian community, these Muslims regarded the emergent Muslim communities as "refuges" where true Islam could be built from scratch.[50] Mabuluka, an African location or township lying twenty miles from Brits, has been the focus of most of their activities. Dr. Ahmad began providing some medical care and other assistance to a few converts and Malawian families living in Mabuluka. This developed into a more substantial project, and soon a small community of some twenty families took shape. A piece of ground was negotiated from the local chief, and a mosque and imām quarters were built with the assistance of the Brits Jamāt Committee. In addition, Ahmad motivated a number of other members of the Brits Mosque to contribute to and occasionally visit the new, growing community. Women sometimes baked cookies and made lunches for sale to raise funds for the Muslim community in Mabuluka township.

Ahmad tried to encourage greater interaction and even integration between the two communities, but his efforts proved less than successful. Mabuluka residents were encouraged at least to perform the Friday worship in their town, and occasionally the Mabuluka imām was invited to address the Brits congregation. This was in itself a significant gesture, which the apartheid racial boundaries in the country had anathematized. However, the contradictions of class and ethnicity between the two communities were not so easily overcome. The Muslims of Mabuluka found it difficult to identify with the demands made on them. Islam was considered an Indian religion in the township. Many were reluctant to adopt the hat, scarf, cloak, and other marks associated with Islam, for fear of being called "Indians." At the same time, however, they also came to rely on the charity emanating from the Brits Mosque. Hence, when a material or financial need had to be met in the township, the "Islamic" symbols were conveniently adopted. It was much easier to procure assistance, financial or otherwise, wearing the proper religious garb. A dissimulated rejection of some Indian cultural practices became part of how the Mabuluka community related to Islam.

Some youth in the township, however, began to reject this attitude and dependence. Therefore, praying in the mosque without a head covering or other symbols they clearly identified as Indian, they began to signal their rejection of Indian culture. In this context of rejection and dissimulation, it was not long before a group called the Murābiṭūn appeared in the township. Founded in Norwich, England, by Shaykh Abd al-Qadir al-Murābiṭ, the movement in South Africa rejected Indian and Malay identities and adopted a deliberately African Muslim identity by following Malikism. Due to its dominance in West and North Africa, Malikism was thought to be an "African" way within Islam. Adoption of Malikism meant rejecting the prevailing Ḥanafism and Shafiʿism of the Indian and Cape Muslims respectively.[51] More directly for Mabuluka, Ali Siphanda, the imām of the Mabuluka Jamāt in 1986, joined the Murābiṭūn, immediately took control of the mosque, and completely barred Indians from attending. During his leadership, the mosque attracted wider interest in the township as it engaged in a more active proselytization campaign by debating with local Christian priests. This brief spell of independence did not last long, however. Some of the Muslims in the township complained to the Indians that the center was being neglected, partly recognizing the fact that the Indian sources of badly needed material aid had dwindled. Ahmad and some residents of Mabuluka called in the police to evict the Murābiṭūn for trespassing. It was highly ironical that Muslims who were most critical of apartheid also relied on its officers to serve them. The ambiguity and contradiction of Islam in the political landscape of South Africa penetrated Muslim institutions deeply.[52]

The Indian-African dynamics were not the only problem facing the new community. The Muslims of Mabuluka were a community of double marginalization: they were not only marginal to the Indian discourse but also to the tribal management of apartheid. Most Muslims in Mabuluka were neither original residents of the township nor part of the Tswana tribal network of Brits. The mother of one student I interviewed came originally from Matatiele in the eastern Cape, having fled a witch hunt there. The student informed me that the other Muslim families were also displaced from other parts of the country and some were married to Malawian Muslims.[53] The "foreign" composition of this Muslim community, whether Malawian or from other areas of South Africa, implied that they could not enjoy the support of township elders and apartheid officials, whose first responsibility lay with the Tswana. Islam, for the Muslims of Mabuluka, provided an opportunity for a new identity and new sense of belonging. It was a community of Muslims in extreme desperation, which those promoting Islamic resurgence hardly recognized as they sought a space for their own discourse. Here was conversion in an African community but not from a three-tiered cosmology to a two-tiered cosmology, as suggested by Horton. It was a community simply in need of another set of cosmological and social coordinates.[54] In fact, conversion did not produce anything; it was a measure of hope that it would.

Addressing women's experiences was as difficult in Brits as was creating an integrated Muslim community. Among the tenets of Islamic resurgence in South Africa has been that Islam not be discriminatory toward women. Islamic resurgent organizations have found that —unlike conversion—there is little support for improving the role of women in the Islamic institutions of the Transvaal. A brief survey of women's Islamic practices reveals that their roles in the community as a whole were significantly curtailed with the rise of Deobandi hegemony. Women in the Transvaal had not enjoyed any prominence in the founding of the mosques. Men often came without their families, in search of better economic prospects, and were joined only later by wives and families. Nevertheless, women in the Transvaal engaged in specific domestic patterns of Islamic life, which they brought from India. While this meant a domesticated lifestyle, it did not eliminate all public participation and practices. Many women, not only those in the households of religious leaders, played a significant role in the education of children, especially girls. With the rise of Deobandi 'ulamā' in the region, women's roles progressively diminished. As the focus shifted to expertise in religious law and theology obtained at institutions abroad, women teachers were vulnerable to firing and replacement. Often with scant regard to their actual contributions, women were systematically replaced by "qualified" men.

The 'ulamā' criticism of general Islamic practices in the mosques directly affected women's religious activities as well. On the special Big Nights, women generally provided boys and men with clean clothes and often with an extra-sumptuous meal and sweets. When the men were gone, however, they dedicated themselves to specially designated recitations of the Qur'ān and other optional prayers for the particular evening. Often, they would immerse themselves in these with much devotion and seriousness. For them, it was a more individual commitment and devotion than were the social gatherings of the men. The criticisms against the Big Nights were not directly addressed at these aspects, but one popular women's public celebration was severely discredited. Women in Brits regularly convened a Muḥarram Majlis, a gathering popular in India, to commemorate the martyrdom of the Prophet's grandson Husayn.[55] For ten days, they would meet at a house and listen to the epic journey of Husayn from Mecca to Kufah in opposition to the Umayyad dynasty. Two or three of the women would be chosen as the lead reciters of the epic. Each reciting would conclude with a salāmī invocation similar to that described earlier for the dhikr jamāt. The ten-day ceremony was criticized for a number of reasons, the most prominent being that women adorned themselves at these meetings with makeup and lipstick! Some discouraged any women's gathering outside their own homes; others encouraged women to join special teaching circles (taʿlīm) where the principles and teachings of the Tablīghī Jamāt were rehearsed. Occasionally, special women's groups consisting of the sisters and wives of Tablīghī men also went out "in the path of Islam." Always, however, these women's meetings were arranged by the male members of the Tablīghī Jamāt in the town. Women were weaned from their independent practices and introduced to the teachings of Islam under the patronage of the ʿulamā'. They lost the little independence they had enjoyed in the former gatherings. In this regard, the Brelvi ʿulamā' did not challenge the diminished role of women, and they also complained that women sometimes arrived with makeup and lipstick. Women were invited to the Mīlād celebrations only when these did not take place inside the mosque. Moreover, apart from their reserved place in a completely different section of the community hall, they did not play any role in the celebration—not even in the cooking of the auspicious food.

In the town of Brits, the study circle of the Muslim Youth Movement did not fare much better, but it suggested how public meetings provided a faint hope for women to explore a different interpretation of Islam. At the time of its establishment in 1983, the Muslim Youth Movement was overly concerned about establishing its own orthodoxy of Islamism through syllabi and regional and national meetings.[56] This was the time when the organization was at pains to prove its credentials to the ʿulamā' in South Africa. Women in Brits could not attend these regional meetings, which were usually held in the cities. Eventually, they dissociated themselves from this organization, though they continued with their weekly study groups. Hence, unlike the Muslim Youth Movement study groups, which were highly structured and ideologically motivated, the groups in Brits tended to be much more accommodating to diverse tendencies. The study group became a place where women commanded complete authority, not dictated to by men from either the Tablīghī Jamāt or the Muslim Youth Movement. Of course, the group generated leadership disputes among women, but that is another story. The study group, in some sense, represented the irony and subtle control of Kenyan women depicted in the classic "Utendi wa Mwana Kupona." This is a poem that appears to be prescribing what the ideal submissive woman ought to do but that describes men as childlike and fragile: "Care for him like a child who doesn't know how to speak"; and "You should praise your husband so his reputation spreads but you should not insist of him that which he cannot produce."[57] The study group similarly appeared to be reproducing the triumph of Islamic patriarchy but at the same time disclosed the subtlety with which women created spaces for themselves. Neither the Islamic resurgent groups nor the 'ulamā' were aware of these unexpected consequences.

Conclusion

Islamic life in the town of Brits was constituted by a hierarchy of groups. The jamāt committee, through its material resources and its relations with the state, ensured the maintenance and building of the mosque and the religious school. Wealthy and influential Muslims played an inordinate role in the community through the Jamāt. The 'ulamā', particularly those trained in the Deoband network of schools, laid the foundations for the fulfillment of religious responsibilities as laid down in Islamic legal codes. Each for their respective services, the Jamāt and the 'ulamā' were indispensable to the community. In the 1960s, they both contributed to the modernization of religious education and the bureaucratization of religious leadership. Over time, the 'ulamā' managed to gain prominence inside the mosques, assisted in no small measure by the Tablīghī Jamāt's discursive occupation of the mosque. The Brits Jamāt Committee, in spite of its fundraising activities, had to concede to the authority of Islamic knowledge.

The Brelvis nurtured an alternative Islam by withdrawing from the center. Shaking hands with one another outside the mosque, they defined a muted discourse inside the mosque, expressed more boldly in homes and community halls. On their own terms, they promoted a different understanding of Islam in terms of presence rather than text, efficacy rather than rewards. The second alternative discourse, of Islamic resurgence, was even more marginalized, lacking the capacity to make a difference within the community. Nevertheless, like the Brelvi opposition, it succeeded in founding a new community on the periphery. Both peripheral discourses illuminated important dimensions of Islamic life in the town. The Brelvi focused on alternative approaches to the Prophet apart from emulating his physical habits and behavior. They stressed the efficacy of the Prophet's being and creation, expressed in the Mīlād gatherings, the dhikr, and the salāmī invocations. Islamic resurgence, on the other hand, focused on the forgotten Muslim communities in the townships and the muted voices of women.

6

The Sermons:
Ritual Inscription of Space

The mosques in South Africa were established and constructed in Muslim discourses. Within the relevant political contexts, the independent Cape mosque provided an opportunity for a new interpretation to flourish, while the Transvaal mosque tolerated peripheral interpretations under the umbrella of political accommodation with the apartheid state. With this detailed historical and discursive background, I now turn to the sermon as a ritual within the mosques. Sermons are shown in this chapter to produce mosques in the same way as discourses. The architectural use of space and the performance of both preachers and listeners reproduce and elaborate these respective discursive voices. The chapter concludes with brief notes on the preachers and their sermons in order to prepare the ground for the re-citation of the Qur'ān analyzed in the next chapter.

The Spatial Production of Sermons

The classical notion of sacred space in the study of religion has been identified by Eliade as the locus of experiencing ultimate reality. According to Eliade, the modern world of homogeneity was threatened by absolute chaos and relativity. In contrast, sacred space, best exemplified in religion, provided a sense of absolute value. This was achieved by setting aside a space distinct from everyday usage: the key difference between sacred and profane. Second, sacred space was intrinsically better than profane space. In addition to these qualities of demarcation and hierarchy, sacred space signified hierophany, a divine intervention in history. Sacred space provided an opportunity to recall and realize contact between horizontal (historical) and vertical (divine-human) dimensions of reality. Eliade regarded sacred space as he did time—as extrahistorical dimensions relived in intense moments of ritual. In the ritual articulation of the sacred space, Eliade rejected the idea that human action was involved: "In reality, the ritual by which he constructs a sacred space is efficacious in the measure in which it reproduces the work of the gods."[1] The Eliadean identification of hierophany in ritual has been variously condemned as theological and as impossible to validate in an empirical study of religion.[2] According to this critique, the study of religion cannot assume or prove the transition from social dimensions to absolute hierophanies. These are privileged and subjective assertions that cannot be proved or falsified by the social scientific study of religion.

Jonathan Z. Smith accepted the category of sacred space but argued that it was not a primordial, timeless entity that could be recalled and remembered for its encounter with the divine. This particular quality of sacred space was an illusory understanding of the nature of "place" as a fixed and changeless entity. When returning to a place where something significant had taken place, it would be a mistake to assume that the experience was duplicated by returning to the same place. Such a return or recollection reproduced a new encounter with the "same mathematical location." The total encounter was thus an experience of a new place. Similarly, sacred places in religious experiences, according to Smith, were continually founded and produced in collective ritual activity and the human acts of remembrance and recollection. "Place" was never given; it was valued and produced in social contexts: "place is not best conceived as a particular location with an idiosyncratic physiognomy or as a uniquely individualistic node of sentiment, but rather as a social position within a hierarchical system."[3] Taking this notion of a socially delineated and hierarchically organized place one step further, Chidester and Linenthal insisted that sacred places were located and articulated in culturally contested contexts. Accordingly, the primary means of remembering the holy or the real or the divine at a place was as much open to inversion and hybridization as it was to recollection and definition.[4] Symbols, including sacred spaces, were open to competition and contestation, two processes that defined sacred spaces as much as the hope or memory of the supreme, ultimate encounter. Applying these insights to the study of contemporary Islam, Gilsenan examined mosques as they were defined and articulated by various religious activities. Contrasting two mosques in a Lebanese village, Gilsenan discussed their spatial definition by the ablution and morgue facilities, the prayer areas, and the way in which worshipers approached them. The village mosque was generally a meeting place reflecting tensions and contradictions in the village itself, while the salon mosque situated at a distance exuded deliberate power, authority, and remoteness.[5]

The Islamic sermon delivered from a particular place on Friday defined the space in the process of taking place. The sermon as a ritual produced space as the preacher spoke, others listened, some walked in late, and others simply ignored the entire proceedings. These acts were all part of sermons and constructed different kinds of spaces in the two mosques under examination in this study. The spaces thus produced were not sacred in an Eliadean sense but were created in the process of the ritual taking place. Each encounter was different and could not be defined by its eternal duplication. However, as I show in the next chapter, neither was the space thus produced totally devoid of religiosity, as Smith, Chidester, Linenthal, and Gilsenan seem to suggest in their social and political examination of sacred spaces. Here, I want to show that the ritual production of the space reproduced and embodied the discourses in the two mosques under consideration. The particular space thus defined was not only based on the architecture and physical organization of the mosque but also produced by worshipers doing things in accordance with the discursive practices discussed in the previous chapters.

Both the Claremont and Brits mosques were clearly identifiable as mosques. Both have pulpits, niches showing the direction of Mecca, central and peripheral prayer areas, ablution facilities, and places for removing and keeping one's shoes. In this regard, they both fulfilled the basic structural and functional requirements of what mosques are supposed to be. These basic architectural and Islamic legal requirements, however, did not exhaust the ritual definition of the mosques as a sermon was delivered. In Claremont, the preacher ascends the pulpit in order to address the people. In Brits, the preacher occupies a prominent place beside the pulpit for a sermon delivered in a non-Arabic language, usually English or Urdu. In both cases, the preachers draw the attention of worshipers to themselves. The orientation generated by the sermon contrasts with the orientation generated by regular worship. The latter leads the congregants away from the mosque toward Mecca, while the former concentrates all attention on the preacher. Ultimately sacredness rests in Mecca, but the Friday sermon's orientation lends some importance to the preachers as well. In Islam, the preacher does not enjoy a sacramental role, but as Waugh has argued, leadership was "infused with and responsible for spiritual norms in the community."[6] More than any other activity in the mosque, the sermon provides the preacher with an opportunity to display and project these norms and values. And the directional focus on him during the sermon exemplifies his central role.

When we turn to how the congregation takes its place during a sermon, the spatial uniqueness of the two mosques becomes clearer. In the Claremont Mosque, women and men take their places in clearly designated areas. Cape mosques have always provided a basement or a mezzanine floor for women. In 1994, moreover, the Claremont Main Road Mosque took one more step in the direction of spatial equity when it divided the main prayer hall longitudinally so that women could take their places next to men. The women's section was much smaller and attracted fewer women, who, according to Islamic Sharī'ah demands, were not obliged to attend Friday prayers. However, the provision of a section of the mosque in Claremont for women was a spatial declaration that women were an integral part of Islamic public space. This participation in Claremont contrasts sharply with the situation in Brits. Here, if and when a woman enters the mosque, she would be politely taken to one of the neighboring homes to join women praying there. In larger cities, women would have to wait in a car or a shopping mall. Women in the Transvaal are positively denied any place in the mosque. The spatial organization within these two mosque traditions reveals distinctly how men and women enter a mosque and how their respective places creat a gendered space of the mosque itself.

This gendered inequality revealed in spatial inequality reflect the respective discourses of the two mosques. In Brits, women are barred from public and visible participation in society; but Claremont challenges this perception in South African society. Claremont's spatial revolution generated a great deal of hostility from Muslim leaders, who quickly called to mind the spatial organization of the Prophet's mosque, where the hierarchy between men and women was upheld by women sitting in the back. This reference, however, only exposed the other mosques' deviation from the Prophet's mosque and the complete elimination of women from public religion. This has not meant, for example, that Transvaal and other Cape mosques opened their doors and admitted women to their "proper" places in the back of the main prayer areas. The textual reference to space was only one manner in which space and other differences were contested for control of the mosque. Interestingly, the mosque in Mabuluka outside Brits, and on its discursive periphery, was allowed to admit women. Mabuluka, and its different spatial organization, does not threaten the discursive hegemony of the central Brits Mosque.

As men prepare and enter the Brits and Claremont mosques, they too highlight the discursive variations between the two. Friday sermons in the town of Brits are attended by about four hundred males. According to Islamic legal prescriptions, failure to attend the service without good reason was likened to apostasy.[7] Attendance for the Friday service was the minimum requirement for being part of the community. In Brits most Muslim males, young and old, attend the Friday prayer, and a few skip it occasionally. To my knowledge, only a few dared the bounds of apostasy by staying away for two consecutive weeks. The determination with which the Friday service is attended in Brits underscored its importance for the definition of the community as far as men were concerned. Their place in the community is defined by their place in the Friday service.

A typical Friday worship begins with the call to prayer at 12:30 P.M. Most Muslim businesses closed a few minutes earlier, while factory workers negotiated time off for an extended lunch break. Women of course went home, while men proceeded to the mosque after collecting clean head coverings. Some also put on long white robes to mark the special occasion of Friday worship. The first section of the mosque was a fully tiled ablution block with small chairs facing the hot and cold water faucets. A few individuals walked straight through, having performed ablution at home. Most others would begin their entrance into the mosque from here. In Brits, the ablution block was also the place where most interaction took place among the worshipers; a place where friends met one another and caught up with the weekly news and gossip. After ablution, one entered a two-tiered prayer area: a covered courtyard lined with beautiful carpets, and the mosque proper, carpeted from wall to wall. The courtyard was not considered to be part of the mosque but served some important ritual purposes. It was a place where latecomers were able to complete their required individual prayers before proceeding inside the mosque proper. The courtyard also served disinterested members of the congregation who chose to remain as far away from the presence and gaze of the preacher as they could. The inner section of the mosque was divided, not by any physical separation but by how worshipers took their places and responded to the preachers. The earliest group of worshipers occupied the first five rows and sat most of the time with bowed heads, listening to the preacher. Immediately behind them was a sparsely occupied empty zone, followed by about seven rows of those who sat and faced the preacher. Those facing the preacher listened more directly and attentively to the sermons, more so than those in the courtyard but perhaps also more so than those in the front rows, whose responses were not visible to the preachers. Toward the end of the sermon, the mosque was filled to capacity, but a significant number of men still continued their discussions in the courtyard and the ablution block. The imām then ascended the pulpit and, after a second call to prayer, proceeded to deliver an Arabic sermon. By now, more men were seated in the central hall and the din in the other areas subsided considerably.

The sermon in Claremont defined a very different religious space during a sermon. In spite of the similar courtyard, central prayer area, and place for ablution, the spatial approach to the sermon defined a different kind of mosque. In Claremont, most people came to the mosque directly from their places of work. Consequently, the distance between work and mosque space was short and unmediated by a stop at home as in Brits. When entering the Claremont Mosque, one did not walk straight into an ablution area but into the courtyard. As at Brits, the ablution area at Claremont also had hot water and towels, but there were no chairs. Ablution was less of a social gathering in Claremont than it was in Brits. After ablution, one took a position in either the central prayer area or the courtyard. In relation to the direction of Mecca, which denoted the front of the mosque, the courtyard in Claremont lay alongside the main prayer area rather than behind it, as in the Brits Mosque. In Claremont, the mosque filled up more evenly than in Brits, even though as at Brits some favored the front rows and some the rear of the mosque.

There were and are two marked differences in the spatial definition of the two mosques. In Brits, entrance into the mosque defines a progressive hierarchy to the most reverent place. One moves from the outside to the ablution block for purification, followed by the courtyard, and then a central prayer area. Worshipers took their places, and therefore defined the spatial significance of the mosque, by choosing one or another area in which to sit and worship. In contrast, the Claremont Main Road Mosque is nonhierarchical. Entrance into the mosque was not graded. In fact, one could step into the main prayer area without going through either the ablution area or the courtyard. This mosque's divisions are horizontal in contrast to the vertical division at Brits. Like the longitudinal division between men's and women's quarters in the central prayer area, the courtyard in Claremont lay alongside the main prayer area. This spatial organization may have been a product of a shortage of space in central Claremont, but it clearly articulates the unique character of the Cape mosque discourse. In this respect, Claremont did not differ much from other mosques in Cape Town. Architecture and practices both constituted the unique Cape mosque.

The space created by worshipers during a sermon, then, duplicated the discourses of the mosques. The spatial hierarchy in the Brits Mosque created a sense of the most deeply religious being farthest away from the outside. In Brits, one went from work to home and then gradually to the front of the mosque, or one stopped along a clearly defined hierarchy if one chose to do so. There were even places for those who did not want to be inside and were happy to grace the edges: the ablution block, the courtyard, and the rear of the mosque. The religious leaders occupied the deepest recesses of the mosque and guarded it with a Deobandi interpretation of Islam. The Claremont Mosque as a whole presented a clearly identifiable space in keeping with the individualistic mosque tradition in the Cape. Its present status as a bold and innovative mosque has enforced this uniqueness and independence. One was either inside or outside. There were no gray and peripheral spaces to occupy in the mosque. In spatial terms, the Claremont Mosque demands a greater degree of commitment from those attending its services. Unlike Brits, the courtyard and ablution block in Claremont does not provide latitudes peripheral to the proceedings in the mosque. There certainly are differences in Claremont between those who proceeded to the front rows and those who occupied the courtyard, but hardly any opportunities exist for the disinterested or the marginalized to occupy certain parts of the mosque.

These differences between the two mosques' spatial organization were reflected in the manner in which the sermons were delivered and received. In Brits, there were in fact two sermons: an official formulaic one in Arabic, usually read from a book of sermons covering every week of the year, and a preacher's "translation." In terms of a majority position in Islamic law, the official sermon in Brits had to be delivered from the pulpit even if only two out of the four hundred or so persons attending understood the language. The Arabic nature of the sermon in particular and Islamic worship in general has been an issue from early Islamic times. Apart from an earlier Ḥanafī position supporting the use of a non-Arab language in worship, the general consensus seems to be an insistence that Islam and Arabness could not be separated.[8] The insistence on Arabic has been fairly consistent, leading Lamin Sanneh to suggest that Islam in general is untranslatable in comparison with Christianity. According to this view, the Arab component of the religion was a major obstacle to its indigenization.[9] There are indeed indications of the progressive Arabicization of Islamic societies, but such a radical identification between Arabic and indigenous alienation ignores the discursive use of Arabic and Arabness for local purposes. Thus in the Transvaal, religious scholars whose orientation in all other respects may be regarded as uncompromisingly Indian insisted on the Arabic nature of the sermon.

As for the scholars' opinion on this issue, they argued that the Arabic sermon represented two cycles (raka'āt) of worship. The normal midday prayer consisted of four obligatory cycles of worship compared to two on Friday, and the difference was accounted for in the sermon. They argued that since the cycles of worship are conducted in Arabic, the sermon must be in Arabic.[10] Some members of the Brits congregation accepted this interpretation, but most did not resort to such rationalization. For them, it was sufficient that Arabic was the language of the Qur'ān and a fitting medium for the official sermon from the top of the pulpit. The Arabic sermon was regarded as an event demanding special devotion. The madrasah training, and occasional reminders from the English sermons, which were understood by all, impressed upon the men the obligatory nature of hearing the Arabic sermons while facing Mecca. An imām not infrequently asked those sitting against the side walls, and therefore not facing Mecca, to change their seating positions during the Arabic sermon. Those lectures intended to be understood by an audience were delivered before the official Arabic sermons.

This sequence of sermons also contributed to the specific creation of space in the two mosques. The translations followed by real sermons created yet another opportunity for hierarchy and distance. In Brits, some sat only to hear the sermons recited in Arabic from the top of the pulpit. The translations could simply be ignored as they were not officially part of the Friday worship. One or two individuals would even open a copy of the Qur'ān for recitation, inaudibly of course, while the preacher spoke in English or Urdu. Such persons would sit up and take note only when the Arabic sermon was announced. In contrast, the Claremont Main Road Mosque, like a few other mosques in the Cape, began a tradition of delivering the sermon in the vernacular from the pulpit. There was consequently only one sermon in the Claremont Mosque; one to which a worshiper could and had to listen. The sermons at Claremont, therefore, demanded attention, devotion, and understanding. Friday worship would not be complete without this particular sermon. The Claremont Main Road Mosque sermon defined a clearly demarcated space in which the sermon was heard and understood. In contrast, the Brits Mosque divided the preaching into two sections: the first was understood but need not be heard, and the other one had to listen to but did not have to understand.

The preachers who delivered the sermons replicated the spatial definition of the two mosques. The Brits Mosque, as I have argued, followed an ascending hierarchy, almost secular at its extremities and hallowed and reserved when the sermon was delivered in classical Qur'ānic Arabic from the top of the pulpit. In keeping with this narrowing gradation, the English sermons in Brits were delivered by individuals who all belonged to one school, Deobandi orthodoxy. For the sermon, we noted how they spatially claimed the innermost part of the mosque. The Claremont Mosque also projected one distinguishable trend. The imām himself was clearly an identifiable tradition, true to the Cape mosque institutional pattern. But unlike the Brits mosque, that at Claremont was not incrementally demarcated. One either stepped into it or one stayed out. Without the presence of a hierarchy inside the mosque, however, the imām often invited the members of the mosque's board of governors, friends, and associates to share the platform. To the consternation of other religious leaders in the country, these people have included women, local politicians, social activists, and occasionally even Christian priests. Some, including the women and the Christian priests, were invited to deliver the presermon talks. In terms of the preachers in the two mosques, then, while the secular was slowly cast off as one approached the pulpit in Brits, it was mediated and sacralized in the Claremont case. The sermon in the two mosques, in short, defined appropriate sacred spaces.

The Preachers

It is time to introduce the preachers and their particular sermons to be examined in the next chapter. These notes identify the background and training of the preachers as well as the particular topics and themes they cover in their sermons. Ḥāfiẓ Abdul Rashied Omar was the official imām and preacher at the Claremont Main Road Mosque. Born in 1959, he went to school in Salt River, Cape Town, and memorized the entire Qur'ān with a well-known teacher, Ḥāfiẓ Shamsuddin. He was in his final year of high school in 1976 when he joined and organized his school's protests against apartheid. Omar was detained for ten days without trial and lost one year of schooling as a result. He then read for a degree in African history and economics at the University of Cape Town. Here, he found himself involved with the Muslim Students Association and thereafter the Muslim Youth Movement. He taught for a while after graduating but then took on the directorship of the Muslim Youth Movement in 1983, followed by its presidency in 1987. Omar's involvement with Islamic resurgence in South Africa placed him in contact with innovative trends in Islamic and political discourses. This, however, did not completely eclipse his emergence as a typical Cape imām. Having completed the memorization of the Qur'ān in 1975, he studied Islamic law with Shaykh Toffar and Qazisaheb in Cape

Town. Later, as a ḥāfiẓ, he became a deputy imām to Hassan Solomons in Claremont in 1978, succeeding him at the end of 1985. In between, he also spent some time in the Sudan at the Africa-Islamic Centre, pursuing higher Islamic studies. This stint could have entitled him to the title of shaykh in Cape Town, but he returned much too quickly and has not made much of his overseas sojourn. On his return, Omar continued his studies at the University of Cape Town, first in the Department of History and then in the Department of Religious Studies, where he obtained a master's degree in comparative religion. While an imām at Claremont, he has also been a research officer with the Institute for Comparative Religions in South Africa, based at the University of Cape Town. Here, he has been involved with the development of multifaith approaches to dialogue and to religious education in South Africa. In summary then, Omar brings to the Claremont Main Road Mosque typical Cape imām qualifications, with some unusual political, academic, and educational experiences.

As noted in chapter 3, Claremont Main Road Mosque was a mosque with a clear political identity in the anti-apartheid movement, providing a platform for political activists to develop themes for Islam against apartheid. The sermons in the mosque covered a variety of topics, but almost all touched in one way or another on the relationship between Islam and the state. Two of the sermons under investigation, one in 1989 and one in 1990, examined *jihād* in the context of apartheid and social reconstruction. In the first, the preacher urged the importance of taking a clear anti-apartheid position, while in the second, he urged members to be engaged in programs of social rehabilitation. A sermon on an Islamic political party in 1990 and on pluralism in 1992 explored an approach to the unfolding new political dispensation in the country. Omar rejected the Islamic party for its idiosyncratic reading of a verse in the Qur'ān. Later in 1992, he even advocated Islamic pluralism for the Muslims in the country. Finally, a set of sermons in 1994 on a program of social reconstruction proposed by the new African National Congress government captured the relationship between the mosque and the new political order. Omar led the first two sermons on this theme and invited noted individuals to reflect on this topic. Shuaib Manjra and Aslam Fataar, both of whom had been active members in the Muslim Youth Movement, and who are regular members of the mosque, each presented a sermon. Manjra is a medical doctor, and Fataar teaches at the University of the Western Cape, outside Cape Town. Adam Samie, chairperson of the mosque board of governors, also preached a sermon on the theme of reconstruction and development. Crowning the series, the mosque invited the then Minister of the Reconstruction and Development

Programme, Jay Naidoo, to address the congregation on February 11, 1996.

I intended to approach the Brits sermons with the same kind of selectivity over a number of years. However, since I knew that in Brits, sermons were not deliberately devoted to topics related to political changes, I decided to collect sermons by different preachers on a single theme. With this in mind, I began my recordings of the sermons in Brits two months before the festival of sacrifice, Eid al-Adhā, in 1990. I was pleasantly surprised when Mawlānā Ebrahim, the first preacher, announced that he would initiate a series on pilgrimage to which the other preachers would contribute. Even though I listened to and recorded many other sermons, I found that this series suited my analysis. Barring one exception on daily worship, presented in Urdu, all the sermons were given in English and dutifully devoted to Abraham, sacrifice, pilgrimage, and the House of God in Mecca. Even though the sermons in the two mosques were devoted to completely different themes, they were amenable to comparison on the issues of politics, sacred spaces, and intra-Muslim relations in South Africa.

Mawlānā Ebrahim, who initiated the series in Brits, lived about seven miles out of town, near the Hartebeespoort Dam. He taught in the madrasah and delivered the sermon once every three or four weeks. He was born in 1955 and attended school in Krugersdorp, west of Johannesburg. At the age of fifteen, he went to the Waterval school of the Jamiatul Ulama Transvaal, where he memorized the Qur'ān. From there, he proceeded to Darbhel, India. After the completion of his studies in 1979, he spent a year with his spiritual mentor before returning home. Mawlānā Ebrahim owned and managed a general store for farm laborers near his home. He operated his business at the two extremities of the day, before sunrise and late in the evening, which suited both his religious obligations in town and his customers. In Mawlānā Ebrahim's first sermon during the period of my recordings, on May 11, 1990, he dealt with the place of pilgrimage in Mecca, deliberating on the establishment of the sacred house and including the story of how Abraham left Haggar and Ismā'īl in the desert. A second sermon, presented on June 8, 1990, continued this narrative and concluded with the suggestion that Abraham's invocation at the founding of Mecca was fulfilled in the person of the Prophet Muḥammad. Mawlānā Ebrahim's third and final sermon took place on the Day of Eid itself, when he demanded sacrifice and commitment: "The Messenger of Allah said that a person who has the ability to make qurbānī [sacrifice] and does not make qurbānī, Rasulullah [the messenger of God] says that such a person is not wanted in our congregation. He must not come to the place of prayer, he must not come to the place of prayer."

Unlike all the other 'ulamā' in Brits, the next preacher, Mawlānā Abu Bakr, was not raised in town. Born in Verulam, in the province now known as KwaZulu-Natal, he attended school in Durban and then worked as a plasterer until 1974. Then he was inspired by the work of Ahmad Deedat, the head of the Islamic Propagation Centre in Durban, to pursue higher Islamic studies in India. On his return, a friend introduced him to the Ermelo community in what is now Mpumalanga, which he served from 1981 to 1989. He came to Brits for a short while and then moved to Nelspruit, also in the same province. Mawlānā Abu Bakr was most actively and directly involved with the Tablīghī Jamāt, often going with them on their journeys to neighboring mosques and communities. This involvement in a social movement may partly be accounted for by the fact that he was a foreigner in the town and is also indicated in his transitory stops in three towns over ten years. None of the other Brits preachers moved as much, and all had extensive family connections in the town. It is interesting to note the effect of marginalization on the kind of religion adopted and practiced. Abu Bakr's position within the Muslim community of Brits corresponded to the Muslims in Mabuluka. Both were on the periphery of their respective societies. Mawlānā Abu Bakr's lecture of May 18, 1990, also focused on Mecca as a place of pilgrimage and on the meaning of sacrifice in a materialistic world. His sermon was distinctive to the extent that he used songs and dramatic expressions to great effect.

The third preacher was Mawlānā Yusuf Bhamjee, who memorized the Qur'ān under the tutorship of Ḥāfiẓ Nana in Brits and Mawlānā Garda in Pretoria. In the absence of a high school matriculation class in Brits at the time, he had to attend school in Laudium, the Indian group area outside Pretoria. It was here that he was given an opportunity to lead the special worship during the nights of Ramaḍān in the central mosque. As a young ḥāfiẓ, Mawlānā Yusuf was proud to join the senior 'ulamā' in the recitation of the entire Qur'ān during Ramaḍān. However, he found himself in the middle of a controversy between the Deobandis and Brelvis on the issue of a supplication at the end of every four cycles of the Ramaḍān worship. The Deobandis condemned this custom as an innovation and refused to lead the congregation in a short supplication. When some congregants in Pretoria insisted that the Deobandis conform to their demands, the young Mawlānā Bhamjee joined his teachers and walked out of the mosque in protest. Mawlānā Yusuf has more recently begun to reflect more critically on the theological divisions in the community, but he continues to be regarded as the bastion of Deobandism in the town.

Mawlānā Yusuf left for Karachi in 1970. Although he came from what anyone in Brits would recognize as a religious family, his father did not regard religious pursuits as the best career choice at the time. Nevertheless, the Mawlānā studied in Pakistan for eight years, and on his return, served the community most of the time since then. His first sermon focused on the House of God in Mecca, and related it to the ethical stance taken by Abraham. The Mawlānā's second sermon on June 14, 1990, recounted the story of the patriarch on the issue of social services in Islam. He rejected the significance of sacrifice for its apparent social benefit, in obvious reference to Islamic resurgence in the town and country. According to Mawlānā Yusuf, sacrifice in the story of Abraham established the priority of the rights of God to obedience and conformity over the rights of human beings. The rights of human beings were to be considered only as a consequence of the rights of God.

The final preacher assessed here was Mawlānā Bhoja, a frequent visitor who served the community in Benoni, east of Johannesburg. Reflecting the similar Deobandi persuasion of most religious leaders, visiting preachers were often invited to present lectures. Mawlānā Bhoja was an excellent storyteller and much appreciated by the audience. His sermon dealt primarily with the journey itself and complemented those of the other preachers who spoke on Mecca, its value, and its mythic history.

The preachers in Brits spoke extensively on Abraham and his relation to the most sacred place in Islam. The person and the place provided clues as to the unique manner in which the most sacred place of Islam, and by extension the mosque of Brits, was articulated. In Claremont, on the other hand, the sermons were articulated in relation to the mosque's place in the context of changing South African politics. Both mosques, Claremont directly and Brits indirectly, explored Muslims' relations with the state and its important transformation. In the next chapter I explore the manner in which the interpretations in both mosques were articulated in the sermons, making use of their discourses and the resources of revelation and disclosure within Islam.

Sermons and the Re-citation of Discourses

It appears as if he is the Reciter of the Qur'ān
In reality, he is the Qur'ān itself.

Muhammad Iqbal

In one of his sermons, Mawlānā Yusuf of Brits recalled the ḥadīth of
the Prophet: "If there were to be any Prophet after me, then it would have
been 'Umar b. al-Khaṭṭāb. He would have been the Prophet." He then
related 'Umar's statement that God granted him the privilege to suggest
three matters that were subsequently confirmed by revelation.[1]

Al-Suyūṭī (d. 911 A.H./1533 A.C.) has collected these and other such
verses under the heading "That which has been revealed on the words
of the companions." In each of these cases, the "Word of God" was antici-
pated by "the word of a companion of the Prophet." The examples from
Mawlānā Yusuf and al-Suyūṭī challenge the notion of a revelation as an
entirely ahistorical, primordial intrusion into the world. It seems that
revelation reflected and confirmed the experiences of the companions. I
argue here that the Friday sermons continued to provide the opportunity
for these divine disclosures. However, unlike the experiences of the first
companions of the Prophet, these disclosures were located in the history of
the Islamic interpretation of the Qur'ān.

It may seem as if this privilege was possible only for the earliest community—and untenable and impossible for later Muslim generations once revelation was completed. While this is true of the Qur'ān as a complete and
closed book, it did not necessarily mean the end of divine disclosures. The
Qur'ān in Muslim society was subjected to two kinds of elaboration. The
first, often regarded as the only legitimate one, was the systematic study
and elaboration of its meaning in the form of *tafsīr*. Taking the Qur'ān as a

book of Prophetic inspiration, the discourse of tafsīr drew on a plethora of tools to explain and extend its relevance to new contexts. History, contexts, language usage, and minute attention to intertextuality were applied to a public discourse of elaborating and explaining the meaning of the Qur'ān as a fixed text. The process of tafsīr brought new insights into a given, closed corpus.

The discourse of tafsīr was matched by another discrete, subjective claim of inspiration that could be applied to the Qur'ān. The notion of *ta'wīl* suggested an esoteric dimension of the text, which was available only to the elect. In contrast to the public elaboration of the text, ta'wīl suggested a text with multiple levels of meaning. It suggested that the meaning of the Qur'ān was in fact expanding through continued divine disclosures. While the text stayed the same on a literal level, its esoteric elaboration was open to expansion. It may be thought that, in comparison with tafsīr, ta'wīl was a later development. An examination of the ḥadīth literature, however, suggested that ta'wīl as an esoteric disclosure was not entirely alien in Islam. As for tafsīr, its foundations appear in the earliest ḥadīth collections. In fact, the following Prophetic statement provides one the possibility of a form of continuing revelation:

> Anas b. Mālik narrated that the Messenger of God said: The good dream of a righteous person is one forty-sixth of prophecy.[2]

> Abū Saʿīd al-Khudrī narrated that the Messenger of God said: If anyone sees a dream which he likes, then it is from God. He should thank God for it, and talk about it. But if he sees something else, that he does not like, then it is from the Devil. He should seek refuge with God from its evil, and not mention it to anybody, for it will harm him.[3]

These Prophetic statements are extremely suggestive for the importance of dreams as a conduit for divine disclosures. In the course of Islamic history, Sufis and Shiʿites concretized this tendency more than any other group of scholars. A brilliant history of Sufi outpourings stands testimony to this phenomenon.[4]

The following opening statement from Ibn al-ʿArabī (d. 638/1240) is typical of the direct inspiration felt by the Sufi from God through the Prophet:

> I saw the Apostle of God in a visitation granted to me during the latter part of the month Muḥarram in the year 627, in the city of Damascus. He had in his hand a book and he said to me, "This the book of the *Bezels of Wisdom;* take it and bring it to men that they might benefit from it."[5]

The saint received an insight into divinity in the same way that the Prophet received the Qur'ān. Ibn al-'Arabī goes much further when he makes a supplication that his composition should be guided directly by God:

> ... so He might favor me with His deposition and spiritual inspiration for my mind and His protective support, that I may be a transmitter and not a composer, so that those of the Folk who read it may be sure that it comes from the Stations of Sanctification and that it is utterly free from all the purposes of the lower soul, which are ever prone to deceive.

It was Ibn al-'Arabī's wish that the *Bezels of Wisdom* (*Fuṣūṣ al-ḥikam*) were nothing short of revelation. Similarly, Shi'ite imāms represented the continuing human-divine contact through their special status. According to Ayoub, "the Imāms did not possess revelation (*waḥy*)" but they "were none the less *muḥdathūn*, that is, people spoken to by angels." After the Prophet, continued Ayoub, they were "the 'speaking' (*nāṭiq*) Qur'ān, while the Qur'ān after the death of the Muḥammad remains the 'silent' (*ṣāmit*) Qur'ān."[6]

The sermon stood at the interstices of these two kinds of Qur'ānic disclosure. The sermon represented a public discourse, which was open to scrutiny and elaboration. Thus, the sermon in Claremont and Brits could not be extricated from the discourses spelt out in previous chapters. These discourses set the range of possibilities for the context, the usage of terms, and the themes to be explored in each mosque. In each mosque, for example, reference to dress codes from the corpus of Islamic texts were negotiated within mosque discourses. In Brits, frequent reference to the dress demands of Islam inscribed the orthopraxis desired by the 'ulamā'. The Claremont sermon in contrast was marked by the total absence of such references. Discourses played an important role in the choice of topics and the range of issues brought into the sermon. They defined disciplinary boundaries and opportunities as to what might or might not be said. Sermons, on the other hand, also offered the opportunity to enshrine and clothe these discourses in convincing and persuasive forms. And this is where the sermon drew on verses and Prophetic statement to do so. As an oral and aural form, the sermon simulated a Qur'ānic recitation and continued the inspirational tradition of the Sufis and Shi'ites in early Islam. I have called this process re-citation to denote the subtle interpretive dimension in the performance of the sermon's citation of Qur'ānic verses.

The Qur'ān as a book, fixed and bounded by numerous rituals, dogmas, and centuries of reflection and painstaking interpretation, was not going to yield easily to infiltration by local contexts. However, sermons provided temporary and spontaneous opportunities for the histories and discourses of the twentieth century to pierce the boundaries of revelation. Coburn has explored this dual notion of sacred literature in Hindu scriptures, the duality between original texts (sruti) and texts of explanation and interpretation (smrti). He argued that the existence of an "Allah Upanishad" meant that the sharp distinctions between the original texts and their interpretations could not easily be maintained. He concluded with a statement that has deep implications for a disclosure in the Qur'ān as well:

> India, it would appear, wants both the literal preservation and the dynamic re-creation of the word, and the movement between these two foci—whether or not they be called sruti and smrti, respectively—is both subtle and continuous.[7]

Original texts and elaborations on them were not clearly separated when placed under scrutiny. This distinction between text and interpretation in the Qur'ān is not as fluid as in the Hindu case. In fact, as I have elaborated in the first chapter, the separation is emphasized in numerous rituals, disciplinary practices, and historical narratives. However, the line of distinction between the Qur'ān and the speaking Qur'ān (Shi'ite imāms) is not as clear as the line of distinction between the Qur'ān and the Egyptian reciter. Depending partly on the context and partly on the religious significance of the reciter, the line of distinction between the Qur'ān as closed corpus and the Qur'ān as interpretation becomes blurred. The quotation given here from Ibn al-'Arabī parallels the Bezels of Wisdom to the Qur'ān. His supplication was a wish that, through the blessing of the Prophet, the Bezels of Wisdom would become another divine disclosure. Some may object that a Shi'ite imām and great Sufis may be as far removed from Cape Town and Brits as can be imagined. In this study I intend no less than to close this gap. I aim to show that the Friday sermons in the mosque traditions discussed provide an almost imperceptible opportunity for preachers to sunder the demarcation between the Qur'ān as closed and the Qur'ān as continued expansion. The sermons constituted creative reading of South African historical discourses into Qur'ānic re-citations.

The Sermon as Re-citation

I begin with some specific examples to elucidate the form of the re-citations. As the preachers translated the verses, they took great liberty in introducing discursive textures into the new renderings. In Brits, both Mawlānās Yusuf and Ebrahim dealt with the following verse in relation to the significance of sacrifice that commemorated the story of Abraham: "Their blood and their meat do not reach Allah, but your piety reaches him" (22:37). Mawlānā Yusuf cited this verse in the context of an extensive argument that the social significance of sacrifice was not as important as the piety implied in the act. This was a direct hint to the Islamic resurgent emphasis in the town and the country on the social significance of Islamic acts. His point was even more specifically directed against those who planned extensively for the distribution of meat among the poor in the townships around Brits. Mawlānā Yusuf's translation was heard as follows: "That the flesh or the blood of your sacrifice does not reach Almighty Allah, it is the *taqwā*, it is the essence, and it is the spirit behind the sacrifice which reached Allah." In the preacher's words, the translation and interpretation were combined to give the effect that this is what God intended in the Qur'ān. Mawlānā Ebrahim's rendering of the same verse was instructive for a different re-citation thereof: "There is this particular *āyah* [verse] where Allah says: . . . That it is not the blood which Allah accepts of yours, or that meat which Allah wants of yours and that skeleton or that body, or that *namāz* [prayer] which Allah wants, or for that matter any practical *'amal* [deed] that we practice, my respected elders, it is not that what Allah wants. But what does Allah want from us? Taqwā, the obedience to Allah. That is: *how* [his emphasis] do we fulfill the obedience and the taqwā of Allah." Mawlānā Ebrahim added many terms to the verse (skeleton, body, namāz) in order to create familiarity. Moreover, he also included obedience to the original taqwā, meaning awe and reverence. Both preachers cited the same verse, and their interpretations could easily be reconciled with each other. However, the point being made here is that their translations spontaneously included extratextual terms and interpretations. What were intended as literal translations turned out to be re-citations. In both, a verse, freely translated, took on a new form as it took on a new reading and a new significance.

In other cases, the preachers in Brits created dialogues and direct speech interjections in the Abrahamic epic. These conversations were placed over the narrative in the Qur'ān, sometimes creating a vivid picture of the stories in question, and sometimes adding dimensions with which the audience could relate immediately. When Mawlānā Ebrahim in Brits emphasized that Abraham was commanded by God to leave his family in the valley of Mecca, he conveyed it in the direct speech of God: "Here Abraham looks at the command of Allah and fulfills what Allah commands . . . that you leave your child, leave your wife, set off and go from here, leave this place." This command was a reflex of Qur'ān 14:37: "O Lord! I have left my family in a barren valley," which Mawlānā Ebrahim reported in the direct speech of God. More dramatically, Haggar's search for water was turned into a divine song, the lyrics being provided by Mawlānā Abu Bakr:

> O Hājrā! I love this sacrifice of yours. I love this running of yours in search of food. And every ḥājī [pilgrim] that's going to come to Mecca, I will make it a compulsory duty on him. If he doesn't make Ṣafā and Marwā, his pilgrimage won't be complete.
>
> Ḥaḍrat Hājra runs up and down. Finally, she goes and lands up there by Ḥaḍrat Ismāʿīl. She sees the baby crying and rubbing his both legs, kicking both legs, hitting on the ground. Allah says:
>
> Jibril, my Hājrā is worried and she is running up and down, my Hājrā is hungry, she is looking for food, my Hājrā is thirsty. She's looking for water. My Ismāʿīl is hungry. Ismāʿīl who is going to be my prophet is hungry. He is thirsty, he is kicking his legs on the ground. Go Jibril to the place where Ismāʾīl is hitting his heel on the ground. Go and spread it out and let water run out from there!

Mawlānā Abu Bakr interspersed the words of God as if they appeared in the Qur'ān, with some standard details Muslims immediately recognized. The narrative turned around important rituals during the pilgrimage, and it located the primeval origins of the well zamzam, from which pilgrims drank water and often brought some home for those who did not make the journey to Mecca. The location of a familiar item in the sermon created a powerful effect, especially when it was retold in the direct speech of God. Similarly, Mawlānā Bhoja also introduced a dialogue in his sermon. When Abraham was ready to "put the knife on the throat," and the angels intervened:

> Third time, he does it, all the angels, all creation is stunned, "Allah, what are you asking for? Are you asking for a life? Are you asking a

father to slaughter his own son? A son born after so much of *du ʿā*
[invocation] and eagerness?"

Allah says: "Yes! I know what I'm asking for, I know what I'm going
to get. I know what I'm asking for, I know what I'm going to get. I'm
asking for sacrifice, I'm getting loyalty, I'm getting sincerity, I'm getting dedication."

Yet . . . Ismāʿīl is on the floor, the mercy of Allah comes into force.

Allah tells Jibril: "Take a ram from paradise and take it to Ibrahim
and say: 'I tested you; you have passed your test with flying colors.
Here is an animal. Slaughter it in place of your son'."

The dialogue and direct speech extended the Abraham narrative in the
Qurʾān and created a sense in which God was speaking directly to
Abraham and to the people of Brits in a language and idiom they fully
comprehended.

Omar in the Claremont Main Road Mosque was equally involved in a
formal re-citation of the Qurʾān in his sermons. Like Mawlānās Yusuf and
Ebrahim, his re-citation was revealed in the translation of key verses. In a
sermon dissuading Muslims from supporting the apartheid state, Omar
recited the entire verse in Arabic, followed by a line-by-line translation:

Wa lā tarkanū
And do not be inclined, do not go forth, rely upon
ila alladhīna ẓalamū
those who are bent on doing wrong, oppressing others
fatamassakum al-nār
or the fire will seize you
And if you want to translate it literally (fatamassakum al-nār) that
    you will be playing with fire
wa mā lakum min dūn Allah min awliyāʾ
You will have no awliyāʾ, no protectors, other than Allah.

The word *awliyāʾ* is the plural of the singular *walī*, a word that Muslims
have not understood. If only we can understand the inner meaning
and implications of the word walī and its plural we will discover what
Allah wants from us in terms of our social relationships with our fellow Muslim brothers and non-Muslim fellow creation.

thumma lā tunṣarūn
Nor should you be helped if you violate the principle enunciated by
    Allah.

The re-citation is as clear in Omar's translation as in the translations of the Brits sermons. First, despite Omar's explicit promise of a literal translation, his was not literal at all. For example, the common expression "you will be playing with fire" for "fatamassakum al-nār" was a colloquialism, which was more immediate and emphatic for the listeners than was a literal rendering of the original Arabic. Moreover, the expression "you will be playing with fire" made human actors the subjects—not the fire, as in the Arabic. This elevation of human agency accorded with Omar's insistence that Muslims reject a fatalistic and acquiescent attitude toward history. Further, Omar promised that a true, inner meaning of the word *protectors* held the key for an understanding of social relations with all those opposed to the apartheid state, irrespective of their religious affiliation. Here again, Omar's translation had to carry the burden of the particular approach of the Muslim Youth Movement and the Call of Islam in the late 1980s to join the anti-apartheid movement. It went against a contending view among other Muslim organizations to abstain from such alliances.[8] The final phrase, "thumma lā tunṣarūn," received an extensive translation. Omar was here also drawing on the new approach of the Muslim Youth Movement, which deemphasized the literal application of Islamic teachings and followed Rahman's option for the application of general principles in varying contexts.[9] In this case, Omar derived a general principle from the verse, namely to shun and keep away from oppressors and evildoers. More important for our purposes here, this principle was incorporated into a re-citation of the verse, as the translation of "thumma lā tunṣarūn" included a reference to a principle: "Nor should you be helped if you violate the principle enunciated by Allah."

These examples illustrate the manner in which verses cited in the sermons were predisposed to being translated and formulated for particular contexts and intentions. In themselves, these idiosyncratic interpretations of verses were not unusual. My purpose here, however, is to indicate the manner in which verses were either literally invented or reread in creative ways. This re-citation of the Qur'ān echoed the oral and aural Qur'ān, the ultimate and supreme word of God. By the techniques of translation and selective emphasis, verses of the Qur'ān related to the story of Abraham and to Islamic politics were re-cited to reveal particular messages in Brits and Claremont respectively. Preachers reenacted new readings of the Qur'ān to produce a spontaneous reading of the Qur'ān in a dynamic, changing society. Re-citation was an oral presentation in a gathering that created the aura of a recitation. More than simply expounding religious obligations and attitudes, the preachers recited a new text of the Qur'ān. In this regard, the sermon—and not the study circle, mosque pillar, or modern Islamic university—may be the original locus of the Qur'ān. Bowman has shown in a short but important contribution that the Qur'ān in early Islamic society was ritually related to *keryane*, a scriptural reading in a gathering.[10] The Qur'ān in a Friday gathering, it seems, continued this tradition of announcing the word of God. The meeting in the mosque on Fridays extended the Prophet's pulpit, not in the recitation of the Qur'ān verbatim but in the aural production of the word of God.

Having demonstrated the Friday sermon as a re-citation of the Qur'ān, I want to return to the discussion in the preceding chapter about the nature of a sacred space. This idea of a place as a locus for the re-citation of a sacred text recalls Eliade's notion of a sacred space, as opposed to the perspectives of Smith, Chidester, and Linenthal. The idea of re-citation argued for here stands midway between the two positions. Unlike for Eliade, the moment of re-citation was not ineffable and undefinable but was directly related to particular interpretations articulating, reflecting, and reinforcing historical discourses. Re-citation was also clearly related to the cultural symbolism of Islam and the notion of a scriptural revelation. Rather than recovering the primordial and ineffable, re-citation brought the primordial (the Qur'ān in this case) to the temporal. On the other hand, re-citation was not simply a reflex of social and political agendas to be grafted onto one single moment of revelation. The religious dimension of the re-citation was not simply a ruse. It was at least important for its power of persuasion. More important, the sermon as re-citation shaped and articulated the metaphors of the historical discourses in the mosque. In this regard, it performed the cosmological function of the original text of Islam.

The Content

The sermons in the two mosques defined contrasting testimonies of the Qur'ān, displaying the discourses and contradictions of the two mosques discussed extensively in earlier chapters. The sermon developed these testimonies into metaphors that confirmed and justified the discourses. These metaphors acted as compelling abstractions of the discourses, easily identified and pursued in a variety of contexts. At the same time, the metaphors could not completely obliterate the contradictions within the discourses that constituted the mosques and the preachers. Between the extremities they tried to bring together, metaphors could not conceal the tensions and difficulties of the artificial construction of outlooks, discourses, and ideologies. Thus, the inspirational dimension of the sermon was not simply overwhelmed and completely determined by the discourses. Given the opportunity of carrying the new interpretations, the sermons disclosed their severe contradictions.

The metaphors of the sermons echoed and reflected the spatial definition of the two mosques, as discussed in chapter 6. There, it was found that the Brits sermons defined a more inclusive space than did those in the distinctive Claremont Main Road Mosque. The Brits sermons defined a hierarchically arranged but more inclusive religious orientation, while Claremont presented a unique, distinct outlook. This contrast was repeated in the metaphors of the sermons as well. The Brits sermons linked the mosque to the house built by Abraham, while the Claremont Main Road Mosque focused on its uniqueness. The sermons in the Brits Mosque extolled a broad, nebulous Islamic law, the Sharī'ah, while the Claremont Mosque advocated specific political action. And third, the Brits Mosque advocated—and even deflected action toward—supplication and invocation, while the Claremont sermons argued for struggle and commitment in society. The sermons at both mosques also revealed some basic contradictions of authority and status within their discursive foundations. At Brits, the fundamental contradictions between knowledge and wealth as competing sources of power could not be eradicated. Claremont, on the other hand, could not quite balance the demands of being progressive with those of being part of an Islamic pluralism in Cape Town.

The Claremont Main Road Mosque came under tremendous criticism for the creative and innovative manner in which it addressed a range of social issues. This criticism has resulted in a self-awareness of being a unique mosque leading the way, not only for mosques within the country but also for mosques throughout the world. The sermon revealed this trailblazing tradition, particularly in the face of continuing pressure to conform. When during Ramaḍān of 1995 the annual general meeting of the mosque was disrupted by protesters, Omar spelled out and committed himself to what he called the "prophetic" role of the mosque in the Eid sermon:

> We began to realize that we should not take for granted what we have striven for during the last few decades at this Masjid. . . . The ideals of this Masjid stand as a beacon of hope and light to Muslims all over the world. We say this with a sense of deep humility.[11]

According to the imām, this was a mosque with a proud history in the face of injustice. Its history justified its continuing to make a unique contribution in the future. From an anti-apartheid past, it pushed forward into the future: "This message of ours does not want to take Muslims back to the seventh century; to a romanticized and nostalgic yearning for the glorious past of Islam. Our message wants to take us forward into the twenty-first century so that we are able to creatively meet the manifold challenges which await us." Continuing this prophetic metaphor, he promised "dispatching . . . our journalists to the front line" where they could "literally humiliate our adversaries in a war of words." These images reinforced uniqueness and the definition of a mosque with a singular mission. Other preachers also reinforced this special mission of the mosque. In his sermon on the Reconstruction and Development Programme, the chairperson of the mosque board, Adam Samie, echoed the imām's metaphor of a trailblazing mosque. Beginning with a recitation of one of the earliest verses of the Qur'ān, namely Muddathir (74:1–5), when the Prophet Muḥammad had little support in Mecca, Samie urged for a similar mission "to confront the society of the day and make a definite break with the past."

The self-awareness of this Cape mosque contrasted sharply with the deliberate obliteration of itself by the Brits Mosque. The sermons in Brits constantly linked the mosque and ordinary Muslim activities to preeminent, primordial events and places associated with Abraham. Religious phrases and symbols used in the community were located in the Abrahamic epic, creating a bond between the Brits Mosque and the sacred house of Mecca. Mawlānā Ebrahim's sermon was not unique for the presence of these linking phrases: "Ibrahim was prepared with the knife. The knife was on the throat. `Bismillah Allah Akbar!' and Allah sent down a sheep for Ḥaḍrat Ibrahim." This Arabic phrase meaning "In the name of God, God is Greatest" must be uttered by Muslims before slaughtering an animal and represents the most important formula for rendering an animal fit for Muslim consumption. Its use in this context was not simply a misplaced anachronism of contemporary ritual in the Abrahamic epic. It provoked and elicited a connection between the Muslims listening to the sermon and the story of Abraham. Furthermore, the preachers all dealt with the House of God in Mecca as a mirror of the Brits Mosque. The epic of Abraham and his sacrifice are mentioned in the Qur'ān without the particular place of sacrifice.[12]

Following extensive exegetical authorization, the preachers in the town all assumed that the place was Mecca and the intended victim was Ishmael. In early Islamic scholarship, the identity of Abraham's intended sacrificial victim was not always unequivocally Ismā'īl; and Abraham's building of the House in Mecca posed a problem to many Muslim historians. During the first Islamic century, Isaac was also mentioned as the intended sacrifice of Abraham, with consensus among scholars converging around Ismāʿīl only in the third century. Firestone has argued that this particular choice provided the narrative support for Islam's independence from Judaism and Christianity.[13]

Obviously, this issue did not arise in Brits in the twentieth century. Instead of the search for the identity of the son, as in early Islamic scholarship, however, the search for Mecca occupied a central part in the Brits sermons. The search for the place by way of a journey provided focused attention on the ongoing journeys made to the sacred house. This important journey always left the town, and the mosque in Brits, and ended at the sacred house in Mecca. Mawlānā Ebrahim recounted Abraham's journey through "villages" and "green places" until they reached the sacred house "just in the form of a hill" surrounded by "rocks, mountains . . . full of thorns." Similarly, Bhoja described the journey in response to God's command, passing "oases" and "tents" until Mecca "slightly elevated, lifted from the ground." For those listening to these sermons in Brits, the journey of Abraham modeled the journeys they themselves had made or wished still to make to the House of God in Mecca. Hence, either by familiar phrases or by the delineation of key motifs in the sacred narratives, the sermons linked the people of Brits and their religious commitments to Abraham. Meaning in Brits was founded in that which existed outside. The mosque of Brits was always in the shadow of the sacred mosque in Mecca. This meaning located outside the Brits Mosque contrasted sharply with the Claremont sermon, which celebrated its own history.

We now turn to the exploration of political ethics in the Brits and Claremont sermons. Since the period in question dealt directly with the political transformation of South African society, it is not surprising to find a clear ethic in each mosque. The preachers in the Claremont Mosque, in particular, were deliberately engaged in the political transformation of the country. They took pride in their stance against the apartheid state and continued to address this issue as South Africa went through a period of transition to a new order. On June 16, 1989, commemorating the Soweto uprisings of 1976 against apartheid, Omar explored the meaning of jihād as a struggle for justice against apartheid, using the Qurʾān 11:113. This position underwent some modification in a sermon delivered on August 31, 1990, when Omar extended the notion of jihād from political struggle to social upliftment. Regarding Qurʾān 4:95–96, he contrasted those who "struggled" (*mujāhidūn*) with those who sat tight (*qāʿidūn*):

Allah, the Almighty, declared that such of the believers who remain passive at home other than the disabled cannot begin to be equal to those who strive in Allah's cause with their possessions and their selves. Allah has exalted those who strive hard with their possessions and their selves far above those who remain passive and sit at home, and Allah has indeed promised ultimate good unto all believers. Yet Allah has exalted above those who remain passive, those who strive hard by promising them a mighty reward many degrees thereof *maghfirah*, forgiveness, and *rahmah*, his grace. Allah is indeed oft forgiving and the dispenser of grace.

As examples of the context where these two sets of believers may be found, Omar referred to the crisis of drug abuse in the community, Muslim membership in liberation movements, and the local Islamic schools. In each of these, he lamented the "indifference, apathy, and complacency" among Muslims with regard to the crucial issues facing the community. The most important question posed to the Claremont community was "Which group do you belong to?" For the imām there were only two groups from which Muslims could choose: "Allah . . . defines some believers as qāʿidūn, staying at home, who refuse to involve themselves for the upliftment of humanity, [and] for the establishment of justice. Those are the qāʿidūn, the pacifists [*sic*], those who are indifferent, who are apathetic, and the mujāhidūn are those who engage themselves in struggle." In Omar's interpretation of the verse, the people who were prepared to involve themselves in the community in various social projects were the mujāhidūn, while the indifferent sat at home. Finally, in 1994, after the first democratic elections, Omar initiated a series of sermons in evaluation of the Reconstruction and Development Programme (RDP) proposed by the state. The sermons endorsed the proposed program, hardly suggesting any unique feature from Islam. Shuayb Manjra, one of the contributors, was succinct: "When asked to speak on the specific role of Muslims within the RDP, I thought long and hard and to be honest could not find a specific role of Muslims, any different from our compatriots of other faiths or none at all." Thus, over the course of six years, the sermons in the Claremont Mosque moved from political jihād to social reconstruction. While the mosque stood as a unique symbol of progressive Islam among Muslims, it was indistinguishable within the larger picture of the rainbow nation. The mosque's ethos corresponded with the civil religion I had found in the Muslim Youth Movement's newspaper from 1990 to 1994. There, as in the Claremont Mosque, the values and symbols of the newspaper coincided with the values and symbols of the new South African nation.[14]

This struggle ethic, compliant to the new nation state, was clearly demonstrated in the mosque's response in August 1996 to the militant jihād of a group called People Against Gangsterism and Drugs. The movement invoked Qur'ānic verses and Islamic slogans against alleged gangsters and druglords.[15] In principle, Omar supported the movement, and a few sermons were devoted to a positive assessment of the rise of a militant Islamic voice on the streets of Cape Town. Yet the Claremont Mosque was also wary of such slogans and endorsed peace initiatives in the city that arrested the confrontational nature of the war against drugs, thereby aiming to "foster a new sense of peace in the city."[16] In particular, on August 30, 1996, Omar joined peace prayers at St. George's Cathedral and in turn invited Rev. Canon Rowan to address the Claremont Mosque. The invitation was met with considerable criticism among Muslims, but it underlined the way in which the mosque's sermons affirmed developments in the new South Africa after the 1994 elections, generally endorsing approaches and directions in civil society, even if critical within the Muslim community.

The particular struggle ethic of Claremont may be contrasted with the stance taken in the Brits Mosque. Here, politics was regarded principally as tainted and best postponed to an eschatological future. Where the Claremont sermons demanded struggle in society, the Brits sermons demanded belief, prayer, and above all invocations. The religious demands toward the House of God had unmistakable political overtones. In the context of Qur'ān 3:95, Mawlānā Yusuf revealed his approach to politics in South Africa: "that surely the first house which was made for humanity, every human being [his emphasis], is most certainly the one in Mecca." He began with an emphasis on the inclusivity in the verse, which he re-cited as "every human being." This universal declaration, straightforward as it may seem, was anathema to the ideology of apartheid, which systematically divided people into different groups. However, in this mawlānā's case, the principle did not translate into a revolutionary political ethic. Yusuf's comparison between the house of God and the houses of politics produced no resemblance:

> And Allah says [!] that while you are in this world, after this house was made for the entire humanity, you will see and you will have seen many houses come into existence, many houses built. Simple and ordinary houses in which people dwell . . . to create influential houses, like parliament houses, Houses of Commons, House of Lords, House of Delegates. You will see many houses coming up. But remember, your emotions and your mental attitudes and your views should al-

ways be centered around this one house of Almighty Allah, which is called the Ka'bah.

All modern political structures, with no distinction made between democratic ones and those created by apartheid, were tainted. The House of Delegates mentioned in the sermon was an apartheid structure, which had made provision for junior Indian membership in the dominant white parliament. By including such a discredited structure in the same breath as "parliament houses, Houses of Commons, House of Lords," the mawlānā made no special distinction for apartheid and paid no attention to the political context of the town. Like Mawlānā Yusuf, Mawlānā Bhoja also denigrated all political structures. Bhoja too obliterated any difference between unjust apartheid and non-apartheid political structures. He posited the house of God as a symbol of primordial value and covenant, and he left little room for a modern political contract and covenant:

> Allah spells it our clearly, crystal clear—no freedom charter, no constitution, nothing whatsoever. In plain and simple words Allah spells it out "lā yanālu 'ahdī al-ẓālimīn" (my favor does not extend to the wrong-doers). If Muslims want to lead the world, the country, that leadership lies in obedience of Allah and his Prophet, otherwise they must forget.

Bhoja dismissed anti-apartheid democratic symbols along with his denigration of modern political structures. The Freedom Charter in his list referred to the basic political manifesto formulated in 1955 by a meeting of organizations devoted to opposing the ideology of apartheid. This manifesto became a symbol of demands made by anti-apartheid organizations in the 1980s and 1990s. In both cases, actual political choices were contrasted with absolute and idealized notions of the house and leadership. And with the selective denigration of the then current political deliberations in the country, neither the house nor the covenant of God could be translated into substantial political activities in South Africa.

The Brits sermons may be contrasted too with the political reading of verses, popular in South African cities during the 1980s as well as in other international contexts. Le Roux has analyzed the hermeneutic switches employed by the Call of Islam in South Africa to relate Moses' fight against the pharaoh in the Qur'ān to the oppressed people's struggle for justice in apartheid South Africa.[17] In a recent study, Hiskett has criticized this political reading of Islam against apartheid South Africa: "One may question whether such ancient decontextualized scriptural references can be successfully adapted to fit modern socio-political contexts—and even whether the attempt to do so is morally honest."[18]

In light of the political experience of apartheid, it seems more important to ask how a religious discourse could be insulated against these readings. The experience of forced removals, and the daily abuse of power, contextualized references to powerful words in the Qur'ān. The lack of political reference in the Brits Mosque requires as much explanation as the political readings that seem morally "dishonest." The former can be related to the compromising socioeconomic role in which the 'ulamā' in the Transvaal found themselves. Apart from changes inside the mosque, they were helpless to affect political developments in the society as a whole. In spite of their dominance in the town, they did not or could not change the political relations obtaining between Muslims and the state.

The preachers in Brits, however, did leave the members with something to do. The sermons focused on the achievements of Abraham, not only in terms of a personal quest or struggle but in terms of supplications and invocations. If activism and struggle pervaded the ethic of the Claremont sermons, supplications and prayers dominated the Brits sermons. The entire epic of Abraham was revealed in an unfolding fulfillment of supplication. The many prayers of Abraham occupied a central position in the sermons of Mawlānā Ebrahim.[19]

Mawlānā Ebrahim in particular used these supplications to recount the epic of Abraham. In his sermons, the sermons themselves became part of an unfolding plan invoked by Abraham at various points of his life. Prayer and supplication moved history, and they could be used by ordinary believers to change the course of their own lives. All the preachers left the people with a message to turn to God in obedience, reverence, and sincerity.

The importance of prayer can be gauged via especially difficult theological and historical problems posed by prayers in the Qur'ān and tackled by Mawlānā Ebrahim in Brits. The examples here underlie the importance prayers posed in the worldview of these preachers, as the object of struggle posed in the Claremont mosque. The first concerned the prayer of Abraham corrected by God in Qur'ān 2:126:

> What du'ā' did he [Abraham] make? For the Muslim only: "That for those who believe in Allah and the hereafter." But Allah adds on to this du'ā': "And those who disbelieve in me, they also will get my sustenance."

The petition of Abraham needed to be explained because a Prophet, chosen and guided by God, could not be contradicted and corrected by

God. Ebrahim, the preacher, tried desperately to find a solution:

> Now why did Ebrahim not make du'ā' here for his other children? Because it is not necessary that the offspring of Ebrahim are all Muslims; there are disbelievers also. In another place Ebrahim makes du'ā' to Allah for the disbelievers and for the Muslims both. And there Allah did not accept the du'ā' of Ḥaḍrat Ibrahim in both cases. He only accepted the du'ā' of the Muslims.

Mawlānā Ebrahim was referring to the following: "My Lord! make me one who establishes the worship; and my progeny also. Our Lord! accept our supplication. Our Lord! forgive me and my parents and the believers on the day of reckoning" (Qur'ān 14:40–41). Taking these two supplications together, Mawlānā Ebrahim wanted to show that Abraham was not wrong for excluding the disbelievers in his first du'ā'. These deliberations by Mawlānā Ebrahim were concerned not only with theological dilemmas. In spite of a neat exegetical solution, Abraham's supplication still posed a problem as to how disbelievers, contrary to God's wish, were presently excluded from Mecca. The mawlānā's solution included a vision of the future determined by the invocation: "But there the reason was that Allah accepted the du'ā' of the Muslims as far as command and rule of the place of Mecca was concerned. That this rule of Mecca will only be in the hands of the Muslimīn. Yes! What is the meaning of this? That before the day of judgment—the Ka'bah will be demolished and destroyed by the non-Muslims. But that will be just before the day of judgment." The disbelievers, according to God's promise, would certainly enjoy the fruits of Mecca. This, however, should not be read as an argument for Muslims to allow them to enter the sacred city. Their presence in Mecca could only be possible in the distant future as part of God's unfolding plan. The point being made here is that prayers and supplications in the Brits sermons provided a foundation for understanding the forces of history as well as events in the future. History and life on earth in general were a kind of map in which primordial events were unfolding according to a plan controlled by supplications. It is not surprising to see, therefore, the repeated emphasis by all the preachers on prayers and supplications.

Bowen has dealt with the issue of supplication in Indonesia, comparing scripturalist and nonscripturalist orientations in society. Those with a closer affinity with the textual tradition in Islam regarded du'ā' as a means by which God may be petitioned, while the *doas* of folk traditions were closely related to the spells and incantations addressed to village spirits. Bowen tried to draw sharp contrasts between the two, representing contrasting discourses, one from the Islamic textual tradition and the other a remnant of folk religion. At the same time, however, Bowen also showed how the doa, as a manipulation of reality, was related to the metaphysics of Ibn 'Arabī's unity of being, and its manipulation of nature.[20]

In the Brits example, supplication (du'ā') was clearly related to the scriptural tradition. In this case, though, du'ā' was thought to be capable of transforming and changing history in the same way that spells could transform reality. The magical doa of Indonesia and the Sharī'ah-based du'ā' were closer to each other than they appeared at first glance. In fact, Claremont's ethic of struggle and mobilization also proposed active struggle in order to change and transform history. Struggle was the symbolic means of eradicating apartheid. Hence, social and political activity in their religious symbolic dimension could be located on a continuum with doa and du'ā'. The continuum, moreover, was not devoid of political consideration. In the politics of South Africa and in contrast with the Claremont tradition, the du'ā' of Brits was a conservative approach to politics and Islamic traditions.

The particular ethical stances propounded in the sermons of the two mosques were not without their inherent contradictions. In each mosque, the sermons re-citing the Qur'ān had to resolve the gulf between a universal message (the Qur'ān) and its particular expression. In each case, we find tensions where mosque discourses were patched up from competing interests. The Brits example was clearer because of the contradictions held inside the hierarchically divided mosque. Mawlānā Abu Bakr addressed the increasingly widespread performance of the hajj pilgrimage among Muslims in South Africa. On the one hand, he decried materialism as the new sacrificial altar of Muslims: "There is some 'ibrat, a great lesson, for us to learn. Because we are sacrificing everything for the sake of the world. You are now running behind these materialistic thinkers, this valueless world. We are forgetting we are going to stand tomorrow in front of our Creator and we are going to answer for every sin. The love of the world has overtaken us." At the same time, Abu Bakr upbraided the rich who went on pilgrimage, linking them to Jews and Christians: "Nabi-e-karim said: When a person has the means for hajj and nothing stops him, he should see that he goes for hajj. And if he still stays away it is better for him to die as a Yahūdī [Jew] or a Naṣārā [Christian]." Having identified materialism as the arch vice, and Jews and Christians as the archenemies, Mawlānā Abu Bakr had to confront the fact that the performance of hajj demanded a great deal of wealth; and that modern hajj was performed with conveniences provided by the West, which for Mawlānā Abu Bakr was synonymous with Jews and Christians.

In his sermon, moreover, Mawlānā Abu Bakr undermined the "materialism" demanded for the fulfillment of the pilgrimage in a number of steps. First, following the ḥadīth he quoted, he relegated the wealthy who did not perform pilgrimage to the same category as Jews and Christians. As for those who did take the trouble, he addressed their pilgrimage in an interesting reading of a Prophetic prediction about the kind of people who would be going for pilgrimage: "The noble Prophet said: `The rich will go to Mecca and Medina for holiday.' [They will]) leave Rome and Paris and go to Mecca, Medina. The noble Prophet said: `The next group of people will be those people that will go to Mecca, that will come there to the house of Allah for the sake of business. They will come there and take goods to sell and bring goods to sell.'" Mawlānā Abu Bakr then described this market: "Because when the pilgrims go there, they go to the bazaar. They notice the Christians who supply everything, from the smallest to the biggest. So when the pilgrim goes to the bazaar he gets so occupied in looking at those things that he forgets his worship." According to Mawlānā Abu Bakr, the Christians were present in Mecca by virtue of their goods, through which they undermined the pilgrimage. The wealthy who went on pilgrimage, in his view, spent their time engrossed in the bazaar stocked by Jews and Christians. The pilgrim admittedly did more than shop in Mecca, however. She spent at least some of the time performing the rites of the pilgrimage. The following comments by Mawlānā Abu Bakr placed even that devotion in jeopardy: "One hājī pilgrim was into such a rage, he threw the sandal so fast he himself went and fell on top of the Devil. They had to take him off from the Devil. That same pilgrim, when he lands at the airport, he becomes the Devil's friend again. In which way? As soon as he lands to declare his goods, he starts lying. He starts lying! The pilgrim just went for ḥajj and comes back, he's lying—that same pilgrim is being exposed by the same Christians." Mawlānā Abu Bakr devalued this religious passion by lamenting the pilgrim's exposure by Christians at the airport in Johannesburg. And finally, the mawlānā continued the Prophet's prediction, weaving materialism, Jews, and Christians into the new reading of the Prophet's statement:

And he [the Prophet] said: "The third group of people who will go there, will go there to beg." And you will see today. When you go there to places like Mecca and Medina, if you are not careful, your pocket will be slit, everything will be taken out. That's why Mawlānā Maqda who is always there mentions in his lecture, he says: "Only pilgrims come here, thieves don't come here." He says: "The job of cutting pockets and taking out money is not the job of a Muslim. It is the job of a Jew, a Christian, an infidel, and hypocrites."

Jews and Christians seemed to be an inextricable part of the pilgrimage, even if in the most derogatory way. In Mawlānā Abu Bakr's view, their presence seemed to despoil every act of the pilgrim, from the performance of the rites up to and including events at the airport in South Africa. On another level, Mawlānā Abu Bakr's devaluation of the pilgrimage identified some key anomalies in its performance. He himself could not resolve the contradictions between the materialism he decried and the wealth that made ḥajj obligatory. According to the Qur'ān: "The people's duty to God lies in making pilgrimage to the House, whoever is able to undertake it" (Qur'ān 3:97). According to Mawlānā Abu Bakr, however, the duty of pilgrimage, possible for the rich, was also despoiled by the rich. In his sermon, he tried to salvage the pilgrimage by abusing the actions of those who actually performed it. By introducing the malevolent notions of materialism, Jews, and Christians, he gave a new, though strange, sense and meaning to the Qur'ānic obligation. This contradiction can only be understood when we keep in mind the fact that religious leaders and wealthy traders were engaged in constant sparring in the Transvaal. The preacher was not only highlighting the existential contradictions of performing one of the most important rites in a Muslim's life; he was inscribing the doubtful value of a trader's religious worship.

The tensions within Claremont sermons related to mosque's position within the Muslim community (*ummah*) and its much publicized nature as a unique mosque. Claremont took pride in its status as a progressive mosque, which I have contrasted with the Brits Mosque in the assembly of Abraham's sacred house. And yet, Claremont did not give up its place entirely in this assembly. On the one hand, it made bold assertions (rituals, pronouncements, and practices) that set it apart from other mosques in South Africa. On the other hand, it had to find some way of continuing to be part of the universal assembly of mosques. Thus, Omar propounded the notion of an Islamic pluralism wherein his own progressive voice was one among many. While he was not prepared to capitulate to Muslim criticism on the issues raised in the mosque, pluralism provided a mechanism for ensuring a place in the broader house of Islam. It was not simply a voice of tolerance toward other views but a demand for itself to be counted among the other mosques in spite of its unique nature.

Omar expounded on Islamic pluralism on a number of occasions. He called this an "intrinsic pluralism," by which he meant a host of interpretations within Islam. He urged Muslims to respect other views and to realize that one's own view may always be subject to correction. A closer look at the Islamic pluralism in the context of one sermon revealed the manner in which Omar used the multiple meanings of hermeneutic theory to deflect and dissipate the force of verses used by parties in Cape Town. Second, it also showed how even pluralism did not preclude a hierarchy in the context of a post-apartheid mosque. In a sermon delivered on September 21, 1990, Omar discussed the issue of pluralism in Islam. He related his sermon directly to a proposed Islamic political party in an advertisement in a daily paper. Omar did not reject the advertised goals of the party, namely the promotion of Islamic ideology, Muslim interests, and pan-Islamism. He argued that these could be achieved through other political strategies. Using the inherent and necessary multiplicity of interpretations of the Qur'ān, he dissipated the key verse cited by the Islamic party, Qur'ān 3:104: "Let there arise among you an ummah, a community of believers, a band of people," First, Omar took dubious recourse to Arabic: "The word party in terms of the Qur'ān is usually translated as `ḥizb,' ḥizb Allah, the party of Allah." According to Omar, since the specific word for "party" was not used, one could not justify an Islamic political party on this basis. Omar's literal reading of a verse went against a contextual reading, which Claremont seemed to advocate. Such an approach did not depend on specific terms and verses in the Qur'ān but on the principles and spirit thereof in the light of text and context. Omar was obviously opposed to the Islamic party's approach to Muslim political interests, and he brought that rejection to bear in a linguistic analysis that he did not in principle support. His second approach to the verse indicated the multiple readings of the verse within the South African community. In particular, he pointed out that the Tablīghī Jamāt in South Africa used the very same verse to call for roving groups of people to call other Muslims to adhere to their program. Omar's third line of attack did not involve Qur'ānic exegesis. Here, he questioned the particular quarter from which the proposal to form an Islamic party came. He hinted that it came from those who did not participate in the anti-apartheid struggle:

> The only way to protect the interest of Islam and Muslims in South Africa is by participating against oppression. Therefore, no Muslim who has been turning a blind eye to the anti-apartheid struggle, who has said that I do not want to participate . . . [deserves] . . . a place in a post-apartheid South Africa.

Using a variety of interpretive strategies, then, Omar tried to use pluralism to give Claremont pride of place. A dubious reference to language usage and a keen sense of how various groups in South Africa appropriate the verse established pluralism. But participation in the anti-apartheid struggle placed Claremont at an advantage. We can criticize the preacher for a selective invocation of Arabic, or an expedient appeal to multiple readings of the Qur'ān. But, taking these dimensions together, the sermon recorded the mosque's own place in the history of apartheid resistance. The notion of pluralism could not be reconciled with the mosque's self-awareness as a trailblazer. The self-effacement of pluralism had clear limits in a Cape discourse that produced unique mosques.

Conclusion

The sermon within South Africa was connected with the basic forms of Qur'ānic interpretation in Islam. I have argued in this chapter that the sermon was both a disciplinary elaboration of the Qur'ānic text in light of the discursive traditions in mosques and also a spontaneous, even inspirational, expansion of the text. The particular reading of the Qur'ān, as the Word of God, reflected the discourses of the mosques and imāms. As a re-cited aural word of God, the sermon as re-citation produced a place and a moment where the participants could relive a moment of divine contact. Preachers in South Africa reenacted the moment of recitation in creative but culturally specific ways. In particular, the sermons promoted their respective discourses in metaphors that encapsulated their place in relation to other mosques and their contrasting political ethics in relation to the politics of apartheid. Claremont's unique anti-apartheid mosque differed from the submersion of the mosque at Brits in the assembly of primordial mosques. While the Claremont sermons urged struggle, Brits sermons enveloped history in efficacious prayers. The sermons of the mosques could not escape their inherent contradictions. The Brits 'ulamā' challenged their wealthy patrons in the practice of one of the fundamental pillars of Islam. Claremont tried to search for Islamicity as well as a unique South Africanism through Islamic pluralism.

8

Conclusions

This fledgling pigeon essayed the air and flew off when he heard a
whistle and a call from the unseen.

Rumi

This study has recovered the history of two Muslim communities and
their institutions under the impact of colonialism and apartheid. Since
1990, when South African liberation movements were unbanned, the full
range of political activities in the past has been slowly coming to light.
This disclosure has illustrated the extent to which European hegemony
disrupted and altered individual aspirations and the textures of societies
and communities in South Africa. The struggle against white domination
was not simply about an alternative political order. Colonialism and apartheid deeply affected the meanings of self, identity, and community institutions. They had impact upon the full range of human emotions and notions
of what an individual and a society could be. For societies that predated
European presence in the region, colonialism and apartheid systematically
dismantled their political institutions and substituted others that favored
the new ruling classes. For those groups who came to South Africa
subsequent to European control, like Muslims, colonialism and apartheid
affected the selves and institutions formed from the day people arrived on
the shores of the country. I have argued that we need to pay greater attention to the history and experience of the many smaller communities that
constitute the South African nation. They disclose the full impact of the
past and the possibilities for the future. These stories, moreover, reveal that
South Africans have not simply been recipients of discriminatory laws and
parliamentary bills; they are not stories that simply evoke applause, pity, or
indignation. Communities also created institutions, discourses, and oppor-

tunities in the face of the most debilitating measures instituted by the state. In short, rather than simply being historical objects, communities were also historical subjects. Painful and heroic at the same time, the stories of communities under apartheid bear testimony to the human spirit. For South Africans, understanding these stories may hold the key for the future of post-apartheid society. For others, they at least offer tremendous insights for understanding communities under extremely difficult conditions.

The sermon has been used here as a prism to understand religious symbols and institutions in two South African Muslim communities. The sermon symbol was shown to be historically grounded in the contexts of colonialism and apartheid, discursively constituted in mosque and imām complexes, and religiously powerful in its simulation of revelation. Study of the South African sermon in each of these three aspects suggested far-reaching implications for understanding religion in South Africa and Islam in context. The historicity of the sermon was located at different levels. Broadly speaking, the symbol was founded in the context of communities established during colonialism and apartheid. In this sense, these two historical movements and their institutions equally affected all religious symbols. The Muslims of Cape Town came as slaves, exiles, and convicts during Dutch company rule and lived through slavery, freedom, British colonialism, and then apartheid. Muslims in the Transvaal region came from India as indentured workers, hawkers, and traders during British colonialism and also lived through the gold rush, the unified government of the former British colonies and Boer republics as one nation, and apartheid. Both the general context of colonialism and apartheid and the Muslims' histories within this setting had direct influences on their religious symbols. The mosques in Cape Town represented the aspirations of leaders who took advantage of opportunities at the end of the eighteenth century to build communities and structures for the underclasses of Cape Town. Through education and ritual services, they provided some semblance of community for slaves and free blacks on the margins of Cape society. Mosques in the Transvaal were built against a background of specific legal opposition and represented the aspirations of Muslims who were determined to make South Africa a home. Both mosque traditions were products of marginality in social, cultural, and political terms. However proud and triumphant, they were always responding to pressures in the political and social contexts of South Africa.

Both Cape and Transvaal Muslims and mosques were often trapped in ambiguous political positions in South Africa. As minorities and/or branded foreign, Indian and Coloured Muslims did not bear the worst forms of subjugation and deprivation. Often, their survival and sometimes their prosperity rested on this middle position in the political economy of South Africa. On the one hand, mosques faced extreme prejudice and political obstacles. On the other hand, authorities left the door slightly ajar for political compromise. It cannot be denied that both the nineteenth-century Cape mosque and the Transvaal mosque were founded in the midst of these ironies. The Cape mosque, with its vocal imām, was able to disguise this relationship when representing the aspirations of its congregation. The Transvaal mosque leadership left political control, and the resultant compromise, in the hands of the traders.

A closer look at the two mosque institutions revealed more detailed configurations of authority, power, and community prerogatives. Mosques and leaders were not merely alternative havens from the ravages of displacement and marginalization. Attention to the place of the imāms, the communities, and the state authorities disclosed the formation of discourses within mosque and imām institutions. The discourses were constructed out of symbols, composed of religious, social, and political elements. The products, recognizable religious symbols in the mosques, were neither inherent and essential traits of human religiosity nor simply maps of cosmologies and worldviews. They were resources within group identities that were effectively employed to construct selves and communities. The establishment of mosques in the context of colonialism and apartheid founded such powerful discourses, which were concretized in regular patterns of language, political attitudes, and actions that enabled and empowered social acts. Communities in the two regions recognized these patterns, which they used to forge acts, leaders, and identities. Sermons could not be divorced from these historically grounded discourses. The sermons reflected and shaped them.

The establishment of the first mosque in the Cape entrenched the central role taken by the imām at the expense of lay persons. Moreover, educational opportunities and ritual services guaranteed the loyalty and commitment of the community to the imām. In contrast, Transvaal mosques emerged in the absence of imāms. The people who founded the mosques, the hawkers and traders, played a dominant role in these mosques and have since maintained that position. Their authority and power was founded in the context of racial prejudice and anti-Indian legislation. Traders and mosque communities alleviated these obstacles through special concessions and relations with the state. When the imām did become established in the

Transvaal, therefore, it was not in the likeness of the Cape community leader. The imām in the Transvaal was ideally an *ʿālim,* a scholar, who employed knowledge to balance or neutralize the financial power and political advantage of the traders.

In the Cape, the imām's effective leadership at the level of the individual mosque was often used to claim leadership over the entire Muslim community. This was not generally successful, but there were numerous attempts to find appropriate mosque-transcendent leadership standards. The first claim to such communitywide leadership was made on the basis of connection to the first mosque, the Awwal Mosque of Tuan Guru. In the twentieth century, the Muslim Judicial Council claimed this leadership on the basis of the Sharīʿah. Like membership in the Awwal Mosque, the Sharīʿah was presumed to provide a clear and unambiguous standard for communitywide leadership. The problem, however, lay in reconciling the place of the individual mosque—the real source of leadership and loyalty—and mosque-transcendent sources of power. The example of the Claremont Main Road Mosque illustrated how the Muslim Judicial Council facilitated the emergence of a dynamic mosque but also felt threatened by it. The council was threatened not only by Claremont's innovative reforms; it was structurally vulnerable to a mosque that undermined its Sharīʿah-centered authority with the leadership mechanisms inherent in the Cape mosque tradition.

In spite of the absence of an acceptable and recognizable criterion for communitywide leadership, the Cape mosque benefited from the ambitions and aspirations of its leadership. Despite competing claims, the Cape mosque remained a religious and civil space. The anti-apartheid political aspirations of the Claremont Mosque presented a striking example of this civic involvement, but this was true of other Cape mosques as well. Since the inception of the Cape mosque, there has always been one or another imām taking the Cape mosque into civil society. Tuan Guru and Frans van Bengalen represented Muslims in the battle between the Dutch and the English. Since then, one can trace a long line of mosques and imāms aspiring to represent Muslims in commissions of inquiry, in courts, in political uprisings, in resistance politics, and now finally in the first democratic state of South Africa. The representation has been challenged, fraught as it was with the contradictions of the discourse itself. However, Cape mosques have never been completely severed from social and political conflicts and challenges. One imām has always risen to the challenge, or exercised the temerity, of claiming Muslim representation in civil society. Some mosques may appear to have withdrawn from civil society to cultivate social and political isolation. The isolation was real, but from the perspective of leadership in the community, it was but a period for cultivating leadership capacity that could be applied in civil society. When state repression increased in the 1980s, the Cape mosque was more easily invoked as a site of opposition and struggle. At first sight, it may appear that the anti-apartheid potential of the Cape mosque must be related to the socioeconomic class of Cape Muslims compared to the relatively better off Indian Muslims in the Transvaal. Without denying the validity of this relationship, it seems to me that the particular mosque tradition predisposed the Cape mosque toward direct involvement in political developments. While the socioeconomic position of Cape Muslims may have predisposed them to resistance or to rejection of apartheid, the particular mosque tradition and its imām provided the vehicle for this protest. The imām, as head of the mosque, was always potentially a social and political leader.

In contrast to the Cape mosque, the Transvaal mosque was not involved in general community leadership, particularly political leadership. By claiming the mosque of the town, the religious scholars in the Transvaal accepted a clear division of labor. Traders and prominent individuals negotiated with the state, while religious scholars determined the religious ethos of the mosque. Following the division of labor to its logical conclusion, Transvaal religious scholars abandoned social and political leadership. The Transvaal mosque remained insulated and closed in order to skirt a political regime that tried to close it down. The Transvaal mosque did not face political disfavor because of its religious disposition but because it represented a despised immigrant group. The mosque became a misrepresented target of discrimination and suffered the particular political relations produced as a consequence. The Transvaal mosque suffered not because of its political statement; it rarely became the site of a civil discourse. The brief moments when Transvaal mosques were used for political campaigns, early in the twentieth century by Gandhi and during anti-apartheid protests in the 1980s, do not alter the general character of the Transvaal mosque. The mosque was founded on the basis of a political compromise entrenched by religious leaders separating the political from the religious. When the 'ulamā' took control of the religious dimension of the Transvaal mosque, they merely confirmed its particular character as a "religious" space, far removed from the civil debates raging in the society.

This does not mean that religion was never invoked in secular space in the Transvaal. This particular element within the Islamic tradition was represented in the Brits Mosque by peripheral interpretations of Islam. Unlike the Cape mosque, the periphery in the Transvaal could easily invoke Sufism, women, African Muslims, and resurgent Islam. In the face of religious control, these sectors found some haven on the periphery of the mosque. As the mosque in Brits become the prerogative of the Deobandi ideological school, it was progressively emptied of dissenting voices, who found sacred enclaves elsewhere. Bowen and Eickelman pointed correctly to the peripheralization of discontent in Islamic society. Bowen related a systematic dissimulation of village traditions in the presence of textual hegemony, while Eickelman showed how reformist traditions in Morocco made inroads into traditional modes of learning. In contrast, people in disagreement with the Claremont Mosque had recourse to other mosques in the Islamic pluralism that prevailed in Cape Town. Thus, the two mosques examined here present contrasting traditions of Islamic ideology and its periphery. In Brits, the mosque's innermost space was controlled by a theologically unassailable worldview, which one could negotiate through dissimulation. The Claremont Main Road Mosque presented a strong ideological position, which one either accepted or rejected.

There is no doubt that the Claremont Mosque, like other Cape mosques, provided significantly better opportunities for women. The Brits Mosque not only excluded women from the mosque grounds; its discursive practices also eliminated independent women's voices in the town. Subtle anthropological studies on Muslim women in historical context have pointed to their power in what appear to be extremely marginalized conditions. The Lindholms' study of women's authority in the North Western Frontier Province in Pakistan and El Guindi's analysis of veiled Egyptian students have urged greater sensitivity to women's experiences in cultural contexts.[1] In Brits, however, the elimination of independent women's religious traditions may require an even more perceptive study of what strategies women adopt in this extreme form of marginalization. Perhaps we will see a greater degree of secularization or a greater degree of dissimulation than Bowen observed in village customs in Indonesia. Claremont, in contrast to the Transvaal mosques, revolutionized the spatial organization of the mosque and provided a greater degree of participation for women. The constraints of the Islamic legal discourse, however, meant that it too had to tread much more cautiously than its leaders wanted to in this regard. Interestingly, women in the Cape played a prominent role in the folk tradition of rampiesny during the Mīlād. On the afternoon preceding the celebration of the Mīlād, women literally took over the mosque when they prepared potpourri sachets for distribution to the men. This spatial occupation of the mosque, and temporary exclusion of males, was replete with many contradictions and confirmed the marginalization of women in the mosques.

Omar in Claremont was ambivalent about this folk custom. Perhaps its partial recovery would provide an avenue for one more step in the direction of an equitable spatial and ideological organization of the Claremont Main Road Mosque.

Leadership in Islam resides with those knowledgeable in the Sharī'ah. This study has highlighted the place of the Sharī'ah in the discursive competitions of the mosque traditions. The relative place of the Sharī'ah in the repertoire of imāms in the Cape and the Transvaal facilitated different kinds of leadership. In both cases, Sharī'ah was a standard of judgment, yet it was applied in the two traditions with opposite effects as far as leadership of the mosque was concerned. In the Transvaal, religious leaders based their leadership on expertise in the Sharī'ah, which they effectively used to acquire leadership of the mosque and religious schools. The Sharī'ah of the religious scholars in the Transvaal did not compete with the authority of other religious leaders—instead it recovered mosques from the traders. The Sharī'ah played a central and dominating part in the leadership of the Transvaal imām, as the cornerstone of a gestural and rhetorical discourse claiming the mosque from traders. For the Cape imām, Sharī'ah was one among many other claims to leadership. Alongside ritual services, the imām employed Sharī'ah in his teaching capacity, and the Muslim Judicial Council tried to entrench communitywide leadership on the basis of its apparent uniformity.

For both the Transvaal and the Cape mosque traditions, Sharī'ah represented the divine and immutable legal code in Islam. In spite of the common understanding of the Sharī'ah in each mosque, its historical and discursive force varied widely. The Sharī'ah in the two contexts was part of mosque discourses. The particular location of Sharī'ah in the mosques has important implications for the development of modern legal reforms within Islam. A number of modern Muslim commentators make a distinction between Sharī'ah as the essential value of Islam, and *fiqh* as the historical record of those values in time and space. This new approach has often been founded on a careful reinterpretation of verses of the Qur'ān implying that God instituted different guidelines for different people in history. It is a view often shared by people of widely differing ideological persuasions. As is explained by Rahman in his seminal book *Islam*:

> Whereas the spirit of the Qur'ānic legislation exhibits an obvious direction towards the progressive embodiment of the fundamental human values of freedom and responsibility in fresh legislation, nevertheless the actual legislation of the Qur'ān had partly to accept the

then existing society as a term of reference. This clearly means that the actual legislation of the Qur'ān cannot have been meant to be literally eternal by the Qur'ān itself."[2]

Rahman's approach to the Qur'ān is not unexpected. However, this so-called modernist viewpoint is also reflected in Al Fārūqī, the champion of the Islamization of the social sciences and a renewal of traditional theology:

> The law is susceptible to change in time and place, conditioned as it must be by the status quo of the addressees. The needs of various societies must determine the nature of the laws they may be expected to observe. The principles of the law and its ends, on the other hand, stand above change and must remain the same throughout creation, since they represent the ultimate purposes of the Creator.[3]

The new interpretations have often assumed that the immutability of all aspects of Islamic law stood in the way of reforms. These new approaches to Islamic law, however, fail to take into account the difference between Sharī'ah as a symbol of immutability and its actual employment in historically grounded contexts. The Sharī'ah as immutable is an idea ultimately inexpressible but nevertheless inherent in every Muslim's response to the divine will. But employing the Sharī'ah in particular settings involves its power in social contexts, making it attainable and always present. As an absolute value, Sharī'ah could not easily be separated from a set of rules and regulations (fiqh). At the level of individual belief and action, detailed rules and rituals express values. The examples of Brits and Claremont illustrate how acts and values manifested specific ideological purposes. Antibid'ah gestures, for example, were deeper and more effective than textual sources. The application of Sharī'ah in historical context served idiosyncratic needs. At the very least, legal reforms had to begin by appreciating the complex nature of religious symbols and discourses in ritual and in moving ideological trajectories. New values imposed upon ritual often ignored the link between ritual and its contextual configuration of values.

These complex configurations between imāms, the Sharī'ah, and other powerful mosque members were reflected in the sermons. In the first instance, the sermon inscribed space during its performance. As men and women approached the Friday service, the space of the mosque took on its discursive form. Space was gendered as women occupied a different place or no place at all, as in Brits. The Claremont Mosque was a relatively nonhierarchical space, though clearly differentiated from the outside. Its ablution facilities, its lateral organization of floor space, and the very language of the sermons delineated a clear, unequivocal space for worshipers inside. The spatial inscription of the sermon exuded the mosque's distinctiveness and uniqueness. Discourse was inscribed in the Brits Mosque as well. Worshipers entered a graded and hierarchical space. Starting from the profane, the mosque gradually became more sacred. Worshipers progressed through the ablution block, the courtyard, and the English translation of the sermon to the Arabic sermon from the pulpit, the locus of an inaccessible word of God understood by a select few. This gradation toward the pure reflected the hegemony of the Sharīʿah as invoked by the religious scholars within the mosque. The sermon symbolized the emptying of the profane, which was a parallel and progressive suspension of the traders and the jamāt committee from the mosque. At the same time, the presence of a periphery in the Brits Mosque represented the place of dissent in Transvaal mosques. At both Claremont and Brits, then, the performance of the sermon inscribed a space that echoed the discourses within the mosques.

The content of the sermons reflected the discourses in appropriate metaphors. The sermons of Brits linked the mosque to the house built by Abraham, while the Claremont Mosque developed its trailblazing identity. The Brits Mosque tried hard to obliterate its individuality and uniqueness. Moreover, the sermons in the Brits Mosque promoted a permanent, unchanging Sharīʿah, supported by supplication and invocation. In political terms, the sermon's metaphors were the religious version of political acquiescence to authority championed by the traders in the Transvaal. The Claremont Mosque sermons advocated political action and argued for struggle and commitment in society. While proud of its identity, it was attentive to establishing its place amid the pluralist voices of Islam in Cape Town.

The sermons at both mosques also revealed some basic contradictions of authority and status within their discursive foundations. As a unique trailblazing institution, the Claremont Main Road Mosque was saddled with its own contradictions in the assembly of Cape mosques. On the one hand, Claremont illustrated how a Cape mosque was able to bring about innovations on the basis of an inherited discourse. The mosque used the ritual forms, the educational structures, and community loyalty to relate the mosque to political and social issues in the society. Anti-apartheid struggle and then post-apartheid reconstruction became the conceptual hallmark of the mosque, although located within familiar forms. On the other hand, on the basis of these innovative ideas, this mosque community regarded itself as a leader in the field, distinct from other mosques. While members paid homage to other leadership structures in the society, they regarded their own mosque community in a special and unique light. In Brits, the fundamental contradictions between knowledge and wealth as competing sources of power could not be eradicated. One of the preachers, as noted, explored the contradictions between religion and power in the performance of pilgrimage. Requiring both wealth and religiosity, pilgrimage was the ideal occasion for revealing the discursive tension between religious and financial power within society and within the mosque.

I now turn to the religious significance of the Islamic sermon. In this regard, I have no doubt that it must be interpreted as the location where the message of God was renewed in the sermon's re-citation. The Qur'ān appeared to be a revelation pronounced only once to the Prophet Muḥammad. According to traditional theology, the Prophet Muḥammad was simply conveying the heavenly message from the preserved tablet into the form of the Qur'ān. To speak of the creativity of the Qur'ān in the context of the Prophet's historical experience, not to mention in the experience of the preachers in South Africa, comes dangerously close to evaluating the Qur'ān as a creative moment in a particular context. Ash'arī theologians generally insisted that the Qur'ān was the "speech of God" and not his creation. And yet, the act of "transmission" (balāgh), which was assumed to have been the sole responsibility of the Prophet Muḥammad, did not exhaust the meaning and function of a sermon or a "reading" of the Qur'ān in a gathering. The reading and recitation was part of a contextual complex of reciter, semantics, and social space. When a new context replaced the old, one expected a new re-citation.

Moreover, the Islamic notions of inspiration (ilhām) of the Sufis, dreams of God and the Prophet to the pious, and the hope for union with God signified that divine contact had not been completely broken with the revelation of the Qur'ān. Rahman's work on the notion of prophecy among Islamic philosophers has shown the porous boundaries between human society and divine effulgence, and Friedmann has followed this notion in the case of one sectarian Islamic group in the twentieth century.[4] These studies certainly indicated that orthodox formulations of the nature of the Qur'ān did not preclude individuals from reproducing revelatory experience. In the present study, the notion of renewing the Qur'ānic recitation has been shown to be present in a common Muslim ritual, the Friday sermon. Unlike the early philosophers and Sufis or the modern religionists in the comparative study of religions, however, I am not inclined to argue that the perception of the divine in a sermon was an ineffable and inexpressible intuition. Rather, mosque discourses, specific metaphors, and contradictions abounded in the re-citation of the Qur'ān. The divine word was couched in typical South African English and in the deep contradictions of being an imām in Brits or Claremont. I have called such a divine irruption re-citation because it combines both an interpretation and a performance.

The series of sermons at Brits on the story of Abraham illustrated the creative re-citation of the Qur'ān in the Transvaal. It was an echo of the revelation recited by the Prophet Muḥammad to his seventh-century audience. As much as that recitation related Biblical stories to the Arabs of seventh-century Arabia, the preachers in Brits repeated and re-cited the epic in the town at the end of the twentieth century. Week after week, the preachers were able to bring the message of the Qur'ān to the men, not by a careful exegetical activity but by a dramatic enactment of Prophetic experience. The preachers localized the story by inserting common religious phrases and contemporary social and political images into an understanding of the epic. The story of Abraham was an opportunity to relate the Qur'ān to the town and reflect on the political situation in the country. One preacher in Brits also subverted the presence of the rich performing the pilgrimage, and another castigated the activists for sacrificing animals for social goals. Similarly, the Claremont sermon re-cited its relations with the state of the day, first developing a Qur'ānic perspective against apartheid and then struggling with a redefinition of its role in the new South Africa. No doubt, the Claremont Main Road Mosque embarked more self-consciously on a new interpretation of various Islamic practices and doctrines, while the Brits reinterpretation was concealed in familiar conclusions. It too, however, had to renew these familiar forms in contemporary re-citations. Most important, the new interpretations in both simulated God's divine revelation to the mosque and the congregation in question.

In terms of Gaffney's literary analysis of sermons in a particular political context, the South African sermons seemed more metonymic than metaphoric.[5] I have shown that sermons in both the mosques examined worked with metaphors. In terms of performance, however, neither of the two sets of sermons tried to bridge metaphorical points of tension. Both were engaged in moments of re-citation from the pulpit. The difference between the two was more a matter of degree than of substance. Gaffney also warned of the danger of metonymic sermons in polarizing Egyptian society, leading to conflict and terror. The polarization was evident in South Africa as well. However, in the Brits Mosque, where metonymy of the sermons was most in evidence, the least political danger was forthcoming. Unlike in Cairo, the Indian Muslim 'ulamā' in Brits had insulated their metonymic re-citations within the mosque against the alternative Islamic voices in the town. The perception of dangerous or benign sermons, therefore, should take into account both the historical circumstance in which they emerged and the competition of the Islamic discourses in ritual and symbolic gestures.

In conclusion, then, this study is located within three intersecting areas of academic debate and discourse. I have been concerned to uncover the vibrant history of Muslim communities within South Africa, not as discursive importations from beyond the shores but as integral and authentic voices of South African history. Second, I seek to highlight and locate modern Islamic reformist discourse in both its ritual and social dimensions. Not merely driven by enlightened ideas, Islamic reinterpretation has been a continuous process at the heart of key rituals in Islamic societies—not merely the special privilege or the damned blight of Westernized modernists; the most conservative also engage in reinterpretation to make sense of the world and create it anew. And third, this study has been an attempt to understand a key Islamic symbol in its deeply religious and mystical dimension. When least expected, and without denying the validity of historical location and explanation, the residual dimension of the sermon as divine word came to the fore. This does not mean that all who read this work have to accept it as such, but I doubt if it can be ignored.

NOTES

Chapter 1. The Sermon in Islam

1. Abu-Lughod, "Anthropology's Orient," 88.
2. Geertz, "Religion," 4.
3. Geertz, *Islam Observed*, 97.
4. Ibid., 98.
5. Ibid., 15.
6. Combs-Schilling, *Sacred Performances*, xiii; quotation at 158.
7. Ibid., 29, 158.
8. Ibid., 40–44.
9. The following represent only a small sample of critical comments directed at Eliade and other essentialists in the study of religion: Wiebe, "Phenomenology of Religion"; Strenski, *Religion in Relation;* Chidester, "The Poetics and Politics of Sacred Space."
10. Combs-Schilling, *Sacred Performances*, 57.
11. Ibid., 70.
12. Ibid., 57, 158, 172.
13. Ibid., xvi–xvii.
14. Asad, "The Idea," 7.
15. Asad, *Genealogies*, 126, 138.
16. Ibid., 214.
17. For an interesting variation of the use of moderate 'ulamā' by Saudis against militant 'ulamā', see Webster, "Hijra."
18. Asad, *Genealogies*, 226.
19. Asad, "The Idea," 15.

20. Ibid., 17.

21. Eickelman, *Moroccan Islam.*

22. Gilsenan, *Recognizing Islam,* 189, 205–6.

23. Leveau, "The Islamic Presence in France," 114; Basteiner, "Islam in Belgium," 136–37.

24. Gilsenan, *Recognizing Islam,* 182, 185.

25. Lindholm, "Leadership Categories," 3–4; see also Gilsenan's *Recognizing Islam* (chap. 2) for a discussion of the changing nature of the scholar in a nation-state.

26. Platvoet, "Definers," 180.

27. Ibid., 187.

28. Borthwick, "The Islamic Sermon," 311.

29. Antoun, *Muslim Preacher,* 1–15.

30. Ibid., 133–36.

31. Gaffney, "The Local Preacher," 35–63.

32. Gaffney, *The Prophet's Pulpit,* 52–55.

33. Ibid., 120, passim.

34. Graham, *Beyond the Written Word;* Denny, "Exegesis and Recitation."

35. Hodgson, *Venture,* 1:367.

36. Smith, *What Is Scripture?* 70.

37. See, for example, Denny, "Exegesis and Recitation," for a brief introduction to this phenomenon.

38. Antoun, *Muslim Preacher,* 6.

39. Fisher and Abedi, *Debating Muslims,* 102.

40. Van Ess, "Verbal Inspiration?" 182, passim.

Chapter 2. Creation of the Cape Mosque Discourse

1. Davids, *Mosques,* 35; Bradlow, "Exploring the Roots of Islam," 15.

2. Bradlow and Cairns, *Early Cape Muslims,* 92, 103–4.

3. Dangor, article rewritten by Y. da Costa with the permission of the author, "Footsteps," 19.

4. Rafudeen, "Muslim Exiles," 63.

5. Jeffreys, "Holy Circle," 157.

6. Dangor, "A Critical Biography," 24.

7. Jeppie has discussed the quandaries of Muslim identity around the symbol of Shaykh Yusuf in "Politics and Identities."

8. Davenport, *South Africa: A Modern History,* 40.

9. Davids, "Alternative Education," 48.

10. Davids, *Mosques,* 45; Barrow, *Travels,* 427. Barrow visited the Cape in 1797–98, when he reported on Muslims praying in the open air while the Calvinist monopoly of public religion was slowly being whittled away.

11. Davids, *Mosques,* 98, 100.

12. Bradlow and Cairns, *Early Cape Muslims,* 22.

13. Quoted ibid., 20.

14. Ibid., 22.

15. Davids, *Mosques*, 89, 101

16. Bradlow and Cairns, *Early Cape Muslims*, 12–13, 20; Davids, *Mosques*, 47.

17. Examples of this relationship between patrons and 'ulamā' are legion, but see at least Makdisi, *Rise of Colleges*; Repp, "Ottoman Learned Hierarchy"; Burke, "The Moroccan Ulama."

18. Davids, *Mosques*, 101.

19. Letters appearing in the *South African Commercial Advertiser*, February 13, 1836, quoted in Davids, *Mosques*, 118, 208.

20. Ibid., 101, 118.

21. Davids, "Alternative Education," 51.

22. Davids and Von Selms disagree on the date of the first published work in Afrikaans in Arabic characters. Von Selms, basing his evidence on an advertisement in 1856, believes that this was the first such text. Davids argues that the first text was printed in 1877. Nevertheless, Davids accepts that unpublished texts had been used since the 1930s. See his "My Religion," 68–69; "The Kitab," 56; "Early Afrikaans Publications," 67.

23. Eickelman, *Knowledge*, 63–64.

24. Colebrooke, *British Parliamentary Papers*, 207–10.

25. Davids, *Mosques*, 118; Bradlow and Cairns, *Early Cape Muslims*, 14–16.

26. Bradlow and Cairns, *Early Cape Muslims*, 87.

27. Nasr, *Living Sufism*, 57.

28. According to Shell, the imāms in Cape Town did not use the rites of passage to create an isolated community. It was an "impressive network of social, educational, and religious institutions . . . [which] . . . attracted many individuals in an economically or socially marginal position" ("Rites and Rebellion").

29. Davids, *Mosques*, 121.

30. Ibid., 164, 167–71.

31. Da Costa, "From Social Cohesion," 106.

32. Davids, *Mosques*, 150–53.

33. The Pilgrim Mosque became the Boerhaanol Islam Mosque in 1949 (ibid., 162–64).

34. Geertz, *Islam Observed*, 67; Bowen, "Western Studies."

35. Bulliet has shown how pilgrimage formed an important reorientation rite for Sunni religious leaders in the eleventh century (*View*, 174–77).

36. Davids, "The Afrikaans."

37. Comaroff and Comaroff, "Introduction," xix.

38. Davids, *Mosques*, 104.

39. Ibid., Annexure A, 208–9.

40. Ibid., 216–17.

41. Much to the consternation of Achmat van Bengalen and Saartjie van de Kaap, both their sons and the sons of Tuan Guru founded the Mohammedan Shafee Con-

gregation in 1830. Abdol Rakiep, the eldest son of Tuan Guru, was its first leader, followed in 1834 by Abdol Roef, the author of the letter. However, it was only in 1843, after the well-publicized dispute between Achmat van Bengalen and Jan van Boughies, that Abdol Roef himself began to be listed in the Cape directories as a "Malay Priest" and presided over a mosque on Buitengracht Street, called the Nurul Islam Mosque.

42. Davids, *Mosques*, 140.

43. Davids, "Imam Achmat," 73.

44. Davids, *Mosques*, 141.

45. Ibid., 69.

46. Bradlow, "Islam," 232, 239.

Chapter 3. The Claremont Main Road Mosque

1. The following pamphlets were widely distributed: "The Forces behind the Wadud Issue: Modernity and Its Implication" and "Muslims Irate at American Woman's Sermon in Mosque."

2. "A Step Forward as U.S. Muslim Woman Gives Sermon at Claremont Mosque," *Argus*, August 13–14, 1994; "Woman Makes Islam History at City Mosque," *Cape Times*, August 13, 1994.

3. "A First for Muslim Women," *South*, August 19–23, 1994.

4. "Masjid Sanctity Desecrated—Say Local Ulema," *Muslim Views* 7, no. 7, Rabil Awwal 1415, August 1994.

5. Resolutions and Recommendations of the Message of the Mosque Conference, Held in Mecca at the Invitation of the Muslim World League from 15th to 18th Ramadan, 1395 (20th to 23rd September, 1975), p. 12.

6. Shell, "Tender Ties."

7. Davids, *Mosques*, 118.

8. Da Costa, "From Social Cohesion," 106–11.

9. Warley, "Mosques of Wynberg."

10. Initially, the mosque was established by Muslims of Indian descent because they felt uncomfortable and excluded in the "Malay" Yusufiyyah Mosque. Ajam, "Hajee Sulaiman Shah Mohamed," 74.

11. Warley, "Mosques of Wynberg."

12. A survey of mosques in apartheid-created Coloured townships was undertaken by Jabaar, Abrahams, Umar, Jubayer, Inglis, and Jardine, "Mosques of the Cape Flats."

13. For the extent and proliferation of adult Islamic education, see Ebrahim, "Muslim Mosque-Based Adult Classes," 8, 34–40.

14. Lubbe, "Custodian or Catalyst?"

15. Murray, *Claremont*.

16. Quoted in judgment by Justice A.J.P. Watermeyer, Supreme Court judgment of

July 25, 1977, in the matter between the Board of Trustees and Sheik Abdullah Abdol Roef and Sheik Cassiem Abdol Roef (hereafter cited as *Trustees v. Abderoefs*).

17. There seems to be uncertainty about the year of Abderoef's death. Davids says he served the Buitengracht Mosque (established in 1844) for twenty-five years, making the year of death 1869, but elsewhere Davids gives Abderoef's date of death as 1859 (*Mosques*, 129, 131). Watermeyer's judgment in the case of *Trustees v. the Abderoefs* (1977) gives his year of death as late as 1895, which seems unlikely.

18. In the first half of the twentieth century, the Stegman Road Mosque and the Claremont Main Road Mosque served the Cape "Malay" Muslims and the Indians, respectively. With increasing miscegenation between the two groups, and the fact that the congregants themselves often crossed the ethnic lines, the commitment to the imāms had to find a more transcendental source for the distinction. In this case, an Islamic legal decree clarified the difference between the two mosques. The racial and ethnic identities did not completely disappear, but the legal approach based on Islamic knowledge was more acceptable to a community conscious of its allegiance to divine law.

19. Interview with Ahmad Gamieldien, Cassiem Saban, and Abu Bakar Hattas, October 14, 1994. The payment of the *zakāt al-fiṭr* became a contentious one in the community in the 1950s, when some religious leaders questioned the legitimacy of collecting it from each and every individual and paying it to the imāms. The charity appeared to constitute an important means of livelihood for the imāms, who were understandably reluctant to accept any change. The Shāfiʿī position, on which the prevailing practice in the Cape was based, did not require the possession of *niṣāb*, a stipulated amount of money one had to have to be declared reasonably wealthy. Any person who possessed money sufficient for the particular day was expected to pay the zakāt al-fiṭr. The Ḥanafīs stipulated that one had to be in possession of niṣāb before the charity became obligatory. Abdullah Haron, who was at the time the imām of the Stegman Road Mosque, criticized the practice at the Main Road Mosque. As a result of his criticism, the practice whereby the proceeds went to the religious leaders came to an end, but the Shāfiʿī legal position as to who should pay prevailed. Haron, "Imam Abdullah Haron," 66; al-Jazāʾirī, *Kitāb al-Fiqh*, 1:626–27.

20. Supreme Court judgment, July 25, 1977, *Trustees v. Abderoefs*, 3.

21. Davids, *Mosques*, 188.

22. Ibid., 127–37.

23. Appeal court judgment delivered November 14, 1978; Supreme Court judgment, July 25, 1977, *Trustees v. Abderoefs*, 38.

24. Judgment by A.J.A. Viljoen in the matter between Sheikh Abdullah Abdol Roef and Sheikh Cassiem Abdol Roef and the Board of Trustees of the Claremont Main Road Mosque Congregation, heard September 11, 1978, delivered November 14, 1978.

25. Letter, August 10, 1992, from O'Sullivan and Co., representing Cassiem Abdol Roef.

26. Supreme Court Case No. 10100/92 in the matter of Sheik Cassiem Abdol Roef and Imaam Rashied Omar and the Board of Trustees of the Claremont Main Road Mosque Congregation, dated October 20, 1992; Second Respondent's supplementary opposing affidavits containing statements of Najjar and Gamieldien; Notice of Withdrawal by Sheik Cassiem Abdol Roef, dated April 13, 1993.

27. Lubbe, "Analytic Investigation," 169.

28. Supreme Court judgment, July 25, 1977, *Trustees v. Abderoefs*, 55.

29. Ibid., 14, 25.

30. Omar, "Impact," 24.

31. Lubbe, "Custodian or Catalyst?" 55.

32. See my "Paradigm of Knowledge of Modern Islamic Resurgence" for an outline of this movement.

33. Davids's brother Salim, a teacher at the mosque, also supported "Sep" Davids. Information from M. Haron, October 28, 1994.

34. Interview with Ahmad Savahl, September 27, 1994.

35. *Muslim News*, August 5, 1977, quoted in Plaintiffs' Articulars of Claim in which Cassiem Abderoef sued Abu Bakr Fakier, the newspaper, and the printers for defamation, dated September 6, 1977.

36. Omar, "Impact," 35.

Chapter 4. Transvaal Mosques

1. Davids, *Mosques*, 186.

2. Bhana and Brain, *Setting Down Roots*, 105–6, 121, 126.

3. A concerted attempt was made by the Zuid Afrikaanse Republiek to define Indians as "natives" in terms of the Pretoria Convention (1881) and hence as precluded from acquiring property. Indians, in turn, fought for their trading rights as British subjects and sought protection from the British Empire. Pillay, *British Indians in the Transvaal*, xiv, 238.

4. Ibid., xiii.

5. See, for example, Johnson, "Indians and Apartheid"; Calpin, *Indians*.

6. An undated government notice: Gov. 143; gen. 864/003. The first mosque built in Durban (Natal) dates to 1884, preceded by a temporary prayer room (*jamāt khānah*) on the site from 1881. Jamal, "West Street Mosque," 10.

7. Pretoria State Archives: CS 260 ref. 2501/03.

8. I have explored the legislation and Indian responses in *Transvaal in Islamic Resurgence*, 59–61.

9. Bulbulia, "Wakf," 157.

10. Calpin, *Indians*, 81–93.

11. A full record of correspondence between the jamāt committee, Effendi, and the assistant colonial secretary is contained in the Pretoria State Archives: Gov. 662, ps 15/04 (6/4–7/4).

12. Naudé, "The 'Ulamā'," 25.

13. Abduh's responses elicited negative reaction in Cairo. See al-Shubrā al-Bukhūmī, *al-Ta'ādīl al-islāmiyyah.*

14. Bhana and Brain, *Setting Down Roots,* 79.

15. Tayob, *Islamic Resurgence,* 65.

16. In 1968, for example, the Brits Jamāt Committee still had to seek the permission of the Indian immigration officer to obtain an imām from Natal. Brits Jamāt Committee Meeting, August 18, 1968.

17. Naudé, "The 'Ulamā'," p. 27.

18. Le Roux, "Die Hanafitiese Ulama," 62.

19. Metcalf, *Deoband,* 16–45.

20. The Young Men's Muslim Association of Benoni became the major publisher and distributor of Deobandi literature in South Africa. It was established by young Indian Muslims in Johannesburg in 1955. As a result of the Group Areas removals, the organization in Johannesburg split into Lenasia and Benoni branches. The Lenasia branch petered out, but the Benoni branch became a major force for conservatism. "Young Men's Muslim Association: Glimpses into the Past," in *Awake to the Call of Islam* 5, no. 2 (Ramadan 1413/February–March 1993):4–6.

21. Rispler-Chaim, "An Old Bid'a," 86–87.

22. Bowen, "Salat"; and his *Muslims through Discourse,* 77–82.

23. See also Shinar, "Traditional and Reformist Mawlid," for traditionalist and reformist views of the Mawlid celebration in Morocco.

24. The selectivity of the interpretation of the Qur'ān was beyond doubt. The following report quoted by Bukhārī, one the most authoritative collectors of the Prophet's statements, indicates that audible supplication was permitted: "On the authority of 'Ā'ishah, [The verse] 'Neither be too loud nor too soft in your ṣalāh' (Qur'ān 18:110), referred to supplication." Ibn Ḥajar, *Fatḥ,* Kitāb al-da'awāt, 11:31.

25. For a general description of these festivals, see Von Grunebaum, *Muhammadan Festivals.*

26. Sābiq, *Fiqh al-Sunnah,* 3:386; Makdisi, *Rise of Colleges,* 35–74.

27. Sanneh, "Translatability," 41.

28. Douglas, *Purity and Danger,* 64.

Chapter 5. The Brits Mosque

1. Eickelman, *Knowledge,* 96–98.

2. Bowen, *Muslims through Discourse,* 180.

3. Thompson, "High Veld," 411–12.

4. Hickey, *Album,* 15. In place of the political and social instability of the war and strife, the Afrikaners in their turn instituted systematic measures to produce servile workers. For example, labor of orphans, often produced by raids against "unruly" chiefs, was mandatory up to the age of twenty-five. In addition, the poll and hut taxes, imposed in 1864 and 1870 respectively, ensured a regular supply of cheap labor. Peires, "Black Political Communities," 25.

5. Lawyers for Human Rights, "Commission of Inquiry into Oukasie Violence"; Morris, *Oukasie*; Stengel, *January Sun*.

6. Interview with I.A.M. Tayob, December 28, 1990.

7. Clearly, the Brits Mosque pioneered religious establishments in the town. The Apostoliese Geloofsending van Suid Afrika built a church in Brits in 1925; a Nederduitse Gereformeerde Kerk had been established in 1910 nearby (1928 in Brits) and a Gereformeerde Kerk in 1911 (1936 in Brits); a Methodist Church was built only in 1944. Hickey, *Album*, 91–92.

8. Ibid., 21.

9. I have had access to the minutes of the committee meetings since January 23, 1959, and have based my analysis of the Brits Jamāt Committee on these and numerous interviews and conversations between 1990 and 1994.

10. Jamāt committee meeting, November 11, 1965.

11. Attempts to raise funds specifically for an imām in 1969 were met with objections. Jamāt committee meeting, August 5, 1969.

12. A resolution claims to have two-thirds of the community's support to "debar" children from Islamic education if their parents do not pay school fees (committee meeting, November 13, 1959). In a committee meeting of January 15, 1960, a newly appointed imām had to collect some additional dues. The issue was raised again on July 4 and November 23, 1973.

13. Paying for a part of a mosque, especially a prayer mat, would ensure some spiritual reward for every person who subsequently used it. Also, the building of a mosque would be reciprocated with a heavenly home in the Hereafter: "On the authority of 'Uthmān, the Prophet said: Whosoever builds a mosque desiring thereby the pleasure of God, God will build a house for that person in paradise." Sābiq, *Fiqh al-Sunnah*, 1:208.

14. Jamāt committee meeting, May 18, 1983.

15. The jamāt committee (July 11, 1984) had to pay the costs for the old plan as well.

16. Jamāt committee meetings, January 23 and November 13, 1959. The process was repeated for the mosque in 1973. Jamāt committee meetings, August 10, 1973, and June 13, 1975.

17. Members of the community recall a man called Arabsāb, literally Mr. Arab, whose recitation was unique and quite different from that of imāms who read Arabic with strong Indian accents. He served the community of Brits around 1941 and the older people in the town remember him with a Fiat car that always had to be pushed. Then there was the imām Jamal al-Din Osmani, who served Brits from around 1945 to 1947, and who is remembered for being the first person to deliver the translation of the Friday sermon in English. That was a revolutionary gesture, as Urdu continued to be regarded by many as the preferred religious language. Osmani was involved in dispensing herbal medicine, probably as his main source of income. These imāms, however, were temporary sojourners who passed through the town for a couple of years.

18. Jamāt committee meetings reported the clashes, sometimes in the public, between members and the Nana family. See meeting minutes of November 13, 1959, when one of the Nana family members was accused of being visited by a "lady" and allowing his sister to teach; August 13, 1962, when the committee received a complaint about credit given to minors; and November 9, 1962, when a committee member was told by an unnamed Nana that he was not that member's "slave."

19. Jamāt committee meetings, September 10, 1963, and February 13, 1964. Also see the meeting of January 15, 1960, for the decision to dismiss "ladies."

20. Children who attended such "independent" madrasahs were prevented from joining the "official" madrasah during midterm. Jamāt committee meeting, July 5, 1964.

21. Jamāt committee meeting, March 29, 1969.

22. Jamāt committee meetings, June 28 and August 13, 1962, and August 10, 1973. The committee complained that the sermons were unacceptable (June 28, 1992), failed to keep to the point (August 15, 1973), or were presented in "too high Urdu" (November 9, 1974).

23. Jamāt committee meeting, January 14, 1981.

24. In his sermon, a visitor in 1992 apparently condemned the entire Muslim community for apostasy. The Jamāt asked the local imāms not to invite him to the mosque in future.

25. Jamāt committee meeting, August 5, 1969.

26. Imām Kassiem resigned but then reapplied for a second time. He was not taken back immediately; but when another teacher left on short notice, Kassiem's application was at hand. He stayed only for another year.

27. Repp, "Ottoman Learned Hierarchy," 20.

28. Jamāt committee meetings, July 10, 18, August 14, 1968.

29. In 1976, after repeated requests and threats to resign, Adamjee did eventually receive a salary raise from R200 to R350 per month but eventually left the town for better prospects in Barberton. Jamāt committee meetings, February 2, 1976, February 11, 1977.

30. The 'ulamā' in Brits adopted this position from at least 1973, when Mawlānā Mobin al-Haq refused to accept the job, which included leading the worship. The jamāt committee tried to include an additional monetary incentive for Ḥāfiẓ Osman in 1982, and for Mawlānā Yusuf in 1983, both of whom refused in principle. Jamāt committee meetings, March 27, 1973, March 10, 1978, October 11, 1982, and March 23, 1983.

31. Interview, Imran Moḥammad, December 31, 1990.

32. Metcalf, Deoband, 296–314.

33. A Sunni Jamiyat-e-Ulama was formed in 1978 in Durban.

34. As in other "black" areas in South Africa, a management committee was responsible for the public amenities of the township.

35. Chidester, "Religious Studies," 15–16.

36. Jamāt committee specially convened for this issue, November 10, 14, 1986.

37. Separate interviews with Mawlānā Abbas Khan and Imām ʿAbd al-Raʾūf Soofie of the Sunni Jamiyat-e-Ulama, July 11, 1992. See pamphlet issued by the latter, "Confusion or Conclusion: Answer to 'Who Are the People of Sunnah?'"

38. The following pamphlets were typical of the textual war between the two parties: "Who Are the People of Sunnah?" by the Eastern Cape Majlisul Ulama and a rebuttal titled "Confusion or Conclusion: Answer to 'Who Are the People of Sunnah?'" by Sunni Jamiyat-e-Ulama SA (n.d.).

39. A Mīlād celebrating the birth of the Prophet was held in the Brits Cinema on September 10, 1961. The annual Jamāt gathering together with Mīlād celebrations was held on September 8, 1961.

40. The Brits Jamāt Committee later became an affiliate of the Islamic Council of South Africa (formed in 1976), a splinter group of the Muslim Youth Movement.

41. Pretoria State Archives: LTG 97 97/5/92.

42. Jamāt committee meeting, February 13, 1959.

43. Jamāt committee meetings, August 18, 1973, July 12, October 17, 1975. The Bantu commissioner, usually a white man, was part of the apartheid bureaucracy to control the free movement of Africans in white towns. The Africans in South Africa have been called a variety of names, including natives, Bantu (meaning people), nonwhites, and blacks.

44. Jamāt committee meeting, October 26, 1977.

45. The jamāt committee in 1969 increased the bāngī's salary from twenty-four rands per month to thirty rands per month and warned him to "stop fafi." Mohammed Said Hanafi contemplated opening a *muti* (African herb) shop in the Jamāt's old school classrooms to supplement his income. Interview, October 15, 1993.

46. At the Jamāt committee meeting of March 18, 1979, the issue was raised of the bāngī's residence and the employment of a "girl" to clean the mosque.

47. Sitoto, "African 'Conversion'."

48. Oosthuizen has discussed the Islamic practices of African Muslims in Durban in "The Muslim Zanzibaris". Thorold has discussed the Qādari Sufi foundation of most Malawian Islamic practices in "Yao Muslims."

49. For an exception, see Vawda, "Islam in an African Township," for the study of a small community outside Durban in the context of Malay and Indian dominance. Also see Abrahams, "The Growth and Spread of Islam," for a survey of Islam in the African communities of Langa, Nyanga, and Guguletu near Cape Town. In the far northern parts of the country, some evidence of Arabic inscriptions has suggested that perhaps the accepted details of the first appearance of Islam in South Africa at Cape Town may have to be slightly altered. A community in the far northern part of the country, the Lemba, may have had Islamic roots through contact with traders in the sixteenth century. This seems to echo what Mandivenga (*Islam in Zimbabwe*, 30) has identified among the Varemba in Zimbabwe, whom Muslims have also claimed as an original Zimbabwean Muslim community.

50. The notion of withdrawal in this case reflects the approach of frustrated Islamists elsewhere in modern Islam. Roy, *Failure*, 79.

51. Tayob, *Islamic Resurgence*, 150–51.

52. Interview, Akbar Ahmad, January 3, 1991.

53. Interview, Luqman Oliver Sumnani, January 10, 1994.

54. Horton, *Patterns*, 37–40.

55. Jaffri, "Muḥarram."

56. Tayob, *Islamic Resurgence*, 154–55.

57. Biersteker, "Language, Poetry, and Power," 68.

Chapter 6. The Sermons

1. Eliade, *The Sacred and the Profane*, 29.

2. Platvoet, "Definers."

3. Smith, *To Take Place*, 45.

4. Chidester, "The Poetics and Politics of Sacred Space"; Chidester and Linenthal, "Introduction."

5. Gilsenan, *Recognizing Islam*, 180–214.

6. Waugh, "The Imam in the New World," 124.

7. Sābiq, *Fiqh al-Sunnah*, 1:255.

8. For a brief exposition of non-Arabic sermons, see al-Jazā'irī, *Kitāb al-Fiqh*, 1:387. The Ḥanafī openness to non-Arabic was not confined to early Islam. When Muslims in sixteenth-century Christian Spain asked Sunni jurists in Cairo about the permissibility of reading the khuṭbah in Spanish, only the Ḥanafī representative permitted it. Koningsveld and Wiegers, "Islam in Spain," 141, 144, 146.

9. Sanneh, "Translatability."

10. The South African Deobandi position on the issue was expounded in an undated booklet entitled "The Position of the Friday Khutbah in Islam, Mujlisul-Ulama (Port Elizabeth)."

Chapter 7. Sermons and the Re-citation of Discourses

1. The Mawlānā reported two such cases. The first was 'Umar's suggestion that the *maqām Ibrahim* (Abraham's "stand") be adopted as the place of prayer for the Muslims (Qur'ān 2:125); the second was his objection to the Prophet that he should not pray for the hypocrites (Qur'ān 9:84). The third, not mentioned by Mawlānā Yusuf, was 'Umar's suggestion for the veiling of the wives of the Prophet. Al-Suyūṭī, *Itqān*, 1:34.

2. Ibn Ḥajar, *Fatḥ*, Kitāb al-ta'bīr, 12:361.

3. Ibid., 12:369.

4. Chittick presents a brief statement of this revelational sense of Rumi's ideas in *The Sufi Path*, 120.

5. Ibn al-'Arabi, *Bezels*, 45.

6. Ayoub, "The Speaking Qur'an," 181, 183.

7. Coburn, "'Scripture' in India," 117.

8. See Moosa, "Muslim Conservatism," for a brief appraisal of Islamic conservative approaches in South Africa.

9. Rahman, *Modernity*, 143–44.

10. Bowman, "Holy Scriptures," 29–37.

11. "'Id al-Fiṭr Khuṭbah Focus," Friday, March 3, 1995.

12. The Qur'ān does not deal in detail with Abraham's journey but with the "building of the house" (2:127), its purification (2:125), and the "desolation of the valley" (14:37).

13. Firestone, "Abraham's Son," 95–131.

14. Tayob, "Civil Religion."

15. Tayob, "Jihād."

16. "Peace in the City: Interfaith Vigil of Prayer and Fasting," Friday, August 30, 1996, Claremont Main Road Mosque.

17. Le Roux, "Hermeneutics."

18. Hiskett, *Course*, 175.

19. See Qur'ān 2:125–29, 14:35–41.

20. Bowen, "Salat," and his *Muslims through Discourse*, 77–82.

Chapter 8. Conclusions

1. Lindholm and Lindholm, "Life behind the Veil"; El Guindi, "Veiling"; Bennet, *In Search*.

2. Rahman, *Islam*, 39.

3. Al Fārūqī and Al Fārūqī, *Cultural Atlas*, 108.

4. Rahman, *Prophecy*; Friedmann, *Prophecy Continuous*.

5. Gaffney, *The Prophet's Pulpit*, 120 and passim.

WORKS CITED

Books and Journals

Abrahams, Zainulghoes'n. 1981. "The Growth and Spread of Islam in Langa, Nyanga and Guguletu in Cape Town." B.A. honors thesis, University of Cape Town.

Abu-Lughod, Lila. 1990. "Anthropology's Orient: The Boundaries of Theory on the Arab World." In *Theory, Politics and the Arab World: Critical Responses*, ed. Hisham Sharabi, 81–131. New York: Routledge.

Ajam, M. T. 1990. "Hajee Sulaiman Shah Mohamed: A South African philanthropist (d. 1929)." *Journal for Islamic Studies* 10:68–76.

Antoun, Richard T. 1989. *Muslim Preacher in the Modern World*. Princeton: Princeton University Press.

Asad, Talal. 1986. "The Idea of an Anthropology of Islam." Occasional Papers Series. Washington, D.C.: Center for Contemporary Arab Studies, Georgetown University.

———. 1993. *Genealogies of Religion: Discipline and Reasons of Power in Christianity and Islam*. Baltimore: Johns Hopkins University Press.

Austin, J. L. 1986. "How to Do Things with Words." In *Literary Theory since 1965*, ed. Hazard Adams and Leroy Searle, 832–38. Tallahassee: University Presses of Florida.

Ayoub, Mahmoud. 1988. "The Speaking Qur'ān and the Silent Qur'ān: A Study of the Principles and Development of Imami Shiʿi tafsīr." In *Approaches to the History of the Interpretation of the Qur'ān*, ed. Andrew Rippin, 177–98. Oxford: Clarendon Press.

Barrow, John. 1804. *An Account of Travels into the Interior of Southern Africa in the Years 1797 and 1798*. London.

Basteiner, Albert. 1990. "Islam in Belgium: Contradictions and Perspectives." In *The New Islamic Presence in Western Europe*, ed. Tomas Gerholm and Yngve Georg Lithman, 133–43. London: Mansell.

Bennet, Clinton. 1990. *In Search of the Sacred: Anthropology and the Study of Religions.* London: Cassell.

Bhana, Surendra. 1985. "Indian Trade and Trader in Colonial Natal." In *Enterprise and Exploitation in a Victorian Colony: Aspects of the Economic and Social History of Colonial Natal,* ed. Bill Guest and John M. Sellers, 223–51. Pietermaritzburg: University of Natal Press.

Bhana, Surendra, and Joy Brain. 1990. *Setting Down Roots: Indian Migrants in South Africa, 1860–1911.* Johannesburg: Wiwatersrand University Press.

Biersteker, Ann. 1991. "Language, Poetry, and Power: A Reconsideration of 'Utendi wa Mwana Kupona'." In *Faces of Islam in African Literature,* ed. Kenneth W. Harrow, 59–77. London: James Currey.

Borthwick, Bruce M. 1967. "The Islamic Sermon as a Channel of Political Communication." *Middle East Journal* 21 (Summer):299–311.

Bowen, John R. 1989. "Salat in Indonesia: The Social Meaning of an Islamic ritual." *Man* (n.s.) 24:600–19.

———. 1993. *Muslims Through Discourse: Religion and Ritual in Gayo Societies.* Princeton: Princeton University Press.

———. 1995. "Western Studies of Southeast Asian Islam: Problem of Theory and Practice." *Studia Islamica: Indonesian Journal for Islamic Studies* 2(4):69–86.

Bowman, John. n.d. "Holy Scriptures, Lectionaries and the Qur'ān." In *International Congress for the Study of the Qur'ān: Australian National University, Canberra, May 8–13, 1980,* 29–37. Canberra: Australian National University.

Bradlow, Adil. 1984. "Islam, the Colonial State and South African History: The 1886 Uprisings." B.A. honors thesis, University of Cape Town.

———. 1989. "Exploring the Roots of Islam in Cape Town in the 18th Century: State, Hegemony and Tariqa." Conference presentation, August 10–11, University of Cape Town.

Bradlow, Frank, and Margaret Cairns. 1978. *The Early Cape Muslims: A Study of Their Mosques, Genealogy and Origins.* Cape Town: A. A. Balkema.

Bulbulia, M.A.E. 1982. "Application of the Concept of Wakf in South Africa." *De Rebus* (April):155–57.

Bulliet, Richard. 1994. *Islam: The View from the Edge.* New York: Columbia University Press.

Burke, Edmund III. 1972. "The Moroccan Ulama, 1860–1912: An Introduction." In *Scholars, Saints, and Sufis: Muslim Religious Institutions in the Middle East since 1500,* ed. Nikki R. Keddie, 93–125. Berkeley: University of California Press.

Calpin, George H. 1949. *Indians in South Africa.* Pietermaritzburg: Shuter & Shooter.

Chidester, David. 1987. "Religious Studies as Political Practice in South Africa." *Journal of Theology for Southern Africa* 58 (March):4–17.

———. 1992. *Shots in the Streets: Violence and Religion in South Africa.* Contemporary South African Debates. Cape Town: Oxford University Press.

———. 1994. "The Poetics and Politics of Sacred Space: Towards a Critical Phenomenology of Religion." In *Analecta Husserliana*, ed. A.-T. Tymieniecka, 211–31. Netherlands: Kluwer Academic Publishers.

Chidester, David, and Edward T. Linenthal. 1995. Introduction. *American Sacred Space*, ed. David Chidester and Edward T. Linenthal, 1–42. Bloomington and Indianapolis: Indiana University Press.

Chittick, William C. 1983. *The Sufi Path of Love: The Spiritual Teachings of Rumi*. Albany: State University of New York Press.

Coburn, Thomas B. 1989. "'Scripture' in India: Towards a Typology of the Word in Hindu Life." In *Rethinking Scripture: Essays from a Comparative Perspective*, ed. Miriam Levering, 102–28. Albany: State University of New York Press.

Colebrooke 1834\08\14, comp. 1968–71. "Papers Relative to the Condition and Treatment of the Native Inhabitants of the Cape of Good Hope." In *British Parliamentary Papers: Colonies: Africa*, v. 20; xxxxix (50) and (252), 207–10. Irish University Press Series. Shannon: Irish University Press.

Comaroff, Jean, and John Comaroff. 1993. Introduction. *Modernity and Its Malcontents: Ritual and Power in Postcolonial Africa*, ed. Jean Comaroff and John Comaroff, xi–xxvii. Chicago: University of Chicago Press.

Combs-Schilling, M. E. 1989. *Sacred Performances: Islam, Sexuality, and Sacrifice*. New York: Columbia University Press.

Da Costa, Yusuf. 1994. "From Social Cohesion to Religious Discord: The Life and Times of Shaykh Muhammad Salih Hendricks (1871–1945)." In *Pages from Cape Muslim History*, ed. Yusuf da Costa and Achmat Davids, 103–13. Pietermaritzburg: Shuter & Shooter.

Dangor, S., rewritten by Yusuf da Costa. 1994. "In the Footsteps of the Companions: Shaykh Yusuf of Macasser (1626–1699)." In *Pages from Cape Muslim History*, ed. Yusuf da Costa and Achmat Davids, 19–46. Pietermaritzburg: Shuter & Shooter.

Dangor, Suleiman E. 1981. "A Critical Biography of Shaykh Yusuf." Master's thesis, University of Durban-Westville.

Davenport, T.R.H. 1987. *South Africa: A Modern History*. 3d ed. Johannesburg: Macmillan.

Davids, Achmat. 1980. *The Mosques of Bo-Kaap: A Social History of Islam at the Cape*. Cape Town: South African Institute of Arabic and Islamic Research.

———. 1989. "The Kitab 'l-Qawl'l-Matini: A Response to 'Problems of Identification' by Professor P.F.D. Weiss." *Journal of Islamic Studies* 9:55–69.

———. 1991. "The Afrikaans of the Cape Muslims from 1815 to 1915: A Socio-Linguistic Study." Master's thesis, University of Natal.

———. 1993. "The Early Afrikaans Publications and Manuscripts in Arabic Script." In *Festschrift in Honour of Frank Bradlow*, comp. and ed. Pieter E. Westra and Brian Warner, 67–82. Cape Town: Friends of the South African Library.

———. 1994a. "Alternative Education: Tuan Guru and the Formation of the Cape Muslim Community." In *Pages from Cape Muslim History*, ed. Yusuf da Costa and Achmat Davids, 47–56. Pietermaritzburg: Shuter & Shooter.

———. 1994b. "Imam Achmat Sadik Achmat (1813–1879): Imam, Soldier, Politician and Educator." In *Pages from Cape Muslim History*, ed. Yusuf da Costa and Achmat Davids, 71–79. Pietermaritzburg: Shuter & Shooter.

———. 1994c. "'My Religion Is Superior to the Law': The Survival of Islam at the Cape of Good Hope." In *Pages from Cape Muslim History*, ed. Yusuf Da Costa and Achmat Davids, 57–70. Pietermaritzburg: Shuter & Shooter.

Denny, Frederick M. 1980. "Exegesis and Recitation: Their Development as Classical Forms of Qur'ānic Piety." In *Transitions and Transformations in the History of Religions: Essays in Honor of Joseph M. Kitagawa*, ed. Frank E. Reynolds and Theodore M. Ludwig, 91–123. Studies in the History of Religions (supplements to Numen). Leiden: E. J. Brill.

Douglas, Mary. 1970. *Purity and Danger: An Analysis of Concepts of Pollution and Taboo.* London: Pelican Books.

Ebrahim, Muhammad Reza. 1991. "An Analytical Survey of Muslim Mosque-Based Adult Classes in the Western Cape Region." B.A. honors thesis, University of Cape Town.

Eickelman, Dale F. 1976. *Moroccan Islam: Tradition and Society in a Pilgrimage Centre.* Austin: University of Texas Press.

———. 1981. *The Middle East: An Anthropological Reader.* New Jersey: Prentice-Hall.

———. 1985. *Knowledge and Power in Morocco: The Education of a Twentieth-century Noble.* Princeton: Princeton University Press.

El Guindi, Fadwa. 1981. "Veiling Infitah with Muslim Ethic: Egypt's Contemporary Islamic Movement." *Social Problems* 28 (April):465–85.

Eliade, Mircea. 1959. *The Sacred and the Profane: The Nature of Religion.* Trans. Willard R. Trask. New York: Harcourt, Brace & World.

al Fārūqī, Ismā'īl, and Lois lamya al Fārūqī. *The Cultural Atlas of Islam.* London, New York: Macmillan, 1986.

Firestone, Reuven. 1989. "Abraham's Son as the Intended Sacrifice (al-dhabīḥ, Qur'ān 37:99–113): Issues in Qur'ānic Exegesis." *Journal of Semitic Studies* 34:95–131.

Fisher, Michael J., and Mehdi Abedi. 1990. *Debating Muslims: Cultural Dialogics in Postmodernity and Modernity.* Madison: University of Wisconsin Press.

Freitag, Sandra B. 1988. "The Roots of Muslim Separatism in South Asia: Personal Practice and Public Structure in Kanpur and Bombay." In *Islam, Politics and Social Movements*, ed. Edmund Burke III and Ira M. Lapidus, 115–45. Berkeley: University of California Press.

Friedmann, Yohanan. 1989. *Prophecy Continuous: Aspects of Ahmadi Religious Thought and Its Medieval Background.* Berkeley: University of California Press.

Gaffney, Patrick. D. 1988. "Magic, Miracle and the Politics of Narration in the Contemporary Islamic Sermon." *Religion & Literature* 20 (Spring):111–37.

———. 1987. "The Local Preacher and Islamic Resurgence in Upper Egypt: An Anthropological Perspective." In *Religious Resurgence: Contemporary Cases in*

Islam, Christianity, and Judaism, ed. Richard T. Antoun and Mary Elaine Hegland, 35–63. Syracuse: Syracuse University Press.

———. 1994. *The Prophet's Pulpit: Islamic Preaching in Contemporary Egypt.* Berkeley: University of California Press.

Geertz, Clifford. 1966. "Religion as a Cultural System." In *Anthropological Approaches to the Study of Religion,* ed. Michael Banton, 1–45. London: Tavistock Publications.

———. 1968. *Islam Observed: Religious Development in Morocco and Indonesia.* Dwight Harrington Terry Foundation Lectures on Religion in the Light of Science and Philosophy. New Haven: Yale University Press.

Gilsenan, Michael. 1990. *Recognizing Islam: Religion and Society in the Modern Middle East.* New York and London: I. B. Taurus.

Graham, William A. 1987. *Beyond the Written Word: Oral Aspects of Scripture in the History of Religion.* Cambridge: Cambridge University Press.

Green, A. H. 1984. "A Tunisian Reply to a Wahhabi Proclamation: Texts and Contexts." In *Quest of an Islamic Humanism: Arabic and Islamic Studies in Memory of Mohamed al-Nowaihi,* ed. A. H. Green, 155–77. Cairo: American University of Cairo Press.

Haron, Muhammed. 1986. "Imam Abdullah Haron: Life, Ideas, and Impact." Master's thesis, University of Cape Town.

Harries, Patrick. 1979. "Mozbiekers: The Immigration of an African Community to the Western Cape, 1876–1882." In *Studies in the History of Cape Town,* 6 vols., ed. Christopher Saunders, 1:153–64. Cape Town: University of Cape Town, History Department.

Hickey, W. A., comp. 1973–74. *Gedenkalbum: Souvenir Album, 1924–1974.* Brits: Tafelberg, Town Council of Brits.

Hiskett, Mervyn. 1994. *The Course of Islam in Africa.* Islamic Surveys 15. Edinburgh: University Press.

Hodgson, Marshall G. S. 1974. *The Venture of Islam: Conscience and History in a World Civilization.* 3 vols. Chicago: University of Chicago Press.

Horton, Robin. 1993. *Patterns of Thought in Africa and the West.* Cambridge: Cambridge University Press.

Ibn al-'Arabī. 1980. *The Bezels of Wisdom.* Trans. R. W. J. Austin. Preface by Titus Burckhardt. New York: Paulist Press.

Ibn Ḥajar 'Asqalānī, Aḥmad b. 'Alī (773–852). n.d. *Fatḥ al-bārī bi sharḥ Ṣaḥīḥ al-Imām Abī 'Abd Allah Muḥammad b. Ismā'īl al-Bukhārī (d. 240/870).* Ed. Muḥammad Fu'ād 'Abd al-Bāqī. Cairo: al-Maktabah al-Salafiyyah.

Jabaar, M. C., Ismail Abrahams, Hassan Umar, Nawaal Jubayer, Hoosain Inglis, and Amien Jardine. 1994. "Mosques of the Cape Flats (Economically Depressed Areas)." Cape Town: Muslim History Project, Islamic College of South Africa.

Jaffri, Syed Husain Ali. 1979. "Muḥarram Ceremonies in India." In *Ta'ziyeh Rituals and Drama in India,* 222–27. New York: New York University Press.

Jamal, Riaz Cassim. 1987. "A Study of the West Street Mosque in Durban." B.A. honors thesis, University of Durban-Westville.

al-Jazā'irī, 'Abd al-Raḥmān. n.d. Kitāb al-Fiqh 'alā ul-madhāhib al-arba'ah. 5 vols. Cairo: Dār al-Fikr.

Jeffreys, K. M. 1938a. "The Malay Tombs of the Holy Circle: 5. The Kramat at Zandvliet, Faure." Cape Naturalist 1 (June): 157–63.

———. 1938b. "The Malay Tombs of the Holy Circle: 5. The Kramat at Zandvliet, Faure (Concluded)." Cape Naturalist 1 (July): 195–99.

Jeppie, Shamil. 1995. "Politics and Identities in South Africa: Reflections on the 1994 Tri-centenary Celebrations of Islam in South Africa." 12th Annual Conference of the American Council for the Study of Islamic Societies, Villanova University, Philadelphia.

Johnson, R. E. 1973. "Indians and Apartheid in South Africa: The Failure of Resistance." Ph.D. diss., University of Massachusetts.

Koningsveld, P. S. van, and G. A. Wiegers. 1997. "Islam in Spain during the Early Sixteenth Century: The Views of the Four Chief Judges in Cairo (Introduction, Translation and Arabic text)." In Poetry, Politics and Polemics: Cultural Transfer between the Iberian Peninsula and North Africa, ed. Otto Zwartjes, Jan van Gelder, and Ed de Moor, 132–52. Amsterdam: Rodopi.

Le Roux, Charles. 1977. "Die Hanafitiese Ulama: Hulle Rol in die Suid-Afrikaanse Konteks." Master's thesis, Randse Afrikaanse Universiteit.

———. 1990. "Hermeneutics: Islam and the South African Context." Journal for Islamic Studies 10:23–31.

Leveau, Remy. 1990. "The Islamic Presence in France." In The New Islamic Presence in Western Europe, ed. Tomas Gerholm and Yngve Georg Lithman, 107–22. London: Mansell.

Lindholm, Charles. 1986. "Leadership Categories and Social Processes in Islam: The Cases of Dir and Swat." Journal of Anthropological Research 42 (Spring): 1–13.

Lindholm, Charles, and Cherry Lindholm. 1993. "Life behind the Veil." In Anthropology: Contemporary Perspectives, ed. P. Whitten and D. E. K. Hunter, 231–34. New York: Harper Collins College Publishers.

Lubbe, G. J. A. 1994. "The Muslim Judicial Council: Custodian or Catalyst?" Journal for Islamic Studies 14:34–62.

———. 1989. "The Muslim Judicial Council: A Descriptive and Analytic Investigation." Ph.D. diss., University of South Africa.

Maasdorp, Gavin, and Nesen Pillay. 1979. "Indians in the Political Economy of South Africa." In South Africa's Indians: The Evolution of a Minority, ed. Bridglal Pachai, 209–54. Washington: University Press of America.

Mahida, Ebrahim Mahomed. 1993. History of Muslims in South Africa: A Chronology. Durban: Arabic Study Circle.

Makdisi, George. 1981. The Rise of Colleges: Institutions of Learning in Islam and the West. Edinburgh: Edinburgh University Press.

Mandivenga, Ephraim. 1983. Islam in Zimbabwe. Gweru, Zimbabwe: Mambo Press.

Martin, Richard C. 1984. "Clifford Geertz Observed: Understanding Islam as Cultural Symbolism." In *Anthropology and the Study of Religion*, ed. Robert L. Moore and Frank E. Reynolds, 11–30. Chicago: Center for the Scientific Study of Religion.

Metcalf, Barbara Daly. 1982. *Islamic Revival in British India: Deoband, 1860–1900*. Princeton: Princeton University Press.

Moosa, Ebrahim. 1989. "Muslim Conservatism in South Africa." *Journal of Theology for Southern Africa* 69 (December): 73–81.

Morris, Allan. 1990. *The Complexities of Sustained Urban Struggle: The Case of Oukasie*. University of Witwatersrand: African Studies Institute Seminar.

Murray, Joyce. 1958. *Claremont Album*. Cape Town: A. A. Balkema.

Nasr, Seyyed Hossein. 1980. *Living Sufism*. London: Unwin Paperbacks.

Naudé, Hendrick David. 1990. "Nywerheidsvestiging in die Dekonsentraasie Punte van Brits en Bronkhorspruit/Ekangala: 'n Geografiese Ontleiding." Master's thesis, University of South Africa.

Naudé, J. A. 1982. "The 'Ulamā' in South Africa with Special Reference to the Transvaal 'Ulamā'." *Journal for Islamic Studies* 2:23–39.

Omar, Abdul Rashied. 1987. "The Impact of the Death in Detention of Imam Abdullah Haron on Cape Muslim Political Attitudes." Paper, University of Cape Town.

Oosthuizen, G. C. [1982]. "The Muslim Zanzibaris of South Africa: The Religious Expression of a Minority Group, Descendents of Freed Slaves." Durban: Research Institute, Department of Science of Religion.

Peires, J. 1986. "The Emergence of Black Political Communities." In *A New Illustrated History of South Africa*, ed. Trewhella Cameron, in collaboration with S. B. Spies. Cape Town: Human Rossouw.

Pillay, B. 1977. *British Indians in the Transvaal: Trade, Race Relations and Imperial Policy in Republican and Colonial Transvaal*. London: Longman.

Platvoet, Jan. 1990. "The Definers Defined: Traditions in the Definition of Religion." *Method & Theory in the Study of Religion* 2(2):180–212.

Rafudeen, Mohamed Auwais. 1995. "Government Perceptions of Cape Muslim Exiles: 1652–1806." Master's thesis, University of Cape Town.

Rahman, Fazlur. 1958. *Prophecy in Islam: Philosophy and Orthodoxy*. Midway Reprint. Chicago: University of Chicago Press.

———. 1979. *Islam*. Chicago: University of Chicago Press.

———. 1982. *Islam and Modernity: Transformation of an Intellectual Tradition*. Chicago: University of Chicago Press.

Repp, Richard. 1972. "Some Observations on the Development of the Ottoman Learned Hierarchy." In *Scholars, Saints, and Sufis: Muslim Religious Institutions in the Middle East since 1500*, ed. Nikki R. Keddie, 17–32. Berkeley: University of California Press.

Rex, John. 1990. "The Urban Sociology of Religion and Islam in Birmingham." In *The New Islamic Presence in Western Europe*, ed. Tomas Gerholm and Yngve Georg Lithman, 206–18. London: Mansell.

Rispler-Chaim, Vardit. 1995. "The 20th Century Treatment of an Old Bid'a: Laylat al-niṣf min Sha'bān." *Der Islam* 72(1):82–97.

Roy, Olivier. 1994. *The Failure of Political Islam.* Trans. Carol Volk. Cambridge, Mass.: Harvard University Press.

Sābiq, Sayyid. 1980. *Fiqh al-Sunnah.* 2d ed. Beirut: Dār al-Fikr.

Sanneh, Lamin. 1994. "Translatability in Islam and in Christianity in Africa: A Thematic Approach." In *Religion in Africa: Experience and Expression,* ed. Thomas D. Blakely, Walter E. A. van Beek, and Dennis L. Thomson, 22–45. London: James Curry.

Searle, John R. 1986. "What Is a Speech Act?" In *Literary Theory since 1965,* ed. Hazard Adams and Leroy Searle, 59–69. Tallahassee: University Presses of Florida.

Shell, Robert. 1992. "Tender Ties: Women and the Slave Household, 1652–1834." In *The Societies of Southern Africa in the Nineteenth and Twentieth Centuries,* 1–33. Collected Seminar Papers vol. 17. London: University of London, Institute of Commonwealth Studies.

Shell, Robert C. 1984. "Rites and Rebellion: Islamic Conversion at the Cape, 1808 to 1915." In *Studies in the History of Cape Town,* 6 vols., edited by Christopher Saunders, 5:1–46. Cape Town: University of Cape Town History Deparment.

Shinar, P. 1977. "Traditional and Reformist Mawlid Celebrations in the Maghrib." In *Studies in Memory of Gaston Wiet,* ed. Myriam Rosen-Ayalon, 371–413. Jerusalem: Institute of Asian and African Studies, Hebrew University of Jerusalem.

al-Shubrā al-Bukhūmī, Yūsuf. 1904 / 1322. *al-Ta 'ādīl al-islāmiyyah fi takhṭi'ah ḥizb al-fatāwā al-taransafāliyyah.* Cairo, n.p.

Sitoto, Fuzile Tahir. 1996. "African 'Conversion' to Islam: A Theoretical Analysis with Special Reference to South Africa." B.A. honors thesis, University of Cape Town.

Smith, Jonathan Z. 1978. *Map Is Not Territory: Studies in the History of Religions.* Leiden: E. J. Brill.

———. 1987. *To Take Place: Toward Theory in Ritual.* Chicago: University of Chicago Press.

Smith, Wilfred Cantwell. 1957. *Islam in Modern History.* New York: Mentor Books.

———. 1993. *What Is Scripture?* Fortress Press.

Stengel, Richard. 1990. *January Sun: One Day, Three Lives, a South African Town.* New York: Simon & Schuster.

Strenski, Ivan. 1993. *Religion in Relation: Method, Application and Moral Location.* Studies in Comparative Religion. Columbia: University of South Carolina Press.

al-Suyūṭī, Jalāl al-Din 'Abd al-Raḥman (d. 911/1505). n.d. *al-Itqān fi 'ulūm al-Qur'ān.* Ed. Muḥammad Abū al-Faḍl Ibrāhīm. Cairo: Dār al-Turāth.

Tayob, Abdulkader I. 1995a. "Civil Religion for Muslims in South Africa." *Journal for the Study of Religion* 8(2):23–46.

———. 1995b. *Islamic Resurgence in South Africa: The Muslim Youth Movement.* Cape Town: University of Cape Town Press.

————. 1995c. "The Paradigm of Knowledge of Modern Islamic Resurgence." *American Journal of Islamic Social Sciences* 12 (Summer): 155–69.

————. 1995d. "The Qur'ān in Muslim Society: The Case of Early Islam." In *Religion and the Reconstruction of Civil Society: Papers from the Founding Congress of the South African Academy of Religion (January 1994)*, ed. John W. de Gruchy and S. Martin, 334–52. Pretoria: University of South Africa.

————. 1996. "Jihād against Drugs in Cape Town: A Discourse-Centered Analysis." *Social Dynamics* 22(2):23–29.

Thompson, Leonard. 1969. "Co-operation and Conflict: The High Veld." In *The Oxford History of South Africa*, vol. 1, *South Africa to 1870*. Oxford: Clarendon Press.

Thorold, Alan. 1993. "Metamorphoses of the Yao Muslims." In *Muslim Identity and Social Change in Sub-Saharan Africa*, ed. Louis Brenner, 79–90. London: Hurst & Company.

Turner, Victor. 1974. "Pilgrimages as Social Processes." In *Dramas, Fields, and Metaphors: Symbolic Action in Human Society*, ed. Victor Turner, 166–230. Ithaca: Cornell University Press.

Van Ess, Joseph. 1996. "Verbal Inspiration? Language and Revelation in Classical Islamic Theology." In *The Qur'ān as Text*, ed. Stefan Wild, 177–94. Leiden: E. J. Brill.

Vawda, Shahid. 1994. "The Emergence of Islam in an African Township." *American Journal of Islamic Social Sciences* 11 (Winter): 532–47.

von Grunebaum, Gustav E. 1976. *Muhammadan Festivals*. London: Curzon Press.

Warley, Rushdee. 1994. "Mosques of Wynberg." Paper, University of Cape Town.

Waugh, Earl H. 1980. "The Imam in the New World: Models and Modifications." In *Transitions and Transformations in the History of Religions: Essays in Honor of Joseph M. Kitagawa*, ed. Frank E. Reynolds and Theodore M. Ludwig, 124–49. Studies in the History of Religions (supplements to Numen). Leiden: E. J. Brill.

Webster, Arthur. 1993. "Hijra and the Dissemination of Wahhabi Doctrine in Saudi Arabia." In *Golden Roads: Migration, Pilgrimage and Travel in Mediaeval and Modern Islam*, ed. Ian Richard Netton, 11–27. Richmond, Surrey: Curzon Press.

Wiebe, Donald. 1991. "Phenomenology of Religion as Religio-Cultural Quest: Gerardus van der Leeuw and the Subversion of the Scientific Study of Religion." In *Religionwissenschaft und Kulturkritik: Beitráge zur Konferenze The History of Religions and Critique of Culture in the Days of Gerardus van der Leeuw (1890–1950)*, ed. Hans G. Kippenberg and Brigitte Luchesi, 65–86. Marburg: Diagonal-Verlag.

Pamphlets and Published and Unpublished Reports

"The Forces behind the Wadud Issue: Modernity and Its Implication." Pamphlet issued by Darul Hadith Cape, Cape Town.

"Muslims Irate at American Woman's Sermon in Mosque." Pamphlet issued by the

Muslim Judicial Council and supported by the Jamiatul Ulama Transvaal, Jamiatul Ulama Natal, and Sunni Council of SA.

"Resolutions and Recommendations" of the Message of the Mosque Conference, Held in Mecca at the Invitation of the Muslim World League from 15th to 18th Ramadan, 1395, 20th to 23rd September, 1975. Reproduced in South Africa by the Muslim Youth Movement, Durban, n.d.

"Young Men's Muslim Association: Glimpses into the Past." In *Awake to the Call of Islam* 5, no. 2 (Ramadan 1413/February–March 1993):4–6. Published by the Young Men's Muslim Association, Benoni, South Africa.

Sunni Jamiyat-e-Ulama SA. "Confusion or Conclusion: Answer to 'Who Are the People of Sunnah?'" Durban, n.d.

Majlisul-Ulama. "Who Are the People of Sunnah?" Port Elizabeth, n.d.

———. "The Position of the Friday Khutbah in Islam." Port Elizabeth, n.d.

Claremont Main Road Mosque. Muslims and the RDP (Recontruction and Development Programme). 1994.

———. "'Id al-Fiṭr Khutbah Focus." Friday, March 3, 1995.

———. "Peace in the City: Interfaith Vigil of Prayer and Fasting." Friday, August 30, 1996.

Muslim Views. Muslim monthly published in Cape Town as *Muslim News* since 1960. Name changed name to *Muslim View* in 1986.

Al-Qalam. The monthly newspaper of the Muslim Youth Movement.

Lawyers for Human Rights. 1991. "Commission of Inquiry into Oukasie Violence." Unpublished report, Cape Town.

Pretoria State Archives. Sermons.
Claremont Main Road Mosque

Not recorded by the author. These recordings are kept by Mr. Rashied Arendse who allowed me to use them. No exact dates are known. I also used the transcriptions of the some of the sermons published by the mosque.

1989: Imam Omar, Jihad against apartheid

1990: Imam Omar, Jihad for social reconstruction

1990: Imam Omar, The question of the Islamic political party

1992: Imam Omar, Pluralism within Islam

1994: Imam Omar, Muslims and the RDP (Reconstruction and Development Programme)

Manjra, Shuaib, Creating a New Society

Samie, M. Adam, Making our Dreams a Reality

Fataar, Aslam, Active Participation in the RDP

Brits Mosque

In Brits, the sermons in 1990 formed a cohesive series. I relied on the recording of the sermons by Shahed Tayob and their transcription by Ilham Brey, and I am extremely grateful to both. In addition, I have also listened to, but not recorded, many additional sermons.

May 11: Mawlānā Ebrahim, the place of pilgrimage I
May 18: Mawlānā Abu Bakr, the meaning of sacrifice
May 25: Mawlānā Bhoja, the journey to Mecca
June 1: Mawlānā Yusuf, the place of Ebrahim
June 8: Mawlānā Ebrahim, the place of pilgrimage II
June 15: Mawlānā Yusuf, the social significance of sacrifice

INDEX

Abdol Roef, Abdullah, 48, 49–50
Abdol Roef, Cassiem, 48, 50–51, 52
Abdol Roef, grandson of Tuan Guru, 46, 47–48, 54
Abdol Roef (son of Tuan Guru), 36, 46, 152n.41
Abduh, Muḥammad, 69
Abraham, 112, 119–21
Abu Bakr, Mawlānā, 113
adult education, 56
African National Congress, 111
African township of Oukasie, 79; discriminatory wages in, 95, 158n.45. *See also* Islam: African
Afrikaans, 55; in Arabic script, 28, 33, 151n.22. *See also* religious language
Afrikaners, 61; Christianity among, 66; in Brits, 78–79, 155n.4
Ahmad, Akbar, 95
Antoun, Richard, 15, 34
apartheid, 56, 58; and Islamic institutions, 139; and Islamic resurgence, 98; and Muslims, 9, 135; and religion, 66; in sermons, 127, 128, 129
Arabic-Afrikaans, 28, 33, 151n.22
Arabicization, 76, 108
Asad, Talal, 2, 9–11
Awwal Mosque, 24–27, 28, 29, 36, 45, 52, 140
Ayoub, Mahmoud, 117
Azaadville, 89

bāngī (muezzin) 94, 158n.45
Bassadien, Armien, 49
Bhamjee, Mawlānā Yusuf, 113–14
Bhoja, Mawlānā, 114
bidʿah (religious innovation), 71–74, 78, 85; and Arabicization, 76; in gestures, 72–74, 76
Bowen, 131–32, 142
Bradlow, Frank, 25
Brelvism, 78, 89; and the Prophet, 92; and women, 100
Brits: church in, 79; history of, 78–80; jamāt committees in, 81–82; leadership of mosque in, 86–88; preachers in, 112–14
Buitengracht Street Mosque, 46, 49

Cairo, 69
Call of Islam, 122
Cape of Good Hope, 21
Chidester, David, 103–4
Christianity: churches in Brits, 156n.7; and pilgrimage, 132–34; and priest in mosque, 110; in South Africa, 3
Claremont Main Road Mosque: and apartheid, 56; changes in, 55, 57; constitutionalism in, 57; criticism of, 40–41; establishment of, 46, 47
Claremont (suburb), 46
Coburn, James, 118
Colebrooke and Brigge Commission, 25, 29, 35

174 / Index

Comaroff, Jean, and Comaroff, John, 34
Combs-Schilling, M., 7–8
conversion: during apartheid, 96; at the
   Cape, 22; Horton's theory of, 99; and
   marginalization, 98, 113

Dangor, Suleman, 22
Darul Karar Mosque, 44
Deobandism (Islamic orientation), 70–71, 73,
   90, 101, 155n.20; in Azaadville, 89; in
   sermon, 108; and women in Islam, 100
dhikr, 91
discourse: in bid'ah disputes, 71; fund-
   raising as, 82; gestures in, 85, 91, 92; and
   historical context of, 138; Islam and, 11;
   and modernity, 11; mosques and imams
   as, 139; on the periphery, 77, 101, 141–42;
   space as, 102–4; in supplications, 131–32
Douglas, Mary, 76

Ebrahim, Mawlānā (Brits), 112
Effendi, Abu Bakr, 33, 49, 68, 77, 94
Eickelman, Dale, 142
Eliade, Mircea, 102–3, 123, 149n.9
ethnicity, 68–69, 76–78

Fakier, Abu Bakr, 54–56
Friday worship: obligation of, 106; in
   practice, vii
funeral rites, 39, 47

Gaffney, Patrick, 16–17, 18, 147
Geertz, Clifford, 5–6, 10, 32
Ghandi, 62, 70, 141
Gilsenan, Michael, 11–12
Graham, William, 17
Group Areas Act, 43, 44–45, 47, 48, 55, 64–
   66, 67

Hanafī school, 33
Haron, Imām Abdullah, 54, 57, 153n.19
Hendricks, Shaykh M. S., 43–44, 46
hierarchy: in leadership, 43, 86–88; of space,
   144–45. See also imāms; leadership
Hodgson, Marshall, 17

Ibn al-'Arabī, 116–17, 118

Ibn Kullāb (theologian), 19
imāms: in the Cape, 43, 68–69, 110, 139; in
   contrast with priest, 35; Deobandis, 71; as
   employees, 62; hereditary succession of,
   51; and politics, 75, 76
Iran: and Islamic Revolution, 56; preachers
   in, 13
Islam: African, 94–99, 158n.49; Indian, 97;
   Indonesian, 5; Malawian, 94, 96;
   Moroccan, 5, 6; principles of, 121–22, 143–
   44; scripturalism and universalism of, 5,
   32, 34; women's, 99–100, 105

jamāt committee, 86; constitution of, 62;
   family control over, 63; political
   patronage, 63, 67–68
Jamiatul Ulama Transvaal, 69, 70, 112
Javaansche artillery, 26

khuṭbah. See sermon

leadership: and adult education, 45; in Brits,
   86–88; as chief priest, 35–36, 45; in civil
   society, 36–39, 140–41, 145; hierarchy of,
   43, 86–88; jurists, Sufis and Prophetic
   descendents, 12; and knowledge, 28, 31,
   70, 143; in Morocco, 28; and patronage,
   151n.17; and ritual service, 30, 143; in
   Saudi Arabia, 9–10, 149n.9; and wages,
   87–88, 157nn.29, 30; Weberian categories
   of, 12. See also imāms
legislation, discriminatory, 61–62
Long Street Mosque, 27, 29
Lubbe, Gerrie, 51, 53

Mabuluka, 97–99, 113; the Murabitun in, 98
Malawian workers, 3, 94
Malay Corps, 37, 38
Mardyckers, 22
mawlid. See Mīlād
Mecca: knowledge from, 31, 43; pilgrimage
   to, 112, 125–26
Metcalf, Barbara, 70
Mia family, 70
Mīlād, 142; in cinema, 91, 158n.39;
   Deobandi, 90, 91; food for, 91; in Morocco
   (mawlid), 7–8, 73; Malawian, 96

Mohammed, Shaykh Nazeem, 44
Morocco, 7–8, 28, 142
mosques: and apartheid, 41, 66; board of
governors, 50, 54–55; in civil society, 37,
128, 145; and colonialism, 38; congregations of, 30, 31, 57; constitution for, 50; and
discourse, 52, 62, 74; dress code in, 73; and
ethnic identity, 68–69, 73, 76–78, 153n.18;
fund-raising for, 47, 82–83, 156n.13; and
gender, 105; ḥanafī, 33; and hermeneutics,
57; hierarchy in, 106–8, 124; leadership in,
28, 34, 35–36; in Lebanon, 12, 103; murids
of, 29, 47; as neutral zones, 11; nominee
ownership of, 64–65; organization of, 30,
42; patronage of, 26–27; pilgrimage and,
31–33; pluralism of, 134–36; and primordial link, 124, 125–26, 145; prophetic role
of, 124–26, 134–36; racial laws of apartheid
and, 83–84; as sacred space, 123; and
salon, 12; and traders, 62, 63, 74; women's
contributions to, 41–42, 81
Mozbieker Mosque, 29
Muhsin, Amina Wadud, 40, 57
murids (in Cape Mosque), 29, 47
Muslim Judicial Council, 45, 47, 48, 51–53,
55, 58
Muslim Youth Movement, 56, 122, 158n.40;
in Brits, 93

Najjar, Shaykh Abu Bakr, 21, 51
Nana, Moosa Pir, 84–85, 157n.18
naṣīḥah (admonishment), 9–11

Orange Free State, 61

Palm Tree Mosque, 27, 29, 30, 43
pilgrimage: and Jews and Christians, 132–
34; and mosques, 31–32; in sermons, 126;
and wealth, 132–34
Platvoet, Jan, 13–14
pluralism, within Islam, 135
politics: and exiles, 3; and Islam, 22, 53, 93,
135; and patronage, 67; and religion, 129–
30; and supplications, 128, 130–32
preachers: bio-data of, 110–14; as culture
brokers, 15; in Iran, 13; Islamization
through, 15; radical, 16

Qiblah, 56
Quawatul Islam Mosque, 49, 60
Queen Victoria Mosque, 32, 38
Qur'ān: and companions, 115–16; interpretation of, 117, 119–23, 135, 148; political
interpretation of, 129–30; principles in,
121–22; and re-citation, 17–18, 19, 117,
119–23, 146–47; and Shi'ite, 116–18; and
Sufism, 116–18; and tafsīr, 115–16; and
theology, 19

Rafudeen, Auwais, 22
Rahman, Fazlur, 143, 146
Rama[dad]ān, charity, 47
religion: definition of, 13–14; and Enlightenment, 10; institutionalization of, 42;
political interpretation of, 129–30;
reductionism, 14; ritual in, 76; supplication in, 130–32; as traditions great and
little, 34; as worldviews, 5
religious language, 2, 9; Afrikaans as, 55; in
sermon, 104, 108–9; Urdu as, 95–96. See
also symbols
resurgence, Islamic, 93; and study circles,
93, 99; and women, 99
Rispler-Chaim, Vardit, 72
rites of passage, 30, 39, 47, 131n.28
ritual: and gestures, 85, 91, 92–93; religion
and, 144; Sharī'ah as, 144

sacred (holy) nights, 71, 99
ṣalāh (worship), 13; ḥanafī, 49
salāmī, ritual, 90; women's practice of, 100
Salt River, 110
Sanneh, Lamin, 76, 108
Saudi Arabia, 9–10, 149n.9
scriptures, Hindu, 118
sermons, 157n.22; and apartheid, 127, 128–
29; and Christians, 110; control over, 86;
creativity in, 19; as discursive, 20; in
historical context, viii, 2–4, 132–36; of
Islamism, vii; language of, 104, 106; as
literature, 16, 147; politicized, viii, 126–30;
and presermons, 40–41, 55, 57, 109–10,
159n.8; re-citation of Qur'āan in, 17–18;
religious dimension of, 4, 17–19, 146; in
Saudi Arabia, 9–10; in snapshot analyses,

sermons (*continued*)
viii; social effects of, 15, 132–36;
supplications in, 130–31
Shah Muhammad, Hadjie Sulaiman, 44, 46
Sharī'ah, 52, 53, 58, 71–72, 75, 108–9, 140; its
immutability, 144, 145; leadership
through, 143; ritual location of, 144
shaykh, 43. *See also* imāms; leadership
Shaykh Yusuf, 22–23, 150n.7
Slamdien, 46
smallpox epidemic, 38
Smith, Jonathan Z., 103
Smith, Wilfred Cantwell, 17
Smuts-Ghandi Agreement, 70
Solomons, Imam Hasan, 56
Soomar, Joosub, 79, 85
South Africa: brief history of, 3–4, 137; Indians
in, 60; new and democratic, 40, 127–29
South African Commercial Advertiser, 35, 36
Stegman Road Mosque, 46, 153n.18
study of religion: as discourses, 6; partici-
pants in, ix, 6
Sufism, 12, 29
supplications, 128, 130–32, 155n.24
Suyūṭī al-, Jalāl al-Dīn, 115
symbols: and colors, 7; in conflict and
competition, 103; discursive, 9;
essentialist, 6–7; historical context of, 7;
Islamic, 5; mosques as, ix, 12, 25;
religious nature of, 13; sermons as, 4;
systems of, 5

Tablīghī Jamāt, 70, 74, 88, 113

traders, 83, 141; and patronage of mosques,
83–84, 141; and religious leaders, 87
Transvaal, ix, 61
Tri-centenary Celebrations, 23
Tuan Guru, 24, 26

Union Jack, 37

van Bengalen, Achmat, 25, 27, 29, 35–36, 52
van Bengalen, Frans, 24–26, 34
van Boughies, Jan, 27–28, 29, 34–36, 42, 52,
152n.41
van de Kaap, Saartjie, 24, 42, 151n.41
van Macassar, Salia, 42
Verwoerd, Hendrik, 52
Vos Street Mosque, 31

waqf (endowments), 66
Waterval Islamic Institute, 70, 71
Waugh, Earl, 104
Weber, Max, 12
women: as adornment at religious
gatherings, 100; in Brits, 81, 99; independence of, 100–101; and Islam, 41–42, 100,
142; in religious schools, 99
Wynberg, 44

Xhosa, 37

Young Men's Muslim Association, 155n.20
Yusufiyyah Mosque, 44

zakāt al-fiṭr, 153n.19
Zuid Afrikaanse Republiek, 61
Zulus, 78

Abdulkader Tayob is associate professor of religious studies and warden of residence at the University of Cape Town. His interests cover classical Islamic historiography, theory of the study of religions, and Islam in Africa. He is the author of *Islamic Resurgence in South Africa: The Muslim Youth Movement* (University of Cape Town Press, 1995).

Breinigsville, PA USA
11 January 2010

230513BV00002B/1/A